"This book is many things. It is a guide to biblical reading, meditation, and prayer. It reintroduces the truth that Scripture's sole purpose is to lead us to the living God in Jesus Christ. It lovingly opens up the riches of monastic and scholastic theology. But above all, this book is a work of spiritual instruction by one of the true spiritual masters of our time. Never has the Church more sorely needed theologians who are masters of the spiritual life, and, in our spiritually arid day, God has raised up Hans to direct our minds and hearts toward union with Christ."

—MATTHEW LEVERING,
James N. Jr. and Mary D. Perry Chair of Theology, Mundelein Seminary

"For a contemporary church that has worn away the point of divine love, Hans Boersma sharpens it again with the flint of tradition. In *Pierced by Love*, the title is more than metaphor; it indicates how we should experience lectio divina. The early and medieval church knew that reading the Bible meant being entered into as much as entering the text. Boersma reacquaints us with the dangers and costs as well as the fruits of divine reading."

—JESSICA HOOTEN WILSON,
visiting scholar at Pepperdine University; author, *The Scandal of Holiness*

"Though the Protestant and evangelical churches have begun to recover elements of the Christian tradition, especially patristic sources, the rich history and theology of the Middle Ages remains to be explored in its fullness. Hans Boersma's *Pierced by Love* is an excellent introduction to and exposition of early and medieval writings on sacred reading. The book's deep examination of medieval authors illuminates the Bible-centeredness of medieval theology and the text's many diagrams further reveal the richness of medieval reading and reflection on the Bible. One does not need to be an expert in medieval theology to benefit greatly from Boersma's analysis and his incisive treatment will change the way you read the Bible. Take up and read!"

—GREG PETERS,
Biola University and Nashotah House Theological Seminary

"Love for Christ flies off every page. With gentle profundity, Hans Boersma guides his reader through the healing process of lectio divina with the skill of a master, a master wounded by the arrow of the Master of all."

—ALEXIS TORRANCE,
associate professor and Archbishop Demetrios College Chair
of Byzantine Theology, University of Notre Dame

"Boersma calls Christians back to the ancient and medieval practice of a spiritual immersion into Scripture as the path to deeper union with Christ. By moving through the four steps of lectio, meditatio, oratio, and contemplatio, he shows how formation and encounter flow together as the reader finds Christ in the depths of Scripture's spiritual meanings. Scripture becomes sacrament—the place where we ascend to contemplative vision of Christ as we find him and are formed into him through its pages. Recognizing the need for sure guides in this journey, Boersma moves through ancient and medieval writers to build up a thick account of how lectio divina unfolds. The result is like moving through a medieval garden of delights in which the voices of Christian tradition swirl together to form a holistic vision of the Scriptures. This is theology in the best sense—historically rooted, spiritually alive, and oriented toward Christ as the telos of life."

—DALE COULTER,
professor, Pentecostal Theological Seminary

"The monk in me skips with delight on delving into this comprehensive exploration of lectio divina by Hans Boersma. The book is exceedingly modest, conversational in tone, and yet impressively profound. It is obviously the rich fruit of both long study in the Christian (especially monastic) tradition and long personal practice of lectio. Boersma refuses to dichotomize between exegesis and mysticism, and he rightly loses interest in any approach to the revealed text that is not ultimately headed toward union with God. Desire for God, thirst for the living Christ, is Boersma's key to biblical anthropology, and this vision every-where informs his interpretation and application of the divine words."

—SIMEON LEIVA-MERIKAKIS,
OCSO, St. Joseph's Abbey

PIERCED
BY LOVE

PIERCED BY LOVE

DIVINE READING
WITH THE
CHRISTIAN TRADITION

HANS BOERSMA

LEXHAM PRESS

Pierced by Love: Divine Reading with the Christian Tradition

Copyright 2023 Hans Boersma

Lexham Press, 1313 Commercial St., Bellingham, WA 98225
LexhamPress.com

Unless otherwise noted, Scripture quotations are the author's own translation or are from the Douay-Rheims version. Public domain.

The image on p. 130 of Bonaguida's *Tree of Life* is reprinted with permission © akg-images/ Rabatti & Domingie

Print ISBN 9781683596776
Digital ISBN 9781683596783
Library of Congress Control Number 2022942972

Lexham Editorial: Elliot Ritzema, Jeff Reimer, Kelsey Matthews, Danielle Burlaga
Cover Design: Joshua Hunt, Brittany Schrock
Typesetting: Abigail Stocker

◆

Seduxisti me, Domine, et seductus sum

Tu m'as séduit, ô Seigneur, et moi, je me suis laissé séduire

Thou hast seduced me, O Lord, and I have been seduced

JEREMIAH 20:7

◆

Contents

Prayer for Lectio Divina

+ In the name of the Father, and of the Son, and of the Holy Ghost.
Amen.

My heart hath uttered a good word: I speak my works to the king:
    My tongue is the pen of a scrivener
        that writeth swiftly.   *Ps 45:1*

My heart hath said to thee: My face hath sought thee:
    thy face, O Lord, will I still seek.   *Ps 27:8*

One thing I have asked of the Lord, this will I seek after;
    that I may dwell in the house of the Lord
        all the days of my life.   *Ps 27:4*

My soul hath thirsted after the strong living God;
    when shall I come and appear before the face of God?

My tears have been my bread day and night,
    whilst it is said to me daily: Where is thy God?   *Ps 42:2–3*

How sweet are thy words to my palate!
    more than honey to my mouth.   *Ps 119:103*

If I have remembered thee upon my bed,
    I will meditate on thee in the morning:

Because thou hast been my helper.
    And I will rejoice under the covert of thy wings.   *Ps 63:6–7*

They that sow in tears
> shall reap in joy.

Going they went and wept, casting their seeds.
> But coming they shall come with joyfulness,
>> carrying their sheaves.   *Ps 126:5–6*

Glory be to the Father, and to the Son: and to the Holy Ghost;

As it was in the beginning, is now, and ever shall be;

world without end. Amen.

Blessed Lord,

who hast caused all holy Scriptures to be written for our learning:

Grant that we may in such wise hear them,

read, mark, learn, and inwardly digest them,

that by patience and comfort of thy holy Word,

we may embrace and ever hold fast the blessed hope of everlasting life,

which thou hast given us in our Saviour Jesus Christ.

Amen.

Acknowledgments

IT HAS BEEN a privilege to work on this book over the past number of years. It has matured through various iterations of a course taught at Nashotah House Theological Seminary. Colleagues and friends gave generously of their time in reading an earlier draft and offering numerous improvements. I am grateful to Chiara Bertoglio, Antje Chan, Ron Dart, Alex Fogleman, Micah Hogan, Kasey Kimball, Corine and Jonathan Milad, Dave Nelson, and Pippa Salonius. I want to thank my daughter Meghan for her talented assistance in drawing up the charts in this book. And my TA Joseph Roberts, who kindly and skillfully did the index.

I very much enjoyed the opportunity to try out some of the material for a variety of audiences. I am indebted to the CiRCE Fall Regional Conference; the Augustine Academy in Hartland, Wisconsin; students attending the Ash Wednesday Retreat at Nashotah House Theological Seminary; the Research Seminar Historical and Systematic Theology at the University of St. Andrews; the St. Thomas Mission in Vancouver; the RADVO Conference in Dallas; the Synod of the Reformed Episcopal Church in Dallas; Christ Church in Waco, Texas; and the Touchstone Conference in Chicago. It was an honor and pleasure to deliver the Holmer Lecture for Anselm House at the University of Minnesota.

I would like to thank Jesse Myers from Lexham Press for the enthusiasm with which he embraced this project, and it has been great working with Elliot Ritzema and Jeff Reimer as my editors. I appreciate the permission to republish material from several recent articles: "Memory and Character Formation: The Ark in Hugh of Saint Victor," in *An Introduction to Child Theology*, edited by James M. Houston (Eugene, OR: Cascade, 2022), 139–64; "Let's Talk about Sin: Retrieving Compunction and Introspection," *Touchstone: A Journal of Mere Christianity* 35, no. 2 (March–April 2022); and "Advent Arrow," *First Things*, December 13, 2018, firstthings.com/web-exclusives/2018/12/advent-arrow.

My wife Linda read and commented on the entire manuscript. God is most gracious in piercing my soul with his love, and especially in his skillful use of my wife's loving support as his arrow.

Advent 2021

Abbreviations

ACCS	Ancient Christian Commentary on Scripture
ACW	Ancient Christian Writers
AMMTC	Ancient Mediterranean and Medieval Texts and Contexts
BCCT	Brill's Companions to the Christian Tradition
BRe	*Biblical Reception*
CFS	Cistercian Fathers Series
CSS	Cistercian Studies Series
CWS	Classics of Western Spirituality
FC	Fathers of the Church
HTR	*Harvard Theological Review*
LCL	Loeb Classical Library
MMT	*Medieval Mystical Theology*
MST	Mediaeval Sources in Translation
MWS	Monastic Wisdom Series
NPNF	*Nicene and Post-Nicene Fathers*
PL	*Patrologia Latina*
RB	The Rule of Saint Benedict
SJT	*Scottish Journal of Theology*
SMCH	Studies in Medieval Cistercian History
ST	Studies and Texts
ST	*Summa theologiae*
TAPS	Transactions of the American Philosophical Society
WSA	The Works of Saint Augustine: A Translation for the 21st Century

Figures

Divine Reading of Divine Scripture

LECTIO DIVINA IS nothing out of the ordinary. It is what happens naturally when Christians wrestle with the biblical text. The Latin term *divina* may intimidate us into thinking it is something different from what we typically do in reading the Bible. But *divina* does not mean "esoteric"; it is more akin to our term *holy*. The Scriptures are holy—set aside for a unique purpose. Scripture is divine in the sense that it has a special place within the church. Lectio divina simply means reading the Bible the way it's supposed to be read—as divine Scripture.

Just as Scripture is divine, so our reading must be divine. Our reading must do justice to the purpose for which Scripture has been set aside. Origen makes this point in a letter he probably wrote to Gregory Thaumaturgus around the year 235:

> Devote yourself (*proseche*) first and foremost to reading the holy Scriptures (*theiōn graphōn*); but devote yourself (*proseche*). For when we read holy things (*theia*) we need much attentiveness (*prosochēs*), lest we say or think something hasty about them. And when you are devoting yourself (*prosechōn*) to reading the sacred texts (*theiōn*) with faith and an attitude pleasing to God,

knock on its closed doors, and it will be opened to you [Matt 7:7] by the gatekeeper of whom Jesus spoke: "The gatekeeper opens to him" [John 10:3]. And when you devote yourself (*prosechōn*) to the divine reading (*theia*), uprightly and with a faith fixed firmly on God seek the meaning of the divine (*theiōn*) words which is hidden from most people. Do not stop at knocking and seeking, for the most necessary element is praying to understand the divine words (*theia*).

Two Greek words stand out in this brief excerpt from Origen's letter. First is the term *theios*, which literally translated would yield the English "divine." But the translator rightly uses the terms "holy" and "divine" interchangeably. Origen's point is that holy books call for holy reading; divine books require divine reading.

The second term is *prosochē*, or "attention." Origen advises Gregory to read the biblical text with attention. Here, I'm somewhat less happy with the translator's equation of attention with devotion. Devotion often carries the connotation of piety. Now, attention does include a pious attitude. But Origen probably had more in mind than just what we today call devotion. When monastic authors of the third and fourth centuries spoke of attention (*prosochē*), they had in mind vigilance, watchfulness, and self-awareness. The monk would watch his thoughts, making sure they were focused on God rather than on anything extraneous. Attention was the opposite, therefore, of distraction.

Origen wants Gregory to be attentive when he engages in divine reading. The Scriptures require his utmost attention. He cannot rush the reading, hurrying to quickly finish. No, divine reading requires his single-minded focus on the biblical text, for only such attention will allow him to find its hidden meaning.

Finding this hidden meaning is the purpose of reading the divine Scriptures. Again, we need not think of anything esoteric here. Origen simply has in mind the New Testament realities of Christ and the church. When we knock and seek, we look for the sacramental or real presence of Christ. Raymond Studzinski, a Benedictine monk from St. Meinrad Archabbey in Indiana, puts it this way: "For Origen everything in the Scriptures has meaning for Christian believers because of their life in Christ. Christ is the source, the content, and the meaning of the Scriptures." To read the Scriptures sacramentally is to look for Christ as the content of the biblical text.

What is fascinating in Origen's letter is that he makes absolutely no distinction between lectio divina and regular Bible reading. They are one and the same thing. Origen was hardly alone in this. When we discuss the twelfth-century Carthusian prior Guigo II in chapter 2, we will see that he links the four steps of lectio divina to the four traditional levels of biblical interpretation. For Origen and Guigo—and this holds true for the premodern Christian tradition more broadly— lectio divina is the ordinary, standard way of reading the Scriptures. Proper biblical interpretation requires a divine or spiritual mode of treating the holy text.

It is important, therefore, to appreciate that lectio divina is nothing out of the ordinary. When we do lectio divina, we read Scripture in line with its divine character—as we always should. To be sure, this claim has a polemical edge. It implies that we do *not* find the meaning of Scripture simply by asking what the human author intended with the text. We do *not* find the meaning of Scripture simply by sticking with a proper method, whether of a grammatical or a historical-critical nature. In short, we do *not* find the meaning of Scripture when we think of ourselves first and foremost as historians. We find meanings—note the plural!—of Scripture primarily by looking forward (to its divine purpose) rather than by looking backward (to its human origins).

Of course, we can use Scripture for other purposes. Origen himself famously constructed a critical edition of the Old Testament, the *Hexapla*, in which he placed the Hebrew text alongside a variety of Greek translations in six columns, which allowed for a careful comparison of the various texts. Although this endeavor was quite technical, Origen never lost sight of the primary purpose of searching for Christ as the hidden meaning of the text.

Origen's work on the *Hexapla* was perfectly legitimate, as are historical and archaeological investigations that focus less immediately on the spiritual aim of contemplation. In fact, both Origen's textual analysis and our own historical investigation can *serve* divine reading. But the point is that we shouldn't lose sight of this divine purpose in Bible reading. The search for meaning (that is to say, exegesis) is a search for God, not an attempt at historical reconstruction. And if exegesis is a knocking and searching for God himself, then lectio divina is simply what we do when we rightly handle the word of truth (2 Tim 2:15).

READING THIS BOOK

THIS BOOK IS not a how-to guide for lectio divina. Instead, we'll look at what happens spiritually in our lives when we embark on divine reading. To be sure, I hope this discussion will be helpful also for people who wonder about what to do in lectio divina. That's just not my primary aim. Besides, I'm skeptical of how-to guides, and lectio divina is not the result of a method. The modern preoccupation with method is alien to a sacramental exploration of the divine Scriptures. Method assumes that empirical analysis of the text produces the one (and only) meaning of the text. Such is not the goal of lectio divina.

Still, it's possible to give advice for good reading strategies. Reading ought never to be a purely subjective enterprise, arbitrarily letting the feelings wash over you. Good reading invariably involves an encounter, with meaning occurring within the encounter. Lectio divina, too, aims at encounter. To read the Scriptures without asking how they call us to Christ is to ignore their fundamental purpose. This book will hopefully be a helpful antidote to seeing lectio as an excuse to leave behind our critical faculties and embark on a sentimental psychologizing of the gospel, for this is not at all what earlier generations of spiritual writers had in mind. They thought of it as a robust—indeed, often piercing and painful—process that demands a careful and deliberate reading of Scripture.

If reading means encounter, then the imagination is perhaps the key faculty that allows the encounter to happen. Words, when properly used, stir the imagination. Words make pictures. Words leave a visual imprint (an image) on the mind, which unites us with the external referent. This is why storytelling is indispensable in faith formation. Throughout this book, we will see theologians such as Anselm of Canterbury, Aelred of Rievaulx, and Bernard of Clairvaux using the insight that words make pictures. They recognized that through the imagination we are united with Christ as the one revealed to us in biblical words.

Pictures or images are often counterproductive because they are overly prescriptive. When we depict the scene of an event, we force the reader's imagination down a particular path. Without the illustration, the reader has the freedom to imagine the scene as he wishes. But once the picture is there, this freedom is gone: the only way of imagining the scene is the one the illustration provides. That's why movies based on novels can be such a letdown. They deprive us of the freedom to imagine the narrative for ourselves. Pictures tend to constrain rather than open up the imagination.

This book does include images, but they are not illustrations depicting particular biblical events. They do not, therefore, narrow or prescribe our imaginative faculty. Instead, the images in this book—taken from medieval authors—function in support of the words. That is to say, the images serve as repositories of particular truths or teachings. They are often fairly abstract, and they help us recall the content of Scripture. To give but one example, the image of Noah's ark devised by Hugh of Saint Victor in the twelfth century (and discussed in chapter 4) is more a diagram of salvation history than a visual representation of the historical ark at the time of the flood. Hugh's mural painting, therefore, did not narrow the imagination but opened it up. I have purposely included images (as well as other figures and diagrams) throughout this book because they give a clear impression of how it is that the imagination functions in lectio divina, in part through the judicious use of images.

The four traditional steps of *lectio* (reading), *meditatio* (meditation), *oratio* (prayer), and *contemplatio* (contemplation) form the frame of the practice. Repetitious reading, thoughtful and extended reflection on individual words or phrases, prayerful reflection on our own lives in the light of our meditation, and finally silent resting in the love of God are the four basic elements. If you are looking for a practical way into lectio divina, the first recommendation I'd give is to read Guigo II's *The Ladder of Monks*, which I discuss in some detail in chapter 2. Meanwhile, here are a few simple guidelines to keep in mind:

- Find a quiet place and begin with a short period of silence to properly focus your attention.

- Read the passage repeatedly—perhaps about four times, interspersed with periods of silence.

- Meditate on a word or phrase that strikes you as significant. Ask yourself how it functions within its immediate context and within the Scriptures as a whole. Look for the revelation of Christ within this word or phrase. And ask what all of this has to do with your own situation and circumstances.

- As you pray, God will confront your life with the fruit of meditation. This may cause the pain of repentance. Or it may flood your heart with gratitude. In prayer, we bring our lives before God in response to the reading of the text.

- Take time throughout the process to pause and rest in silence before God. Keep Origen's advice in mind not to be hasty. It is when words and silence alternate that meaning can occur.

The structure of this book follows the four-stage movement of lectio divina. The first two chapters are introductory. I begin in chapter 1 by asking how lectio takes us from sacrament (*sacramentum*) to reality (*res*). The process transfixes or pierces us, and in so doing it transfigures us. Chapter 2 offers a detailed discussion of the four steps of lectio divina by looking at the ladder metaphor in dialogue with Guigo II's *The Ladder of Monks*.

In chapter 3, we turn to the first step, that of reading (*lectio*). I explore how lectio divina offers an antidote to the vice of acedia or sloth, drawing on Augustine's understanding of words as means to overcome acedia and to center our hope on the eternity of God. Chapters 4 through 6 deal with meditation (*meditatio*). We first turn to the link between memory and meditation in chapter 4, looking especially at how Hugh of Saint Victor used Noah's ark to impress biblical truth onto his students' hearts and minds. Medieval theologians often compared reading to eating, so in chapter 5 we consider how they employed various alimentary tropes to make the point that we meditate on Scripture in the hope of tasting the sweetness of the Lord. We next turn to the imagery of the tree of life, which medieval writers such as Bonaventure loved to use in meditating on the cross. We will see in chapter 6 that lectio divina serves to unite us with the suffering of Christ on the cross.

With chapter 7, we turn from meditation to prayer (*oratio*). The piercing grief over sin, which we encounter throughout the tradition—in Augustine, John Cassian, Bernard of Clairvaux, Anselm of Canterbury, and Aelred of Rievaulx—calls us back to a more introspective form of Christianity. Chapter 8 turns to the final step of lectio divina by raising the perennial question of the relation between action (Martha) and contemplation (Mary). Though both are indispensable, we will see in this chapter why, throughout the tradition, Christians have seen contemplation as the final, ultimate step not only of lectio divina but also of the Christian pilgrimage itself. This contemplation takes us to the ineffable mystery of God; the last chapter, therefore, shows that our silence anticipates the Great Silence of God's love in Christ.

This book is somewhat difficult to classify. It has an obvious spiritual component: we will retrieve the practice of lectio divina by going through each of the four steps. But you will also notice a marked historical component, for I will present many illustrations from and discussions of patristic and (especially) medieval tradition. Further, throughout the book, I will be discussing the theology that underlies lectio divina. And in doing all this, I will often appeal to the biblical witness—as did all previous generations of lectio divina practitioners. In short, biblical, historical, theological, and spiritual categories overlap and intertwine. I do so purposely, in the conviction that we need all four, in unison, as we try to read the divine book in a divine manner.

Finally, a comment on the Bible translation used in this book. For the most part, I follow the Douay-Rheims Bible from the late sixteenth and early seventeenth centuries. The reason is that it translates the Latin Vulgate, and the spiritual writers I quote mostly followed the Vulgate. The Douay-Rheims Bible thus keeps us closest to the biblical text as these theologians would have known it. I do, however, make an adjustment for the numbering of the Psalms (and a few other passages). To accommodate current practices, I follow the numbering of most contemporary translations. Therefore, if you search the Douay-Rheims Bible (or the Vulgate or the Septuagint) for a psalm that I quote in this book, you will in many cases have to look for the one prior to the one mentioned in the text. (For example, Psalm 45 in this book is Psalm 44 in the Douay-Rheims Bible.)

Transfiguration

STABAT MATER

Love is the face of God. We see him face-to-face—Jesus, hanging on the cross. When the old man Simeon saw Mary with the child, he burst out in prophecy: "And thy own soul a sword shall pierce (*pertransibit*), that, out of many hearts thoughts may be revealed" (Luke 2:35). The thirteenth-century hymn *Stabat Mater* ponders the fulfillment of Simeon's words as the Savior's "mother stands weeping" (*stabat mater dolorosa*) by the cross. The second stanza describes the piercing of her soul:

Cuius animam gementem,	Through her heart, His sorrow sharing,
contristatam et dolentem	all His bitter anguish bearing,
pertransivit gladius.	now at length the sword has passed.

Singing this hymn, we do not objectively recount Mary's grief from a distance. Instead, we identify with her as she looks on her son being crucified:

Sancta Mater, istud agas,	Holy Mother! pierce me through,
crucifixi fige plagas	in my heart each wound renew
cordi meo valide.	of my Savior crucified:
Tui Nati vulnerati,	Let me share with thee His pain,
tam dignati pro me pati,	who for all my sins was slain,
poenas mecum divide.	who for me in torments died.
Fac me tecum pie flere,	Let me mingle tears with thee,
crucifixo condolere,	mourning Him who mourned for me,
donec ego vixero.	all the days that I may live.

The song beseeches the Holy Mother to nail or drive the wounds of the crucified into our hearts. We ask that we may weep with her and join her in mourning our crucified Lord.

Stabat Mater takes Simeon's words as a prophecy of Mary uniting with her son in his suffering, and the song invites us to identify with him as well. The painful transfixing (*pertransire*) of Mary's soul produces pain within the hearts of those who appropriate Christ's sufferings by meditating on them. The hymn is the outcome of meditative reading—lectio divina—both of Simeon's *Nunc Dimittis* (Luke 2:29–32) and of John's reference to Mary's presence at the foot of the cross. Throughout the centuries, interpreters have linked Luke 2:35 with John 19:25–27, despite the obvious difficulty that Luke's Gospel does not actually mention Mary's presence at the cross. But for attentive readers, such as the composer of *Stabat Mater*, the language of Mary being pierced inescapably echoes Jesus's being pierced on the cross.

The souls of both Mary and the chanter of this song are pierced with grief. In chapter 7, I will discuss in greater detail how compunction—puncturing or piercing of the soul—functions in lectio divina. For now, it is enough to note that it is this type of personal meditation that evokes compunction in *Stabat Mater*. Lectio divina is a form of reflective or meditative reading of Scripture that brings us face-to-face with the subject matter of the text. The subject matter of the Song of Simeon is, at least according to *Stabat Mater*, the crucified son of the Virgin. With Mary, we see him face-to-face. It is the love of God in the face of Christ that both transfixes and transfigures us.

FLESH ON THE CROSS, WORDS ON THE PAGE

WE REACH THE goal of the God who is love only through the pain of the cross. Similarly—and that will be the main point of this chapter—we reach the goal of lectio (contemplation) only through patient reading, meditation, and prayer. The initial stages of lectio divina (the lower rungs of the ladder) are indispensable. Why? Because flesh on the cross and words on the page are God's love in act. Saint Paul extols this love when he speaks of "the breadth and length and height and depth" of the charity of Christ, which surpasses all knowledge (Eph 3:18–19). These four dimensions cannot but remind us of the cross, where we see God's love in action. In John's Gospel, Jesus mentions only one of these four dimensions. He speaks of the height of the cross: "When you shall have lifted up (*hypsōsēte*), the Son of man, then shall you know that I am he (*egō eimi*)" (John 8:28). With these last words, Jesus identifies himself with the God who once revealed himself to Moses in the burning bush as "I am" (Exod 3:14). It is in the height of the cross that we see Jesus as God because it is there that he shows redemptive love.

Jesus uses the language of being lifted up twice more. First, in his nighttime conversation with Nicodemus, he explains that he will be "lifted up" (*hypsōsen*) like Moses lifted up the serpent in the desert

(John 3:14). Jesus links faith in the crucified Son of Man to eternal life (3:15–16). We join this eternal life of God by accepting the love of God displayed on the cross. Second, Jesus explains that it is when he is "lifted up (*hypsōthō*) from the earth" that he is victorious over the ruler of the world and will draw all things to himself (12:31–32). The cross is God's throne. Nothing on earth reaches quite as high as the cross of Christ, for nothing is as high or sublime as the love of God.

Lectio divina starts where God himself begins. Since God manifests himself primarily on the cross, lectio divina also takes this as its starting point. In the human Jesus, lifted up from the earth, we recognize the God whose identity is love. We find God in the words of Scripture—the *Nunc Dimittis*, the "I am" sayings of John's Gospel, the crucifixion scene. The eternal Word is revealed in temporal words—flesh on the cross, words on the page. We don't get to the capital-*W* Word without small-*w* words. We cannot bypass either the incarnate and crucified Jesus or the biblical account that speaks about him. Jesus is God's sacrament. Scripture too is God's sacrament, since both make present the reality or the truth of the love of God.

This chapter offers a word of caution against bypassing either the cross or biblical words. Both are sacraments of God's love for us. Sacraments are indispensable means of salvation. As we will see, the twelfth-century monastic writers Aelred of Rievaulx and William of Saint-Thierry, each in his own way, refused to ignore the sacramental cast of our journey back to the eternal Word of God's love. Friendship, for Aelred, is important because heaven itself is a place of friendship transfigured. In other words, temporal friendship on earth functions as a sacrament of eternal friendship in heaven. Similarly, for William, pictures of Christ's suffering are indispensable because they are sacraments in which we encounter the truth of the love of God. Heaven transfigures suffering into the glorious reality of love. The sacramental reality (*res*) for which we long, therefore, is a transfiguration of the sacramental means (*sacramenta*) that we encounter on our earthly pilgrimage. And perhaps the most amazing truth is this: we ourselves are transfigured as we learn to see the transfiguration of sacraments into the reality of God's love.

We can make the same point by turning to the four steps of lectio divina. The last step is contemplation of the reality (*res*) or the truth (*veritas*) of God's love. But we are temporal, earthly creatures, and so we dare not bypass the initial three steps. We must first turn to the outward sacraments (*sacramenta*): we need to do the reading (*lectio*), the meditation (*meditatio*), the prayer (*oratio*). In these first three steps, we busy ourselves with ordinary words—reading them, thinking on them, and praying over them. Only after much patient exploration of the *sacramenta* do we get a glimpse of the *res* of God's love as he takes us beyond our words into contemplation of the eternal Word. It is typically only after much practice that, with Saint Paul, some are caught up into Paradise itself (2 Cor 12:4).

Lectio divina, therefore, is not a method or technique, which gives us guaranteed, easy access to psychological well-being. Joseph Cardinal Ratzinger cautions against such a mistaken view of contemplation in his 1989 *Orationis Formas*, a "Letter to the Bishops of the Catholic Church on Some Aspects of Christian Meditation." Ratzinger directs us back to the cross: "The love of God, the sole object of Christian contemplation, is a reality which cannot be 'mastered' by any method or technique. On the contrary, we must always have our sights fixed on Jesus Christ, in whom God's love went to the cross for us and there assumed even the condition of estrangement from the Father (cf. Mk 13:34)." This is wise counsel, for it is on the cross that we recognize the face of God.

So, lectio divina is an exercise in patience. It resists the temptation of jumping straight into contemplation. As this book unfolds, it will become clear that lectio divina is a slow and often painful process that takes seriously the sacramental character of God's revelation. Of course, God can reveal himself however, whenever, and to whomever he wants, no matter the path we ourselves have taken. But our job is to turn back, time and again, to the regular practices of reading, meditation, and prayer. It is in the incarnate Christ, made known in biblical words, that we witness the self-revelation of God's love.

In our impatience, we may be inclined to skip the first three stages. To do so would be an act of pride, for it would be an attempt to grasp the reality (*res*) of eternal life without paying due attention to the sacraments (*sacramenta*) that God intends to use to bring us there. Without meditation on the words of Scripture and the incarnate Christ, our attempts at contemplation cannot but flounder. Why? Because the *res* for which we long is embedded within particular, revealed *sacramenta*. We should not try to circumvent the particular ways in which God shows his love for us.

Christians naturally struggle with the tension between sacrament and reality. The reason is that, with Saint Paul, "we know, if our earthly house of this habitation be dissolved, that we have a building of God, a house not made with hands, eternal in heaven. For in this also we groan, desiring to be clothed upon with our habitation that is from heaven" (2 Cor 5:1–2). The groaning and desiring that the apostle notes mark all authentic Christian spirituality. But it is never a groaning and desiring that dispenses with the temporal small-*w* words that God provides to draw us into his eternal capital-*W* Word.

It is true that negative theology requires us to negate all particular, positive statements that we make about God. But the silence that results from this negation is not sheer nothingness; instead, it is God's eternal fullness that escapes our linguistic abilities and so demands our silence. I will have more to say about silence and negative theology in chapter 9, but for now, let me simply observe that the aim of lectio divina is not an empty abyss but the deepening abundance of God's love in Christ. Our heavenly future—eternal contemplation of God— is the *fulfillment* of God's love in Christ, not its opposite.

Nowhere do we get as profound a view of God as on the cross. This is not to say that by looking at God's face on the cross, we fully grasp his eternal mystery. But it is to say that we should spend time with Mary at the foot of the cross, because nowhere else does God reveal his love more clearly. "Greater love than this no man hath, that a man lay down his life for his friends," says Jesus to his disciples (John 15:13). He calls us friends rather than servants because he keeps no secrets from us: he makes known to us everything he has heard from his Father (15:15). On the cross, God reveals himself to us as our friend, as the one who loves us to the point of death.

FRIENDSHIP TRANSFIGURED

BUT THE PROBLEM is this: doesn't lectio divina take us away from the cross and from the friendship it conveys? Sure, we begin with flesh on the cross and words on the page. We read the Scriptures (*lectio*) and we meditate on them (*meditatio*). But lectio divina ends in contemplation and stillness. And heaven is eternal contemplation. So, in the hereafter, we'll never read and meditate on the Scriptures again. Saint Augustine (rightly, I think) suggested that in heaven we will no longer need a Bible because we will have attained to the love of God itself—the aim or purpose of the Scriptures. In contemplation, we are done with meditating on the cross, leave behind the ups and downs of our personal relationships, and center on the unity and eternity of God. In short, the very purpose of lectio divina seems to be to take us away from the particular to the universal. Are the cross of Christ and his friendship mere stepping-stones to contemplative union with an eternal One?

We shouldn't brush off the objection too quickly. Both Augustine and lectio divina work with Plato's ladder. In his *Symposium*, Plato famously describes love as moving from the personal to the universal by climbing up a ladder of five rungs, each with its own type of beauty, so that we climb up from the beauty of a particular body to Beauty Itself. Love—*erōs* in Plato's dialogue—takes us from the first rung up to the fifth, and increasingly we lose the particularity that characterizes the love of individual things. At the very top, Plato figures, we arrive at the world of Forms or Ideas. Does it make any sense, someone might ask, to foster friendships with particular people if Beauty Itself is the only thing that truly matters?

Figure 1.1 suggests certain similarities between Plato's ladder, Augustine's move from biblical words to Love Itself, and the four steps of lectio divina. Plato, Augustine, and lectio divina all move from the particularity and multiplicity of temporal sacramental means (*sacramenta*) to the universality and unity of eternal reality (*res*). The Augustinian tradition—and the Christian practice of lectio divina—has an unmistakable kinship with Plato's ladder.

	Plato		Augustine	Lectio Divina
Reality (*res*)		Beauty Itself	Love Itself	Contemplation
Sacraments (*sacramenta*)		Beauty of different branches of knowledge	Biblical words	Prayer
		Beauty of law and custom		
		Physical beauty in general		Meditation
		Beauty of a particular object		Reading

Figure 1.1: *From Sacraments to Reality:*
Plato, Augustine, and Lectio Divina

We will talk about ladders much more in the next chapter, and I'll
make a more detailed case there for why we need them. Admittedly,
though, the ladder imagery does have its limits. It falls short because
when we climb a ladder, we take one rung at a time. The metaphor
makes it hard to picture ourselves as standing both on the highest
rung ("Beauty Itself") and the lowest rung ("beauty of a particular
body") at the same time. The truth of the matter is that the two are
intertwined: standing on the lowest rung, we already are in touch with
Beauty Itself. (And I think Plato realized this.) It is precisely when
we stand at the top of Plato's ladder that we most truly appreciate the
lowest rung. Why? Because it is Beauty Itself that is present within
individual beautiful things.

Plato—as well as Augustine and the lectio divina tradition—rightly
saw that love (here on earth) does not fully and permanently satisfy.
That problem marks not just erotic love but also charity. And friendship suffers from the same limitation. The joy and peace that friendship

gives make us long for more, because friendship functions like an oasis within the desert; friendship longs for the entire desert to be transformed into an oasis. In our experience, we encounter deserts all over the place, while friendships are fragile and weak. The limitations and particularities of love and friendship cause tension in our lives. This side of eternal life, we keep yearning for the abundance and universality of the love and friendship of God.

The metaphor of friendship with God has its roots in Scripture itself. God calls Abraham his friend (Isa 41:8; cf. 2 Chr 20:7; Jas 2:23), and he speaks with Moses as with a friend (Exod 33:11). Jesus talks about Lazarus as his friend (John 11:11); and, as we have already seen, in John 15 he calls his disciples friends. Friendship, Scripture suggests, is a higher form of love. Jesus explains that it is the particular act of laying down one's life for a friend that demonstrates this love (15:13). It is as though Jesus were saying: the higher up the ladder, the more particular the love; nothing reaches as high as the cross of Christ. The language of friendship reminds us, therefore, that genuine love sticks to particulars. Friendship takes up the personal and particular and dwells with them.

Joseph Cardinal Ratzinger's *Orationis Formas* underscores the importance of particularity in meditative reading. He cautions us to be mindful of how divine revelation functions: God comes to us in particular words (the Bible) and in a particular person (Jesus Christ). Ratzinger then mentions the topic of friendship with God, and he explains that Christianity relies on the particularity of this friendship. "Revelation," he comments, "takes place through words and actions which have a constant mutual reference, one to the other." Words and actions are indispensable for friendships to flourish. In later chapters we will discuss the silence and solitude of contemplation. They, too, are indispensable for lectio divina. But they rely on friendship and community.

Spiritual Friendship, the famous treatise of the Cistercian abbot Aelred of Rievaulx written between 1163 and 1166, likewise points out friendship's particularity. It does so by differentiating friendship from love. Love, Aelred explains, is something we offer to all people, even our enemies, while we restrict friendship to a select few: "By the law of charity we are ordered to welcome into the bosom of love not only our friends but also our enemies. But we call friends only those to whom we have no qualm about entrusting our heart and all its contents." Friendship outshines love because our friends are not "a burden and a bore" to us, unlike enemies to whom we have extended our love. Friendship, therefore, is a particularized kind of love, extended to only a few.

Aelred maintains that true friendship is necessarily friendship in Christ. Cicero may offer a pretty good definition in his book *On Friendship* when he describes friendship as "accord in all things, human and divine, conjoined with mutual goodwill and affection." But the Roman philosopher did not know Christ, and Christians recognize that "accord in all things" is found only in Christ: "Friendship must begin in Christ, continue with Christ, and be perfected by Christ." True friendship, for Aelred, can flourish only within a particular context—that of Christ and fellow Christians.

Finally, Aelred links growth in friendship with growth in virtue. He explains that friendship grows out of love. Only people who are marked by goodness can foster true friendship, for only they have the requisite purity and love of neighbor. The better we are (and the more we are grounded in Christ), the more we are capable of friendship. Only the perfect, therefore, can consummate friendship. Aelred has such high praise for friendship that he ties it directly to wisdom. The two are virtually identical, claims Aelred—which is a significant claim, since God's Word is eternal wisdom. The Cistercian abbot doesn't quite say that God *is* friendship, but it seems the only thing that restrains him from making this claim is that Scripture itself doesn't do it. Of course, Scripture does say that God is love (1 John 4:16), and Aelred seems to assume that just as we can share in God's love, so too we can share in his wisdom and his friendship. Again, it is a particular way of living that is congenial to friendship.

How, then, are we to understand eternal, perfect friendship? Friendship, we saw, is limited, particular, and multiple while God is infinite, universal, and simple. How can friendship be compatible with contemplation of God? Aelred insists that, nonetheless, the two go hand in hand. He draws attention to a key characteristic of friendship: it makes one out of many. "Among perfect friends," he writes, "wisely chosen and carefully proved, whom a true and spiritual friendship has united, no discord can bring about a separation. Since friendship makes one out of two, just as a unity cannot be divided, so also friendship cannot be divided into two." True friends always remain friends because they are no longer two but one. Friendship, by definition, is unbreakable; it creates a lasting, indestructible unity. For Aelred, perfection both consummates friendship and yields true unity; the two are not opposed to each other. Contemplation of God, therefore, perfects rather than destroys friendship—for it is in contemplation of God that the many are taken up into the One.

Earthly friendship, for Aelred, is a harbinger of contemplation. Friendship displays a glimmering of the ineffable union with God that will one day be ours. Friendship, we might also say, is perfected (or transfigured) when we are united in God; friendship is the many made one. Aelred ends his treatise on friendship with a beautiful paragraph that moves from human friendships, via friendship with Christ, to friendship with God:

> Thus rising from that holy love with which a friend embraces a friend to that with which a friend embraces Christ, one may take the spiritual fruit of friendship fully and joyfully into the mouth, while looking forward to all abundance in the life to come. When the fear is dispelled that now fills us with dread and anxiety for one another ... then with the beginning of relief from care we shall rejoice in the supreme and eternal good, when the friendship to which on earth we admit but few will pour out over all and flow back to God from all, for God will be all in all [1 Cor 15:28].

In eternity, our friendship will "pour out over all," insists Aelred. Throughout his book, he has made the point that while love is universal, friendship is particular. But in heaven, love and friendship become identical, for both become universal. What is more, all human friendships will "flow back to God" so that God will be all in all. Friendship remains friendship, even in heaven. But it will be perfected friendship—the many united into one.

Even when we get to the top of the ladder, therefore, we will not simply kick it away. It would be better to say that we will pull up its lower rungs into the top, as if it were an extension ladder. Heavenly *contemplatio* gives us the fullness of the biblical words that we first encountered in *lectio*. The eschaton will give us Love Itself—the love that the biblical words held out to us, every day of our lives. Augustine is no doubt correct that we won't be reading Scripture in heaven, just as we won't be practicing lectio divina any longer. But the reason is not that the ladder was needless or problematic in some way. We may put it this way: in contemplation and in heaven, the small-*w* words of Scripture are transfigured before our eyes, so that all we see is the capital-*W* Word of God—the eternal, divine Word itself.

IMAGES AND IMAGINATION

THE TWELFTH-CENTURY SPIRITUAL writer William of Saint-Thierry repeatedly addresses this same tension between sacrament and reality in his *Meditations*, which he wrote between 1128 and 1135. The Benedictine (and, later, Cistercian) abbot speaks of the mental pictures that he constructs in praying to God. For example, when he thinks of the Trinity, his soul has a "foolish way of picturing (*imaginatio*) things," imagining that there are three bodies, each occupying its own place, and that the unity of God means that somehow the three must be made one. Faith-informed reason refines and replaces such pictures of the mind. William is nervous about treating the phantasms or images of our mind as literal, straightforward descriptions of God. Doing so would turn them into idols (*idola*), claims William. God's unity does not mean solitude, and his threeness does not mean plurality of number. Because the mind's imagination does not give us reality, William longs to move beyond the sacraments of God's revelation. He yearns to move beyond pictures of unity and plurality to the face of God itself.

William does not, however, repudiate mental picturing. He opens Meditation 10, "The Incarnation and Passion of Christ," with a quote from Galatians 6:14: "God forbid that I should glory, save in the cross of our Lord Jesus Christ." William realizes that the angels behold the glory of Christ's divinity. But he himself has not yet attained angelic spiritual maturity:

> Since I have not yet progressed beyond the elementary stage of sensory imagination (*sensualis imaginationis*), you will allow and will be pleased if my still-undeveloped soul dwells naturally on your lowliness by means of some mental picturing (*mentis imaginatione*). You will allow her, for example, to embrace the manger of the newborn babe, to venerate the sacred infancy, to caress the feet of the crucified, to hold and kiss those feet when he is risen, and to put her hand in the print of the nails and cry: "my Lord and my God!" [John 20:28] And in all these things, as Job says, "visiting my beauty, I shall not sin" [Job 5:24], when I worship and adore what I see and hear in my imagination (*imaginando*), and what my hands handle of the Word of life [1 John 1:1]. For I will confidently assert that in the sweet ordering of your wisdom this grace was provided for us for all eternity. It was not the least of the chief reasons for your incarnation that your babes in the Church, who still needed your milk rather than solid food [Heb. 5:12], who are not strong enough spiritually to think of you in your own way, may find in you a form not unfamiliar to themselves.

Regular sense perception enables us to draw pictures or images in our minds. The abbot of Saint-Thierry insists we should use this imagination (*imaginatio*) in matters of spiritual significance. In particular, we should use it whenever we turn to the Gospel stories: the babe in the manger, Jesus's infancy, his crucifixion, his resurrection body. The imagination is a positive good; it is meant to dwell on God-given images.

Still, William straightforwardly admits that it is spiritual immaturity that requires him to use small-*w* words to gain access to the capital-*W* Word. He is one of the babes who need milk and cannot yet handle solid food. William ultimately aims at the truth or inward reality of the biblical stories: "We make a mental picture of your passion for ourselves, so that our bodily eyes may possess something on which to gaze, something to which to cleave, worshiping not the pictured image (*picturæ imaginem*), but in the image (*in imagine*) the truth (*veritatem*) of your passion." Note the careful distinction William makes: it is not beyond or outside but *in* the image (*in imagine*) that we discern the truth (*veritas*) or reality (*res*) of Christ's passion.

A little later, William uses similar sacramental language when he speaks of the river of joy that floods the soul that comes to the Father through Christ the door. He then acclaims Christ: the soul "seems to see you as you are [1 John 3:2]. In sweet meditation on the wonderful sacrament (*sacramento*) of your passion she muses on the good that you have wrought on our behalf, the good that is as great as you yourself are great, the good that is yourself. She seems to herself to see you face-to-face [1 Cor 13:12] when you thus show her, in the cross and in the work of your salvation, the face of the ultimate Good." The passion of Christ is a sacrament, and it is *in* this sacrament—in the cross and in the work of Christ's salvation—that the soul finds the reality or truth: the face of the ultimate Good.

William describes this sacramental reality not only with personal language ("the good that is yourself") but also with the language of love: "When we look more closely at the picture (*imaginem*) of your passion, although it does not speak, we seem to hear you say: 'When I loved you, I loved you to the end' [John 13:1]." When we meditate on the passion of Christ, the crucifixion takes a particular shape or form as an image in the mind, and it is this image that allows us, in turn, to contemplate the reality of Love Itself—the divinity of Christ. Figure 1.2 illustrates how William understands the move from sacrament to reality:

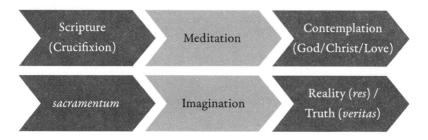

Figure 1.2: *William of Saint-Thierry: From Sacrament to Reality*

The top arrow depicts how lectio divina works: meditation takes us from Scripture to contemplation. The bottom arrow explains that this same process is sacramental in character: the imagination allows us to move from the earthly, temporal sacrament to the heavenly, eternal reality. For William, the biblical story is indispensable in this process. It is the biblical crucifixion narrative that, as sacrament, gives us the material from which our imagination makes forms or images. These images, in turn, allow us to contemplate the reality (*res*) or truth (*veritas*) of Christ—the reality of the God who is love. So, meditation is the process of picturing the crucifixion (or some other biblical event) in our minds. Contemplation takes the image and distills from it the truth or reality that it contains.

The truth or reality of Scripture is beyond words. But William never suggests that in contemplation, we leave Christ behind. When we see the face of the ultimate Good in contemplation, it is still the face of Christ—though contemplation takes us from his humanity to his divinity. Much of Meditation 10 is written in the form of a prayer addressed to Christ, and in the conclusion, William speaks to him about face-to-face union with him in contemplation: "This, Lord, is your face towards us and our face towards you." At the very end, however, the abbot turns from Christ to his reader: "Go, man, whoever you are who find this treasure hidden in the field of your own heart [cf. Matt 13:44]! Sell all that you have, sell yourself as a slave forever, that you may gain this treasure for your own! For then you will be blest and all will be well with you. Christ in your conscience is the treasure that you will possess." For William, Christ is the treasure (the *res*) that we dig up in the field of our heart. Contemplation—though its joy is ineffable—means union with God's eternal love for us in Christ.

CONCLUSION

LECTIO DIVINA CAREFULLY navigates between two extremes—the gnostic impulse and the materialist impulse. The gnostic impulse would have us bypass the messiness of the particularity of the cross and of biblical words. If union with the One is our aim, why bother with reading of and meditation on particular biblical texts? Why not immediately turn inward, there to find the eternal wellspring of eternal being? This gnostic impulse is a tempting one, which lures us with the prospect of attaining to universal truth or reality without having to bother with particular rites, texts, practices, or commitments. However, Christians simply cannot bypass the *sacramenta* in trying to reach for their reality. At the heart of divine self-revelation stands the obstinate reality of the cross.

The materialist impulse, meanwhile, reduces particular objects and events to what we can observe with the senses. Contemplation, from this perspective, would seem to be an erroneous flight from the down-to-earth realities that we can touch and see. When materialism drapes itself in Christian garb, it is often historical study of Scripture—viewed as something altogether different from traditional *lectio* and *meditatio*—that takes center stage. The materialist impulse treats Scripture merely as an object of empirical analysis. But we dare not stare ourselves blind looking for the history *behind* the words, for it is the reality *in* the words that we are meant to adore and worship.

The two approaches may seem each other's opposites. The gnostic impulse aims to secure the reality without bothering with the *sacramentum*; the materialist impulse idolizes the *sacramentum* without recognizing that it contains a deeper reality. But the similarity of the two approaches is greater than the dissimilarity. Both the gnostic and the materialist impulse fail to acknowledge that sensible objects have their deepest reality from God rather than from themselves. In terms of biblical revelation, the flesh on the cross and the words on the page are sacraments. And as sacraments they call us beyond reading and meditation to contemplation of God himself. Lectio divina is a sacramental discipline. It aims to take us more deeply into the life of God.

Neither the gnostic nor the materialist impulse truly values created things and historical events. In the case of the gnostic impulse, this is rather obvious, and generally not a matter of dispute: second-century gnostics treated creation as a fall from the eternal, divine fullness (*plērōma*), and this identification of creation as evil made gnostics treat salvation as an escape from everything bodily and sensible. Saint Irenaeus devoted his five books *Against Heresies* to exposing and defeating this gnostic impulse, rightly insisting on the goodness of God's creation.

It is sometimes difficult for us to recognize that a similar anti-creational logic stamps the materialist impulse. This is because our cultural ethos tends to be materialist and because materialism—at least in its most consistent form—claims that matter is the source of whatever exists. How could materialism *not* value this-worldly, sensible realities? The point is quite straightforward: if creation is not suffused with and upheld by a reality greater than itself, then it has no inherent purpose or significance. In that case, the only significance and meaning it has is what I (or we together) assign to it. As a result, meaning and purpose are mere constructs. In practice, it becomes tempting (often irresistible) to use sensible objects—including human beings—as means that serve our self-constructed ends.

The approach taken by Aelred of Rievaulx and William of Saint-Thierry offers a different way. It has some agreement with both the gnostic and the materialist impulse. It agrees with the former that this-worldly realities are not ultimate and that sensible realities and history are marred by sin. It agrees with the latter that created objects are good and that historical study is valuable. This way, however, is not the result of borrowing the best elements from these two approaches. Rather, the sacramental vision of Aelred, William, and others offers a distinct, third way.

In lectio divina, we unapologetically take our stance with Mary, pierced or transfixed at the foot of the cross. Mary experienced there the pain of the sword piercing her heart, as she identified with her son being pierced by nails and spear. Lectio divina deliberately turns to the sacrament of the cross, for it is in the suffering of Christ that we witness most profoundly the love of God. Of course, lectio divina does not focus only on the cross. Along with the Gospels, the Psalms and the Song of Songs have also served as trusted sources for lectio divina. They all are sacraments that convey the reality of the love of God. Lectio divina is a sacramental practice that—in reading, meditation, and prayer—makes us linger with the flesh of Christ and the words on the page.

Nor does the final stage of contemplation crush these sacraments. Rather, as we have seen, contemplation transfigures earthly sacraments—the cross, human words—into divine truth. Contemplation allows us to clearly see the divine reality that always already shimmers within creation. It is because we ourselves are transfigured in the process of lectio divina—from glory to glory (see 2 Cor 3:18)—that we can see the transfigured Lord in all his glory and that we recognize the divinity of the Word. In contemplation we no longer simply read the words of Scripture; instead, we read the face of God in the eternal Word. In contemplation, it is no longer the human Jesus whose piercing pains our hearts; instead, the Spirit raptures us into Love Itself, the love with which the Father eternally begets his Son.

In short, when lectio divina trans*fixes* us, it also trans*figures* us. Nothing remains the same, for when we ourselves are transfigured, we recognize sacraments for what they really are—manifestations of the eternal love of God.

II

Acrophobia

SPIRITUAL ACROPHOBIA

I AM SCARED OF heights. I have a tall ladder in my garage, but I rarely take it out. I should clean the gutters at least once a year, but after climbing the first four or five rungs of the ladder, my heart begins to pound and my body starts to sweat, as panic crawls into my skin and rattles my bones. I invariably end up sheepishly admitting to my wife that I just cannot do it. Experts call it *acrophobia*—the Greek *akron* meaning "height" or "summit"; hence, fear of heights. Thankfully, my son laughs at my fears and cheerfully does the job for me. Acrophobia is entirely foreign to him.

Physical acrophobia may be irrational, but it is hardly a serious disorder: as long as my son is willing to clean the gutters, I'm alright. Spiritual acrophobia is an altogether different matter. It too is irrational, but unlike physical acrophobia, it is deadly. Much Christian spirituality today is afraid of ladders.

Here's why the issue is pertinent to lectio divina: there's no such thing as divine reading without ladders. In this chapter, my aim is to provide a basic introduction to the practice of lectio divina. For this purpose, we will turn to a little treatise on the topic, written by the Carthusian prior Guigo II (†1188), titled *The Ladder of Monks* (*Scala Claustralium* in Latin). It is an accessible little book, and the title makes clear that for Guigo, divine reading is about going up a ladder.

Guigo treats the four steps of lectio divina as four rungs on a ladder. He introduces the topic of divine reading this way:

> One day when I was busy working with my hands I began to think about our spiritual work, and all at once four stages in spiritual exercise came into my mind: reading, meditation, prayer and contemplation. These make a ladder for monks (*Scala Claustralium*) by which they are lifted up from earth to heaven. It has few rungs (*gradibus*), yet its length is immense and wonderful, for its lower end rests upon the earth, but its top pierces the clouds and touches heavenly secrets.

If the four steps of lectio divina are a ladder that takes us up to heaven, the negative implication is clear: Guigo would treat today's rampant acrophobia as a serious impediment to divine reading. Conversely, without meditative reading we find it more difficult to reach our heavenly goal.

Guigo was hardly alone in linking lectio divina with ladders. Ladders are everywhere among the spiritual writers in Christian tradition. Saint John Chrysostom directs us in one of his homilies on John's Gospel: "Mounting step by step, let us reach heaven by a Jacob's ladder. I say this for it seems to me that by that well-known vision Jacob's ladder was a figure of this, namely, the ascent through virtue, little by little, by which it is possible to ascend from earth to heaven, not by steps apparent to the senses, but by the emending and correcting of one's habits." Saint Augustine, in his *Confessions*, treats the Psalms of Ascent as a ladder on which we go up to God's temple in Jerusalem. Saint Benedict tells the monks in his Rule to "set up that ladder on which Jacob in a dream saw angels descending and ascending." Bernard of Clairvaux's *The Steps of Humility and Pride* outlines the spiritual life as a ladder with twelve rungs on which one can either go up or down. And when Hugh of Saint Victor in his *Mystical Ark* envisions the ark's internal structure, he pictures it as crammed with ladders: "Twelve ladders ascend from the four corners of the Ark: three from each corner, four in each room, different ones in different corners. And each ladder has ten steps, which is 120 steps altogether, 60 and 60." Hugh's ladders allow us to climb by means of the virtues toward perfection. Even where the ladder imagery is not explicitly invoked, the idea of going up toward perfection in steps or stages is ubiquitous in patristic and medieval literature.

LADDERS OF MORALIST ASCENT?

OF COURSE, WE often rationalize our angst about spiritual ladders. Two scruples, in particular, stand out: the dangers of moralism and elitism. To address these concerns, let's take a look at the famous twelfth-century icon *The Ladder of Divine Ascent* in figure 2.1.

The icon, which is kept at Saint Catherine's monastery at Mount Sinai, depicts the Christian life as an ascent up the ladder. As contemporary Christians, we may be intrigued—perhaps even awed—by the otherworldly austerity of the imagery, but we tend to be repulsed by the moralism that the icon seems to convey. Aren't we climbing up by our own strength, while heavenly angels (top left) and earthly believers (bottom right) look on as we do battle with demonic forces? Perhaps

Figure 2.1: *The Ladder of Divine Ascent*

we're relieved at Christ welcoming us at the top, but doesn't his presence there underscore that it is only at the end of the Christian life, not at the beginning, that we experience union with Christ?

Climbing up the ladder also seems inescapably to involve a kind of elitism and hubris, whether subtle or blatant. Certainly, the icon does not envisage an egalitarian or universalist nirvana. Some of the monks climbing the ladder are stronger than others. Demons manage to pick off and drag away those who give in to the passions or evil thoughts (*logismoi*). Only some, therefore, reach Christ, who welcomes them, one by one, into Paradise itself. Perhaps unsurprisingly, John Climacus ("The Holy John of the Ladder," it says above his head) is depicted at the top: the seventh-century saint had spent forty years in the Sinai desert before taking up the leadership of Saint Catherine's monastery. It is his book, *The Ladder of Divine Ascent*, that became the inspiration of the later icon. So, we are probably right to think that it is he who receives from Jesus the crown of victory as he steps off the ladder into heaven. His name seems fitting: the Greek word *klimax* means "ladder," and Saint John has made it to the top. Immediately following John, "the Holy Antonios, Archbishop" is depicted in white. Quite possibly, he was the monastery's abbot at the time when the icon was written. John and Antonios rank above the other monks, who in turn do much better than the ones who altogether fail to make it into the welcoming arms of Jesus. The elitism is unmistakable, or so we may be led to think.

The fear of moralism and elitism that feeds today's spiritual acrophobia is not altogether irrational. Fear of -isms is perfectly rational. If moralism means that we tick off boxes of rules without the help of God, angels, or church, we should avoid it altogether. And if elitism means that we are proud of having ticked off these moral boxes, we simply put on display our own distance from God.

No doubt John Climacus believed that the Christian life truly matters. He depicts a vicious spiritual battle, and the moral life is central to it. We have choices to make, choices that determine whether we will be successful in our ascent up the ladder. John's spirituality is synergistic in character: we must cooperate with the grace that God gives if we are to make it to heaven. Nonetheless, his spirituality is hardly bereft of Christology. The thirty chapters of his book—corresponding to the thirty rungs of the ladder that we can count in the icon—are patterned on the thirty years of the life of Christ before he was baptized; Christ not only welcomes us into heaven, but he also lays out the very ladder that takes us to him. When John describes the virtuous life that takes us to heaven, he treats these virtues not only as an imitation of Christ but also as a participation in him. In other words, small-*v* human virtues share in capital-*V* divine Virtue. The Orthodox scholar Dimitrije Bogdanović helpfully puts it this way: "For Climacus the virtues are not so much qualities of man as qualities of God; they are divine attributes." For Climacus, whatever progress we make is always progress *in Christ*. The Christ that we meet at the end is the very same one who sustained us throughout the journey.

No matter how strongly Climacus may want to defend free will, he also recognizes the need for divine grace. When he arrives at step seven, John speaks powerfully about the "gift of tears"—a mourning over sin. We don't conjure up such tears; they are a gift from God: "When the soul grows tearful, weeps, and is filled with tenderness, and all this without having striven for it, then let us run, for the Lord has arrived uninvited and is holding out to us the sponge of loving sorrow, the cool waters of blessed sadness with which to wipe away the record of our sins." Tears of repentance are an uninvited, gracious gift from God.

Likewise, Climacus warns against pride in his discussion of chastity—"a name common to all virtues"—in step fifteen. He cautions, "Anyone trained in chastity should give himself no credit for any achievements, for a man cannot conquer what he actually is. When nature is overcome, it should be admitted that this is due to Him Who is above nature, since it cannot be denied that the weaker always yields to the stronger." And in step twenty-three, John again cautions against the ever-present danger of pride: "It is sheer lunacy to imagine that one has deserved the gifts of God. You may be proud only of the achievements you had before the time of your birth. But anything after that, indeed the birth itself, is a gift from God. You may claim only those virtues in you that are there independently of your mind, for your mind was bestowed on you by God." Synergy does not preclude divine grace; nor does it give permission to boast.

We can also note that in the icon, the angels above are not uninterested spectators. John Climacus insists, "We have Almighty God, the angels, and the saints to help us toward virtue." He maintains that our prayers depend on angelic mediation: "Our prayer has neither the power of access nor the wings of purity to reach the Lord, unless our angels draw near to us and take it and bring it to the Lord." And repeatedly, John encourages his monks with talk about their "guardian angel." The spiritual struggle is one in which angels are intimately involved. Their stern and watchful eyes depicted in the icon penetrate the hearts and minds of the monks as they climb the ladder.

Nor does the monastic community in the icon's bottom right look on indifferently. Their uplifted hands signal prayerful involvement.

The theme of brotherly love and mutual care permeates *The Ladder of Divine Ascent*. John highlights the sweetness of communal monastic life: "An unbreakable bond of love joined these men together." He suggests that the solitary, anchoritic life should not be lightly undertaken. Especially at the outset, we need the structures of communal or cenobitic life: "It is not safe for an untried soldier to leave the ranks and take up single combat. Equally, it is dangerous for a monk to undertake the solitary life before he has had plenty of experience and practice in the battle with the passions of the soul." What is more, we need a spiritual guide, someone who, like "some Moses," helps us escape from Egypt and serves as our "intermediary with God." Much like angels, fellow monks are indispensable for spiritual progress.

John's spirituality is dependent on Christ, on direct divine intervention, and on angelic as well as communal assistance. His spirituality is hardly moralistic. For John, humans are not autonomous; they do not by themselves determine their outcome in a world of pure nature. In John's universe, God himself, angelic forces, and human beings all join in the fight for salvation. Human freedom does not preclude God—or the supernatural more broadly—from acting and intervening in temporal affairs.

LADDERS OF HUMILITY

NOR IS JOHN'S spirituality elitist—if by that we mean a kind of snobbery that considers a small group of insiders as deserving of special status or treatment. Of course, the icon depicts John Climacus and Holy Antonios as closer to Jesus than others. But the point is not to look down on those who haven't made it to elite status. Precisely the opposite: John's treatise aims to encourage all of his monks to climb the ladder and so to advance in excellence or virtue. (The Greek word *aretē* means both "excellence" and "virtue.") John's universe may well be hierarchical in character. But the ranking of this hierarchy is fluid: by living a life of excellence, we move up the ladder and so attain to our heavenly end.

Elitism—and the pride that invariably accompanies it—is by no means an imaginary danger. But the same monks who talk about ladders also warn against elitist pride. Saint Benedict of Nursia paradoxically links humility and ascent in chapter 7 of his sixth-century Rule. He derives the paradox from two biblical passages: Luke 14:11 ("Every one that exalteth himself shall be humbled: and he that humbleth himself shall be exalted") and Psalm 131:1–2 ("Lord, my heart is not exalted: nor are my eyes lofty. Neither have I walked in great matters, nor in wonderful things above me. If I was not humbly minded, but exalted my soul: As a child that is weaned is towards his mother, so reward in my soul"). Benedict takes these biblical passages as teaching that we ascend to heavenly exaltation through the humility of the present life. Reflecting next on the angels descending and ascending on Jacob's ladder (Gen 28:12), Benedict comments that "we descend by self-exaltation and ascend by humility. Now the ladder erected is our life on earth, and if we humble our hearts the Lord will raise it to heaven." Paradoxically, self-exaltation makes us go down the ladder, while humility makes us go up. It's a paradox that Benedict keeps in mind throughout his Rule.

William of Saint-Thierry, writing his *Golden Epistle* (ca. 1144–1145) to the Carthusian monks of Mont Dieu in the Ardennes of northern France, deeply admired their semi-eremitic (or desert) lifestyle, with monks living in solitary cells around a cloister, while joining together for the major hours and for meals. William was convinced that this solitary life was grounded in Scripture—considering the examples of Elijah, Elisha, John the Baptist, and even the Lord himself. William, therefore, looked to the Egyptian desert fathers as great examples for Western monastics, and he tried assisting them in making the transition from Animal Man, via Rational Man, to Spiritual Man.

But William also recognized the danger of pride accompanying the strict asceticism demanded for this journey into perfection. And so, the Cistercian abbot warns the monks of Mont Dieu that "exalted thoughts are death," and he tells them to treat their monastic calling as a sign of spiritual weakness rather than strength: "Think of yourselves ... as wild beasts shut up in cages, as animals that could not be tamed in any other way." William enjoins the monks to take Paul's words in 1 Timothy 1:15 to heart: "Christ Jesus came into the world to save sinners, of whom I am the chief." Rubbing it in, he writes,

> I would not then have you think that the common light of day shines nowhere but in your cell, that the skies are not clear except above you, that God's grace is at work only in your conscience. Does God belong to solitaries alone? Rather he belongs to all men. For God takes pity on all men and does not hate any of those whom he made. I would prefer you to think that the weather is fine everywhere except with you, and to think worse of yourself than of anyone else.

The contemplation of the Spiritual Man is antithetical to all boasting, according to the Cistercian spiritual master. Only with a pure heart can one see the face of God. William concludes his treatise, therefore, with yet another warning that his readers should abase themselves and should "become of no worth" in their own eyes as they contemplate God. The climactic aim of *visio Dei* (vision of God) can be reached only with a humble heart.

GUIGO'S FOUR STEPS

IT'S TIME TO dust off the ladder and put it back to use, for spiritual acrophobia is no less irrational than physical acrophobia. Guigo II, the twelfth-century prior of the Grande Chartreuse in the French Alps (540 miles south of the Mont Dieu charterhouse) adopted the ladder imagery to illuminate the process of lectio divina. He was convinced that it is through personal, experiential reading of Scripture that we climb the ladder. The second column of the chart of figure 2.2 makes clear that his manual, *The Ladder of Monks*, closely ties the four rungs of the ladder (*lectio, meditatio, oratio, contemplatio*) to the traditional four levels of biblical meaning (literal, allegorical, tropological, and anagogical). This means that for Guigo, Scripture—or, rather, a proper engagement with Scripture—forms the ladder that takes us to God himself.

Let's look in some detail at the chart of Guigo's ladder. On the first rung (*lectio* or reading), beginners engage in the "careful study (*inspectio*) of Scripture." The Carthusian prior treats this rather straightforwardly as reading and trying to understand the outward words of Scripture. Here we explore the text to discover its significance. The process is like eating a grape: beginners first bite its outside skin in reading before they can enjoy the flesh of the grape. Or, we could also say that the reader is simply putting the food in his mouth. The external words or outward senses are all that matters at this point. In short, the basic concern is the literal or historical meaning of the text.

Pierced by Love

RUNGS	LEVEL OF MEANING	FOOD METAPHORS
Lectio	Literal meaning Careful study of Scripture	Seeks Puts food in the mouth Rind
Meditatio	Allegorical meaning Rational search for hidden truth	Perceives Chews and breaks food Smells Digs (for treasure)
Oratio	Tropological meaning Devoted turning to God	Asks Extracts food's flavor
Contemplatio	Anagogical meaning The mind lifted up beyond itself to God	Tastes Sweetness itself Consolation

Figure 2.2: *Guigo II's Ladder of Monks*

CHARACTERISTICS	SPIRITUAL MATURITY	DIVINE ASSISTANCE
Hearing the outward words read Outward senses	Beginners	Natural "The good and the wicked alike can read and meditate."
Goes to the heart Inward understanding	Proficients	
Longing for experiential meaning Sobbings and tears	Devotees	Supernatural "We can do nothing without Him. It is He who achieves our works in us, and yet not entirely without us."
Outstrips every faculty Experience Transfiguration Merely temporary Vision of God	Blessed	

On the second rung (*meditatio*), the reader uses reason to find the hidden truth of the biblical passage. Having made some progress, he is now among the proficients. The reader chews and breaks the food of Scripture and smells it. Or, changing metaphors, we could say the reader digs in the Scriptures for the hidden treasure (cf. Matt 13:44). Guigo does not use the term, but he seems to have in mind the allegorical level of meaning. This deeper level becomes clear to us only through an inward understanding, which reaches the heart. He suggests, however, that this inward grasp of allegory is not yet anything supernatural or spiritual. The last column makes clear that perceiving allegorical truth is an ordinary, rational matter: "The good and the wicked alike can read and meditate."

The next two levels, however, are different. In *oratio* (prayer), God himself confronts us through the Scriptures with our lives. Guigo links prayer, therefore, with the tropological or moral meaning of the text. Prayer, he explains, is "the heart's devoted turning to God to drive away evil and obtain what is good." At this point, the hidden meaning is no longer just a matter of rational knowledge. With deep desire, the devotee now longs to see this hidden or experiential meaning. He cries out to God with sobbings and tears as he reflects on the shortcomings in his life. The steps of reading and meditation have prepared the reader for God's grace, but the experiential desire expressed in prayer is a supernatural gift from God: "We can do nothing without Him. It is He who achieves our works in us." At the same time, with an appeal to 1 Corinthians 3:9 ("we are God's coadjutors"), Guigo immediately adds the qualifier, "and yet not entirely without us." Guigo's synergism is similar to that of John Climacus. We prepare for supernatural grace through reading and meditation, but God himself gives us this grace when, through prayer, we experience a moral turnaround.

The final rung, that of *contemplatio*, is an anticipation of the eschatological face-to-face vision of God. As Guigo puts it, here "the mind is in some sort lifted up to God and held above itself, so that it tastes the joys of everlasting sweetness." From the moment the monk started reading, he had embarked on a process of ascent or anagogy (leading up), for each of the four steps is a rung on the ladder. But the last rung, that of contemplation, is uniquely linked to anagogy, because at this point the reader joins the blessed departed, arriving at the heavenly aim of the ascent. The reader now, finally, tastes the food or the sweetness itself, as he enjoys the consolation of seeing God. Along with Peter, James, and John, he experiences the transfiguration as he sees Christ in his glory. This experience of spiritual vision—though typically of brief duration— "outstrips every faculty," claims Guigo. This is the aim of the longing and desire that animated the entire process.

The heart's longing for an experience of spiritual vision is key. Scripture as such does not take us to God. Purity of heart does, and Scripture's aim is to purify the heart. Only the pure in heart can see God (Matt 5:8). Jesus's beatitude is the central text that Guigo uses to articulate the process of lectio divina. For Guigo, the purpose of Scripture is to purify our hearts so that we may be equipped to see God. We reach the final rung of the ladder (*contemplatio*) only if we are purified through our engagement with Scripture.

Guigo, therefore, takes his readers to the sixth beatitude for an exercise in lectio divina. This text—"Blessed are the clean of heart: they shall see God"—is like a grape filled with many flavors. We first hear these words in *lectio*. Then, in *meditatio*, we turn to numerous other Scripture passages that echo both this requirement of purity and the reward of God's blessing. In this way, we gain a sense of Scripture's multiple flavors.

In prayer (*oratio*), the heart humbles itself and expresses its longing for God—making use of the very language of Scripture, also in prayer. The Lord then graciously stops us in the middle of our prayer, and, like the father of the prodigal son, takes us to the final step of *contemplatio*. He "runs to meet" the soul "in all haste" (cf. Luke 15:20). He graciously "restores the weary soul, He slakes its thirst, He feeds its hunger, He makes the soul forget all earthly things: by making it die to itself He gives it new life in a wonderful way, and by making it drunk He brings it back to its true senses." Guigo describes the reality of seeing God by drawing the reader imaginatively into the parable of the prodigal son: pure in heart, the son sees his father face-to-face.

This lectio divina passage is well chosen. After all, Jesus's words point explicitly to the vision of God, which Guigo believed to be the aim of divine reading. Any other biblical passage can lead to divine contemplation, but not every other passage actually *mentions* this contemplation. By turning to Matthew 5:8, therefore, Guigo accomplishes two things. First, as we just saw, he engages this beatitude to show his readers how the four steps might function if we were to take this verse as our focus text. Second, Guigo also appears to suggest that Jesus's saying itself has lectio divina (or, at least, the steps of *oratio* and *contemplatio*) as its subject matter: it speaks of the transformation and purity that come to us in prayer and of the contemplation that results. In short, Guigo's book is an exercise in lectio divina on a text that already has lectio divina as its topic.

CONCLUSION

GUIGO'S *LADDER OF MONKS* may seem a bit static or rigid, and the four rungs may seem a little too neat and orderly. Is it true, for instance, that only beginners read? Does one ever move beyond the steps of reading and meditating? Do beginners never pray? Is it not true, rather, that all of us, regardless of spiritual maturity, keep going up and down the ladder? Similarly, the tidy division of natural and supernatural activities might make us uneasy. Is it possible to separate natural abilities from supernatural gifts as sharply as Guigo does? And isn't it a little odd for Guigo to classify meditation (along with allegorical meaning) as a natural activity that "the good and the wicked alike" can engage in? After all, many other patristic and medieval authors spoke of allegory as the "spiritual" sense of Scripture in part because they were convinced that only through the gifting of the Spirit could one see the christological or allegorical significance of the biblical text.

I have some sympathy for these objections. Guigo does, perhaps, give the impression of four separate rungs, especially when he states that "one precedes another, not only in the order of time but of causality," and when he links each step with a particular level of spiritual maturity. And we certainly should handle the distinction between natural and supernatural activities with great care. Reading and meditating always already aim at the goal of contemplation—or, at least, they should. The Spirit is at work from the start, and the entire process of lectio divina is marked by his loving guidance of the soul. Conversely, prayer and contemplation do not sideline or destroy the natural faculties: grace perfects or transfigures our natural gifts.

At the same time, we do well to cut the Carthusian monk some slack. Dividing the steps into a chart, as I have done, perhaps makes the four steps look tidier than they appear in the actual *Ladder of Monks*. We also should keep in mind that his treatise, written to his "dear brother Gervase," is a teaching manual. Every good teacher knows that tidy divisions are useful both for the sake of clarity and to impress the contents on students' minds. Most importantly, though, while Guigo does speak of four distinct steps on the ladder and does tie each one to a distinct maturity level, he also insists that the four steps are intertwined. He tells us it's no use taking only the first steps if we don't arrive at the last, and we won't get to the last if we refuse to spend time on the first. For my part, I think of Guigo as a spiritual master, patiently and deliberately offering healing for self-inflicted acrophobia.

III

Paying Attention

JACK BOUGHTON'S ACEDIA

AS A KID, Jack Boughton was different from his seven siblings. Incapable of paying attention for long, he never relaxed. New distractions, invariably troublesome ones, proved irresistible. He would escape family festivities, skip out of church, blow up mailboxes, spend long nights in the bar, and engage in petty theft. His father's supply of generosity seemed endless, though Jack severely tested the old man's ability to forgive after getting a girl pregnant. At that point Robert, a Presbyterian pastor in Gilead, Iowa, "had come to the last inch of his power to forgive, and there was Jack, still far beyond his reach." Jack, always a stranger to stability and never able to accept forgiveness extended to him, withdrew and eventually left the family home.

Marilynne Robinson's 2008 novel *Home* picks up at the point where Jack, after a twenty-year absence, returns in 1956 to the parsonage where his sister Glory cares for their elderly father. Jack constantly apologizes for being in the way. "His father said, 'No need to apologize, Jack! Here you've only been home a few hours and I have you apologizing to me!'" But Jack cannot escape the sense of not belonging. He knows he has not changed over the years. He is an alcoholic, and despite his best intentions, he keeps inflicting hurt on the old Boughton and on his sister. Jack remains a stranger in the home and the town where he grew up; he resigns himself to living without hope. As the old Reverend Boughton puts it, "I always felt it was sadness I was dealing with, a sort of heavyheartedness." Jack, we might say, is the ultimate reprobate, destined to wander outside the realm of faith.

Perhaps the most profound scene in the book is when, over dinner, Jack awkwardly confronts his father's old friend, the neighboring Congregationalist pastor John Ames, about the doctrine of predestination. Jack proves himself to be both very well-versed biblically and razor-sharp intellectually. The conversation moves from the death of the son born from David's sin with Bathsheba (2 Sam 12) to God's promise not to punish the son for the iniquity of the father (Ezek 18) to Jesus's insistence that neither the man born blind nor his parents had sinned (John 9). Brutally honest, Jack admits that he is thinking about himself: "I've wondered from time to time if I might not be an instance of predestination." Reverend Ames's wife Lila reaches out to Jack: "A person can change. Everything can change." But Jack never really does. When Glory invites the siblings to come home in anticipation of their father's death, Jack leaves home, unable to face his siblings, untransformed by the love and forgiveness of his father and his sister.

Robinson doesn't spell it out, but Jack suffers from the vice of acedia. The term is often translated as "sloth," "apathy," "sadness," or "despair." Each of these translations is pretty good, though none fully captures it. The term's etymology points to an absence of care or concern (*kēdeia*). When we cave in to the temptation of acedia, we give up on life. Looking at our past, we cannot face the future. Our memories render us incapable of hope. Acedia arises, therefore, from an inability to forgive ourselves. Or, put more sharply, acedia stems from doubting *God's* ability or willingness to forgive us. Joseph Ratzinger, therefore, links acedia with despair: "In the Christian system of virtues, despair, that is to say, the radical antithesis of faith and hope, is labelled as the sin against the Holy Spirit because it excludes the latter's power to heal and to forgive and thereby rejects salvation." The despair that expresses itself in acedia, according to Ratzinger, is the ultimate sin. Why? Because it succumbs to the darkness of a life without the love of God.

The terms *sadness* and *sloth* highlight two key elements of acedia. Jack Boughton has both. The first is the one that Jack's father Robert observes in him; the second is evident in Jack's inability to hold down a job. Together, Jack's sadness and sloth make clear that he has resigned himself to his apostate state. Jean-Charles Nault, in his book *The Noonday Devil*, perceptively points out that Saint Thomas Aquinas alludes to these same two features when he defines acedia. The Angelic Doctor describes it as "sadness about spiritual good" (*tristitia de bono divino*) and "disgust with activity" (*taedium operandi*). The sadness mentioned both by Aquinas and Jack's father sins against the joy that springs from charity: whereas charity leads to joy, hatred results in sadness—in particular, sadness with respect to the enjoyment of God. The disgust that Jack experiences and Aquinas describes prevents one from reaching the happiness of his final end. Nault explains that it is "a break in the impetus, a paralysis, a halt that cuts us off from God." Acedia, therefore, is a general state of boredom with life.

GOING HOME BY STAYING HOME

THIS IS A chapter on reading (*lectio*), the first of four steps. By attending to the words that we read, we aim to eradicate acedia. I hope to show how attention—the practice of carefully attending to the biblical text—is a means of battling the demon of acedia. Proper attention takes us out of the boredom of a purely temporal, horizontal, this-worldly existence. Proper attention gives us the joy of a vertical orientation toward the eternity of God. Saint Augustine admonishes himself in book 11 of the *Confessions* to turn his attention to God in reading the Scriptures: "Press on, my mind, and pay strong attention (*adtende*). 'God is our help, he has made us and not we ourselves' (Ps. 62:8; 100:3). Pay attention (*adtende*) where the truth begins to dawn." It is Augustine's hopeful resolution that animates this chapter. Why? Because reading the Scriptures contemplatively aims for the truth of God himself. We attend to God when we read, in the hope of overcoming time-induced ennui and lethargy.

Lectio divina, therefore, is grounded in the conviction that words on the page do not imprison us. Let me explain what I mean by drawing on Jean-Charles Nault's distinction between passing through (*passage*) and passing beyond (*dépassement*). When we reduce biblical reading to a linear textual movement, we merely pass through. We may gain some historical or even theological know-how on the journey, but our exercise remains at the level of a purely horizontal passing through. We're always on the move, from word to word, line to line, paragraph to paragraph. Passing through means we never stop to truly pay attention. Aimlessly moving along, we never find a home. We suffer Jack Boughton's acedia. By contrast, when we carefully attend to the biblical text, we recognize that it is capable of taking us beyond itself to God. As I hope to show, when we arrive at God's eternal now, we come to the true source and reality of every temporal event. By passing beyond to God, rather than merely passing through, we take the text as the place where a vertical journey is meant to begin, in hopes of entering into the life of God himself.

It is acedia, explains Nault, that marks out *passage* as distinct from *dépassement*. Acedia, he explains, "is the temptation to reject *passing beyond* and to stick with *passing through*, thus losing sight of the dynamic of desire, which is the dynamic of love." Love takes us from time to eternity. Chiara Bertoglio puts it this way: "Love bridges the chasm between time and eternity, because Love is the matter of which God Himself is made, and it is an experience which permeates every moment of our life." Reading with loving attention takes up the disparate and temporally scattered elements of the story and discerns their point of unity in the God of love. Through reading with the dynamic of love, therefore, we reach God as the telos or aim of our reading and thereby overcome acedia's apathy. It is passing beyond (*dépassement*) that takes us home.

The title of Robinson's novel points to Jack's inability to stay at home. Jack is always on the go, fleeing from one situation to another, incapable of basking in the peace and joy of his home. The spiritual writings of the Benedictine tradition are replete with warnings not to flee one's cell but rather to look for heaven within the confines of the cell. The *Golden Epistle* of William of Saint-Thierry issues this counsel:

> As your vocation demands, dwelling in heaven rather than in cells, you have shut out the world, whole and entire, from yourselves and shut up yourselves, whole and entire, with God. For

the cell (*cella*) and heaven (*celum*) are akin to one another: the resemblance between the words *celum* and *cella* is borne out by the devotion they both involve. For both *celum* and *cella* appear to be derived from *celare*, to hide, and the same thing is hidden in cells as in heaven, the same occupation characterizes both the one and the other. What is this? Leisure devoted to God, the enjoyment of God.

William's etymology may be off, but the point he makes is powerful: the cell (*cela*) can become heaven (*celum*) when the monk takes seriously that his cell is a place of leisure and enjoyment of God. William goes so far as to insist that the cell excels eucharistic celebration: the cell can turn into heaven at any time and continuously offers the monk the reality (*res*) of Christ's body and blood.

William's teaching has a long pedigree. Itchiness to leave one's cell served as a telltale sign of acedia from the fourth century on. Evagrius of Pontus, warning against the demon of acedia, explains that this demon "compels the monk to look constantly towards the windows, to jump out of the cell." The desert father Arsenius advises one of the brothers not to listen to the thoughts of the devil. Instead, "Go: eat, drink and sleep, only do not leave your cell, aware that remaining patiently in one's cell is what brings a monk into line." John Cassian depicts a monk suffering from acedia as fancying "that he will never be well while he stays in that place, unless he leaves his cell (in which he is sure to die if he stops in it any longer)." The entire tradition recognized that abandoning one's cell was identical to abandoning one's spiritual goal.

The vice of acedia is not a uniquely monastic trait. Nault, who is abbot of the Benedictine Abbey of Saint-Wandrille in France, makes clear that acedia is the "uprooting of man from his proper place; in a word, it is man's departure from his dwelling." Marilynne Robinson's character Jack, therefore, suffers from the same malady that has threatened monastics through the centuries. Indeed, the threat has likely become more rather than less disturbing with the onset of modernity. Sadness (*tristitia*) and disgust (*taedium*) have increased: we feel sadness because we no longer take God as our final end, and we experience disgust and become slothful because this loss of purpose renders our activities meaningless.

Nault explains that acedia has a spatial as well as a temporal dimension. Both have to do with an irrepressible penchant for change. We witness the spatial dimension in the multiple and rapid succession of changes in location, occupation, spouse, and church. The loss of continuity in these areas betrays personal as well as cultural instability and loss of identity, fueled by incessant, vapid social networking and web surfing. We suffer the temporal dimension when, over time, we get bored with God's good gifts. Acedia, explains Evagrius, is a "noonday devil." The never-ending heat of the noonday becomes oppressive and seems to last forever. As a result, we settle for mediocrity and turn to distractions of novelty, gossip, curiosity, bodily agitation, and activism.

The Christian life can flourish only through acedia's mirror opposite—namely, stability (*stabilitas*). It is by *staying* home that we *go* home to God, because stability is a precondition for paying attention. Not surprisingly, then, stability serves as a key virtue in Saint Benedict's Rule. Benedict describes four kinds of monks: cenobites (living in community), anchorites (solitary hermits), sarabaites (without a superior or a rule), and gyrovagues (literally "circle wanderers"). It is the last group that interests us here. Saint Benedict's description of "circle wanderers" is like a sketch of modern rootlessness. They "spend their entire lives drifting from region to region, staying as guests for three or four days in different monasteries. Always on the move, they never settle down, and are slaves to their own wills and gross appetites."

To counter the monks' wanderlust, Benedict's Rule would accept a postulant into the community only after he has kept knocking at the door for four or five days, has stayed in the guest room for some time, and has proved his willingness to learn the Scriptures, as well as to eat and sleep in the novice quarters. Only once the novice has clearly accepted the hardships of the monastic life and has repeatedly committed himself to "perseverance in his stability"—first after a two-month period, then after a six-month period, and finally after another four-month period—is he welcomed into the monastery.

At that point, the novice makes his solemn monastic vows, promising "stability, fidelity to monastic life, and obedience." These three vows—stability (*stabilitas*), fidelity (*conversatio*), and obedience (*oboedientia*)—are the foundation of Benedictine spirituality. But they are not just monastic vows. They have broader applicability, offering basic wisdom for a fruitful Christian life. Stability is a precondition for spiritual healing. William of Saint-Thierry explains to his novices that the cell is their infirmary and obedience the treatment that offers healing. He warns them that spatial stability is essential: "To try to escape ill-health of the soul by moving from place to place is like fleeing from one's own shadow. Such a man as he flees from himself carries himself with him. He changes his place, but not his soul." William knows that far too often we move from place to place trying to escape from ourselves. Our flight mechanism makes it impossible to properly fix the soul.

The reading program of lectio divina flounders without stability. Lectio divina is a medicinal practice. The healing requires patient focus and aims at countering the numerous tempting distractions that cause the sickness of acedia. Lectio divina, therefore, is a therapeutic endeavor that prevents or heals the sickness of a wandering mind, teaching it instead to focus on God. Meditative reading does not just teach us the contents of the biblical text (though of course it does that too). It aims at moral change, a change from sadness and disgust to happiness and joy. Lectio divina serves to bring us home to God.

AUGUSTINE: FROM MEMORY
TO INTENTION

LET'S MOVE FROM the spatial to the temporal dimension of acedia. We'll do this by turning to Robinson's Pulitzer Prize–winning novel *Gilead* (2004), which precedes *Home* in her four-book series. In *Gilead*, the Congregationalist reverend John Ames—such a close friend of the old Boughton that Jack was named after him—tells the story of his grandfather, a preacher who had traveled from Maine to Kansas to fight for the abolitionist cause in the 1850s. After the Civil War, John's grandfather moved in with his pacifist son (also a preacher) in Gilead. The result was a tense situation between the two, which ended with John's grandfather's departure from Gilead and his return to Kansas sometime in the 1880s.

John Ames reminisces how his grandfather made the decision to move back to Kansas probably while watching a baseball game in Des Moines, with the little boy admiring Bud Fowler while sitting beside his grandfather in the stands: "There was that old man my grandfather sitting beside me in his ashy coat, trembling just because he did, sharing out the frugal pleasures of his licorice, maybe with Kansas transforming itself from memory to intention in his mind that very afternoon."

The meaning of this last clause is straightforward enough. The old firebrand preacher had sermonized and fought in and around Kansas in support of abolitionism. An acquaintance of insurrectionist John Brown, he had even lost an eye in the Battle of Wilson's Creek in 1861. Sitting in the baseball stands, the old preacher thought back to this time and decided to move away from his pacifist son back to Kansas. Kansas had a place no longer just in his mind's memory but also in its intention. Kansas changed from past to future.

It is worth pausing at the language Robinson uses to describe what went on in the old preacher's mind: Kansas, she writes, transformed itself "from memory to intention." The language is Augustinian—so much so that one is tempted to think Robinson must have had Saint Augustine in the back of her mind as she wrote her novel.

In his autobiographical work *Confessions*, Augustine reflects a great deal on what happens as we move in time from the past to the future, particularly in book 11. Four related terms play a key role in his discussion: distension (*distentio*), attention (*attentio*), intention (*intentio*), and extension (*extensio*). Andrea Nightingale, in her book *Once Out of Nature: Augustine on Time and the Body*, carefully discusses Augustine's use of these terms. In particular, she notes that for Augustine, *distension* has to do with our experience of time. We live in a fallen world, which means that we are in exile. Only since the fall do we experience time. Being temporalized means being removed from the eternity of God.

We undergo two profound consequences of temporal exile. First, our mind is stretched or distended from past to future, from memory to expectation. Nightingale calls this *psychic time* since it is an experience of the mind. Everything we experience in the mind moves from past to future. Nothing is ever stable in the present. Temporal existence, for Augustine, means instability. Second, natural organisms experience aging as they move from birth to death. Nightingale refers to this as *earthly time* because of the natural, bodily developments that all living beings undergo. Augustine regarded both psychic and earthly time as problems. Both mark our lives as pilgrims or alien residents. Both keep us away from God, because they keep us away from the eternal now of God's own life.

Are we forced simply to wait till the end of the pilgrimage to get rid of our temporalized condition and to see the face of God? Augustine wasn't quite so pessimistic. Neither was the later Western tradition. It is the practice of lectio divina that filled them with hope. Lectio divina was a strategy for reaching, already in this life, beyond the distension (*distentio*) of the mind. How? Making the biblical text our home, and so attending meditatively and at length on the reality of which the text speaks, helps us overcome temporal distension and instead turn to God's eternity. Of course, reading relies on temporal plot development, with past and present, memory and expectation playing integral roles. But proper focus (*attentio*) links us to divine eternity. In lectio divina, vertical movement overcomes horizontal distension.

Augustine struggled intensely with how to overcome distension. For example, in discussing the chanting of psalms, he comments,

> Suppose I am about to recite a psalm which I know. Before I begin, my expectation (*expectatio*) is towards the whole. But when I have begun, the verses from it which I take into the past become the object of my memory (*memoria*). The life of this act

of mine is stretched (*distenditur*) two ways, into my memory (*memoriam*) because of the words I have already said and into my expectation (*expectationem*) because of those which I am about to say. But my attention (*attentio*) is on what is present: by that the future is transferred to become the past. As the action advances further and further, the shorter the expectation (*expectatione*) and the longer the memory (*memoria*), until all expectation is consumed, the entire action is finished, and it has passed into the memory (*memoriam*).

Note what Augustine writes about the present: "My attention (*attentio*) is on what is present." His attention, however, does not have staying power. As Nightingale puts it, "The *attentio* is a passive point of transit—it marks the present moment where expected future events move into memories of the past." Augustine finds it difficult to pay attention. The reason is obvious. If we draw a timeline for the chanting of the psalm, the portion that is in our memory touches the portion of our expectation:

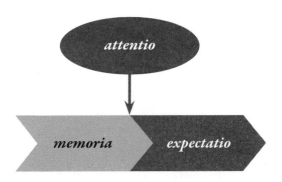

Figure 3.1: *Augustine on Reading*

The reading process moves more and more words from the *expectatio* portion to the *memoria* portion: the gold area gets longer, the purple area shorter, because the words of the psalm are stretched or distended both into the past (through memory) and into the future (by way of expectation). *Attentio* does not have a horizontal space of its own that it can occupy. The transient character of reading seems to render focusing or attending impossible, since the present consistently eludes us.

How, then, can we possibly pay attention? Doesn't the nature of time imply that we experience an inescapable distension (*distentio*) back and forth between past and future, memory and expectation, without ever landing anywhere? Thinking back to the old Reverend Ames, is Kansas always only in the past and in the future? Does it ever become an abiding home? And if we cannot ever reach the stability of home, will we always be distracted by the multiple images of memory and expectation darting through our mind? Are we the hapless victims of impressions that force themselves on us in our pilgrim wanderings?

Despite his struggles, Augustine remains hopeful. The *expectatio* of the future is not a gazing on an unknown field of interminable possibilities. Take the example of reciting a psalm. In the practice of lectio divina, the words of the psalm are prescribed. They channel our expectation so that we can focus and attend as we are guided by the flow of the words. Augustine speaks of this focused attention by using the terms "intention" (*intentio*) and "extension" (*extensio*). For Augustine, while distension imprisons us within horizontal temporal horizons, intention and extension open up a vertical dimension that allows us to attend to God.

How does this process work according to Augustine? Let's look at the terms "intention" and "extension" in turn. Nightingale translates *intentio* as "active-attention," because it deliberately focuses on what lies ahead. In a lovely passage discussing the measurement of sounds, Augustine speaks of the role of this active intending:

> Suppose someone wished to utter a sound lasting a long time, and decided in advance (*praemeditando*) how long that was going to be. He would have planned (*egit*) that space of time in silence. Entrusting that to his memory (*memoriae*) he would begin to utter the sound which continues until it has reached the intended (*propositum*) end. It would be more accurate to say the utterance has sounded and will sound. For the part of it which is complete has sounded, but what remains will sound, and so the action is being accomplished as present attention (*intentio*) transfers the future into the past. The future diminishes as the past grows, until the future has completely gone and everything is in the past.

We actively prepare the words that roll off our tongue. Augustine uses several terms that highlight this active preparation of the mind—*praemeditare*, *agere*, and *propositum*. This planning counters distraction and allows for focus or *intentio*, or, in Nightingale's translation, "active-attention." Needless to say, when we already know the text that we are going to read, *intentio* comes to us more easily, for we already have prior familiarity with the trajectory ahead of us. This is what happened to Reverend Ames: it is his memory (*memoria*) that enabled Kansas to become an intention (*intentio*) in his mind. He already knew the place where he was headed. Similarly, the more often we read the Psalter, the easier we find it to attend to the words of the text.

But are we not still caught in the maelstrom of transience? *Intentio*, Augustine makes clear, transfers the future to the past. In other words, *intentio* still simply moves us along the timeline from *memoria* to *expectatio*. How will we reach the God who is beyond time? This is where Augustine turns to the language of extension (*extensio*). Several times, the African bishop turns to Philippians 3:13–14: "Brethren, I do not count myself to have apprehended. But one thing I do: Forgetting the things that are behind and stretching forth (*extendens*) myself to those that are before, I press towards the mark, to the prize of the supernal vocation of God in Christ Jesus." Saint Paul uses the language of "stretching forth" to describe the spiritual race to which he is committed.

Paul combines horizontal language ("stretching forth to those that are before") with vertical discourse ("supernal vocation"). Augustine is drawn to this peculiarity of the text because it indicates that for the apostle, temporal distension (*distentio*) does not capture every dimension of human existence. The upward call is possible. How? Augustine hints at the solution when he writes,

> But "For your mercy is better than lives" (Ps. 63:3). Behold, my life is a distension (*distentio*), and your right hand upheld me (Ps. 18:35; 63:8) in my Lord, the son of man who is mediator between you the One and us the many, who live among many and through many; so that "I might apprehend through him in whom also I am apprehended" (Phil. 3:12) and, leaving behind the old days, I might be gathered (*colligar*) to follow the One, "forgetting the past" and moving not towards those future things which are transitory but to "the things which are before (*ante*)," not stretched out (*distentus*) but extended

(*extentus*), not by being stretched out (*distentionem*) but by active-attention (*intentionem*).

Augustine draws two key lessons from Philippians 3:12–14. First, the Pauline *extensio* is different from *distentio*. When we strain forward in extension and reach the prize, we find out that the prize was always already there. Those future heavenly things are not transitory but were there before (*ante*) us; they are eternal. The prize is always already there, waiting for us, and the way to get a glimpse of it even now is through active-attention (*intentio*). Deliberate attention, therefore, allows us to overcome the multiple and timebound character of human words (and of human existence in general).

Second, the incarnation is what makes the Pauline *extensio* different from mere temporal *distentio*. Even though life is a temporalized distension, God's right hand upholds us in the mediator—the one who stands between the One and the many. Christ is both God and man. He combines in himself the One and the many. The many, therefore, are joined to the One in Christ. By following him, we are gathered (*colligere*) into the One. For Augustine, God's incarnation in Christ opens up a vertical dimension that allows us to reach beyond the horizontal unfolding of temporal events. Christ connects us to the God who is beyond time. When in our reading of the Scriptures we attend to Christ, by implication we contemplate the eternal now of God himself.

Straining forward is hard work. Neither the life of virtue nor the reading practice of lectio divina takes off without active-attention. And as long as we are in the race, the problem of *distentio* remains. Augustine knows that only in the hereafter will we reach the destination:

You are my eternal Father, but I am scattered (*dissilui*) in times whose order I do not understand. The storms of incoherent events tear to pieces (*dilaniantur*) my thoughts, the inmost entrails of my soul, until that day when, purified and molten by the fire of your love, I flow together to merge (*confluam*) into you.

In this life, the stretching (*distentio*) of time cannot but scatter us and tear us to pieces. The many do join the One in the mediator, but it remains a tough slog. Distraction always threatens to undo our focus. Only in the hereafter are we safe within the unity and eternity of God. We need to pay attention as long as we haven't arrived in Kansas.

CONCLUSION

Time, for Augustine, poses a problem. He contrasts time with eternity and suggests that our aim is to move from the one to the other. He identifies this problem as one of temporal creatures longing for eternity with God as their home. Perhaps we frown on Augustine: Isn't time a good gift from God? And isn't the temporal flow of words likewise a gift from God? Don't we need the movement from memory to expectation (as in figure 3.1) to make sense of the Scriptures? The answer to each of these questions is yes. Time is God's gift, as is the temporal flow of words, and we cannot properly read the Bible without moving from memory to expectation.

Still, we shouldn't be too hard on the African bishop. Augustine did not despise words; he loved them. And he loved thinking and talking about them. Several of the quotes in this chapter make clear that he reveled in pondering how we move from sound to sound as we read the Scriptures. Augustine had no intention of bypassing or ignoring this movement of the words. Quite the opposite. Again, therefore, Augustine loved the words of the biblical text. For Augustine, to read the Bible well was to read it and reread it, and in this way to make our home in it. That is precisely what lectio divina does. It makes the Bible our home.

Moreover, God's eternal now is not simply the negation of temporal distension. God's eternal now includes every moment of time—but at an infinitely higher interval. For Augustine—as for the broader tradition both East and West—time is the unfolding of the eternal now. In some mysterious manner, all of time is included in the eternal now of God's providence. "Our personal stories," writes Chiara Bertoglio, "are embraced, contained, and (at the same time) displayed in God's eternal present; thus, that infinite moment represents the maximum of dynamicity and 'life.'" God's eternity is not everlasting boredom; it is fullness of action—*actus purus*, Aquinas would say.

Fullness of action—how? God's eternal now is the unfolding source of every chronological moment in time. God's eternal now holds time, every moment of it, in its loving embrace. When in lectio divina we overcome the transience of time, time is not lost. Instead, we trace it to its source, which contains it in a higher mode, the providence of God's eternal now. Lectio divina enables us to carefully attend to the present even as we temporally move from memory to expectation.

Lectio divina, therefore, takes temporal creatures into God's eternal now. The maelstrom of time is indispensable for this process—as indispensable as the flow of words. Biblical words, spoken and reflected on within the flow of time, bring us to God. We reach the God beyond words through words, the God beyond time through time. It is *passage* (passing through), not mere *dépassement* (passing beyond), that takes us to God. But Augustine also recognized that when we truly make the Bible our home, the many words of Scripture merge into One. The words of our memory and those of our expectation merge together when we contemplate God, the reality to which all biblical words refer. It is in the unity of our love of God that we arrive at the final meaning of all words.

Unlike us, God is not stretched out in words or in time. God dwells in the eternal present. Contemplation of God in lectio divina, therefore, requires that we move beyond words and beyond time. Paradoxically, it is when we make our home within the temporal flow of words that we find our home within the eternal God who is beyond all words.

IV

Swirling Thoughts

DEMENTIA AND IDENTITY

OUR SOCIETY IS aging rapidly. Many of us, therefore, are confronted with loved ones suffering dementia. We grieve over them as they have difficulty recalling what they've read or experienced. We struggle with how to respond when we hear them repeat themselves yet again within a short time. The damage done to the brain cells has affected our loved ones' ability both to recall things and to think ahead. The most basic routines become difficult. Confusion and fearfulness come to the surface. Sometimes anger, suspicion, and depression result. Those with a spouse suffering from dementia often note that the person they lived with for so long has changed. Spouses experience a sense of loss and frequently are trapped in an increasingly untenable situation, while feelings of resentment induce a sense of guilt.

Dementia is not purely a matter of memory loss, but memory loss is a big part of dementia and a leading cause of some of the attending symptoms. It's not hard to see why. Memories shape who we are. Recollections of people and events, joys of past experiences, as well as regrets about missteps in our lives—they all contribute to who we are.

Without these experiences from the past, we would not be who we are today. No matter what unnerving things we may have gone through, no matter how our outlook on life may have drastically changed, we are still the same person as before. Our memory ties it all together and gives us a sense of continuity and stability. Dementia overturns all this. It robs us of our past and, in so doing, removes the stability of our character—our sense of identity.

Memory loss also affects our ability to plan for the future. Past experiences inform our decision-making process. This is true not just in the superficial sense that past experiences help us navigate similar situations in a new context. Rather, every sentence we speak and every activity we undertake builds on a complex web of skills that allow us to look ahead and sketch out our future. For the most part, we don't give these weaving skills a second thought; we simply take them for granted. But when the web begins to fray and tear, memory loss deprives us of the ability to undertake new actions. Because the door to the past is closed, the road to the future is blocked off as well.

LECTIO DIVINA WITH
A LIVING CONCORDANCE

LECTIO DIVINA RELIES on memory. Patristic and medieval authors knew their Bible. They internalized the Scriptures. They read them over and over, they deliberately committed large chunks to memory, and they were able to call them to mind whenever the need arose. Columba Stewart, in his book *Cassian the Monk*, notes that the fourth-century Egyptian desert fathers spent much of their time memorizing Scripture. They referred to the habit of repeated, attentive reciting of Scripture as *meletē*, a Greek term that later Latin writers translated as *meditatio*. The biblical texts saturated the monks' hearts and minds through constant repetition. As a result, memorizing and meditating were virtually synonymous. For many of these early Christian theologians, the second step of lectio divina—meditation— was primarily a matter of committing the biblical text to memory.

The fourth-century desert father Saint Anthony, for example, was well-known for his memory skills. And early in the next century, John Cassian speaks of striving "with constant repetition to commit these readings to memory." Ammonius, one of the Tall Brothers from Egypt, was legendary: "He had committed to memory the Old and New Testaments, and he knew by heart 6,000,000 verses of the highly reputable writings of Origen, Didymus, Pierius, and Stephen, so the fathers of the desert testify." Saint Jerome, advising his friend Laeta about the education of her daughter Paula, writes famously,

> Let her learn the Psalter first, with these songs let her distract herself, and then let her learn lessons of life in the Proverbs of Solomon. In reading Ecclesiastes let her become accustomed to tread underfoot the things of this world; let her follow the examples of virtue and patience that she will find in Job. Let her then pass on to the Gospels and never again lay them down. Let her drink in the Acts of the Apostles and the Epistles with all the will of her heart. As soon as she has enriched her mind's storehouse (*cellarium*) with these treasures, let her commit to memory the Prophets, the Heptateuch, the books of Kings and the Chronicles, and the rolls of Ezra and Esther. Then at last she may safely read the Song of Songs: if she were to read it at the beginning, she might be harmed by not perceiving that it was the song of a spiritual bridal expressed in fleshly language.

We are perhaps inclined to linger over Jerome's comments on the Song of Songs—not safe for Paula to read if she were to take it in its fleshly sense—but the far more amazing aspect of this passage is the expectation Jerome places on Paula in terms of memorization. When Jerome speaks of "learning" the Psalter, as well as many other books, he has in mind that she is to commit to memory the biblical books she is reading. The result, he tells her mother, is that Paula's heart will become a storehouse (*cellarium*) of biblical treasures.

Monastic rules typically required repeated chanting and memorizing of Scripture. The fourth-century Rules of Pachomius required that, at a minimum, the monks learn by heart the entire Psalter and the New Testament. They were supposed to chant psalms on their way to church and back, and also when they were occupied with basic manual tasks. The Rule of Saint Benedict assumed that biblical lessons could be recited "by heart" (*memoriter*). And when Benedict speaks of "meditating" on Scripture, he has in mind a process of repeated recitation (from memory), which readily invited the monk to reflect on the implications of the biblical text. This type of meditation has rightly been called "the leisurely savoring of biblical texts that were mostly committed to memory." Meditation, here, is not quite identical with memorization, but the two are very closely linked. Memorization is the initial step of meditation and lies at the foundation of all subsequent rumination on the biblical text.

Our society devalues the role of memory. Why memorize if all the information we want is at our fingertips? If I want to know where Scripture uses a particular word, I do a quick word search in my database. My laptop has a copy of Logos Bible Software, which is a truly impressive storehouse or *cellarium* of biblical treasures. In a split second, it gives me the results of whatever Bible search I may want to perform. I wouldn't want to do without. But, of course, the reason this database is indispensable is that the information is on my computer, and not in my head. Where Jerome speaks of Paula's heart as a *cellarium*, I treat my laptop as one.

Jean Leclercq, the twentieth-century French Benedictine monk, discusses in *The Love of Learning and the Desire for God* a monastic type of exegesis that he calls "exegesis by concordance." The way it worked is that the monks would explain "one verse by another verse in which the same word occurs." Leclercq's observation is perceptive: both patristic and medieval authors would often interpret the Bible through this kind of verbal association. They would turn to various biblical texts containing the same word or phrase, and then would check what kind of theological or spiritual connections they could make. It was a rather playful enterprise, grounded in the conviction that the same Spirit had inspired every one of the canonical texts and that God operates in similar ways at various points in salvation history. By constantly going back and forth through Scripture, over time one became what Leclercq calls a "living concordance": the monk's mind contained huge lists of words, which he could match, from memory, with lists of biblical texts in which they occurred. Few of us are a living concordance. My concordance is mostly in my Logos program, and sadly, I suspect, this is true for many of us.

Having a concordance in a laptop is not the same as having it in one's head. What is in my laptop is not part of my past experience; it doesn't shape my character; and I cannot use it to give shape to what lies ahead. Only if—one way or another—the biblical text has entered my mind can it also mold me as a person. Monks memorized Scripture not just because they lacked a concordance on the bookshelf or in the database. They did it because they wanted the biblical text to form their character. They were convinced that once the biblical text was in their minds, it would also seep into their very bones. The process of lectio divina will yield contemplation only once we have allowed the biblical text to become part of who we are.

I mentioned earlier that dementia not only makes it difficult to recall things but also impairs the ability to plan ahead. Loss of the past and loss of the future go hand in hand. Both the classical and the Christian traditions recognized this. The Roman philosopher Cicero, who early in his career wrote a book on rhetoric titled *On Invention* (ca. 87 BC), connects memory to the cardinal virtue of prudence. Prudence, which we may broadly describe as the ability to discern the right thing to do given the circumstances, depends on memory. Cicero explains that memory is one of three elements that make up prudence: "Memory is the faculty by which the mind recalls what has happened. Intelligence is the faculty by which it ascertains what is. Foresight is the faculty by which it is seen that something is going to occur before it occurs." Memory, intelligence, and foresight together give us prudence. Memory has to do with the past, intelligence with the present, and foresight with the future. For Cicero, the reason a lack of memory hampers our decision-making is that memory is one of the three key elements of prudence.

Saint Thomas Aquinas, in the *Summa theologiae*, does something similar. He too deals with memory as part of a larger discussion on the virtue of prudence. In fact, Aquinas is even more insistent than Cicero that memory has to do with the virtues. Cicero discussed memory in a book on *rhetoric*. His idea was that if you want to be a good speaker, you need to know how to store speeches in the mind. But Aquinas deals with memory as a part of *moral theology*. He talks about it in book II-II of the *Summa*, where he elaborates on the virtues. Aquinas agrees with Cicero, though, that we need memory if we want to chart our course of action in a judicious manner. "Experience," claims Aquinas, "is the result of many memories ... and therefore prudence requires the memory of many things." In other words, both Cicero and Aquinas recognized that it's not enough to have a concordance on the laptop. For prudent decision-making—for the life of virtue—we need to become a living concordance.

HUGH OF SAINT VICTOR:
THE CONFUSION OF "SWIRLING THOUGHTS"

HUGH OF SAINT VICTOR worked with the same assumption. As the principal of the school at the Abbey of Saint Victor, the twelfth-century Parisian monk was unreservedly committed to memorization as a key element of the curriculum. He presented his novices with a book of biblical facts called *Chronicle* (ca. 1130). It consists of about thirty-seven lengthy folio pages full of columns and diagrams with names, dates, and events from biblical history and church history as well as the history of Christendom, all of which the novices were supposed to transfer from the book to their heads.

Hugh begins the preface to the book as follows:

> My child, knowledge is a treasury and your heart is its strong-box (*archa*). As you study all of knowledge, you store up for yourselves good treasures, immortal treasures, incorruptible treasures, which never decay nor lose the beauty of their

brightness. In the treasure-house of wisdom are various sorts of wealth, and many filing-places in the store-house (*archa*) of your heart. In one place is put gold, in another silver, in another precious jewels. Their orderly arrangement is clarity of knowledge. Dispose and separate each single thing into its own place, this into its and that into its, so that you may know what has been placed here and what there. Confusion is the mother of ignorance and forgetfulness, but orderly arrangement illuminates the intelligence and secures memory.

Two things stand out in these opening words. First, Hugh speaks of the heart as a strongbox or a storehouse (*archa*)—an "ark," we could also translate. Of course, when the novice opened his textbook for the first time, the treasures would only be in the book, not in the mind. Hugh, however, insists that these treasures belong in the "filing-places" of the heart. The *Chronicle*'s treasures must be transferred. The *archa* of the page is meant to be reproduced in the *archa* of the heart. Second, Hugh is concerned with orderly arrangement. The various treasures need to be filed in their proper place. When we place rulers and popes in the wrong filing-place, confusion rather than clarity is the result. And confusion, in turn, leads to ignorance and forgetfulness. According to Hugh, we avoid confusion and arrive at knowledge by properly transferring the various treasures of the *Chronicle* into the *archa* of the heart.

Around the same time that he wrote the *Chronicle*, Hugh reflected on the image of the ark in a series of lectures that became the four-part treatise *Noah's Ark*. In some respects, the two books are rather different from each other. Whereas the *Chronicle* is a basic textbook

that outlines sacred history, *Noah's Ark* offers a variety of figural inter-
pretations of Noah's ark that aim to bring the monks closer to God.
Hugh recognizes no fewer than four types of arks, which correspond
to historical, allegorical, moral, and eschatological levels of meaning:

> The first is that which Noah made, with hatchets and axes,
> using wood and pitch as his materials. The second is that which
> Christ made through His preachers, by gathering the nations
> into a single confession of faith. The third is that which wisdom
> builds daily in our hearts through continual meditation on the
> law of God. The fourth is that which mother grace effects in us
> by joining together many virtues in a single charity.

Hugh calls the first—the historical ark, which Noah himself built—
simply by the name of "Noah's ark" (*arca Noe*). The second ark, constructed by preachers, is called the "ark of the church" (*arca ecclesiae*).
Here, he allegorizes the ark by explaining that its deeper meaning
concerns the church. The third ark is built by wisdom in our hearts
when we obey God's law. This "ark of wisdom" (*arca sapientiae*) has to
do with the moral or tropological meaning of the ark. Finally, the "ark
of mother grace" (*arca matris gratiae*) brings all the virtues together
in the unity of love. Here Hugh is thinking of the perfection that the
anagogical or eschatological meaning offers.

The wide-ranging and speculative character of *Noah's Ark* gives it a
different feel from the more pedestrian *Chronicle*. Still, the two treatises address the same problem—namely, that of confusion, instability,
distraction, or disorder. Hugh begins *Noah's Ark* with the following
comments:

When I was one day sitting with the assembled brethren, and
replying to the questions which they asked, many matters came
up for discussion. Finally, the conversation was so directed that
we began with one accord to marvel at the instability and rest-
lessness (*instabilitate et inquietudine*) of the human heart, and
to sigh over it. And the brethren earnestly entreated that they
might be shown the cause of these swirling thoughts (*cogita-
tionum fluctuationes*) in man's heart, and further particularly
begged to be taught if such a serious evil as this could be coun-
tered by any skill or by the practice of some discipline.

Hugh's fellow monks are troubled by the heart's instability and rest-
lessness, which he describes using the language of "swirling thoughts."
Like swirling or billowing waves, thoughts come and go; they take
hold of our mind only to be replaced by others. Disordered thoughts—
which Hugh recognizes go back to disordered desires—reach out to
an endless array of objects, mistaking them for our ultimate good. Our
thoughts reach out to so many different objects that the soul loses its
stability and fails to find rest. By so exchanging the love of God with
love of the world, we lose the stability of our heart.

The solution, to Hugh, seems clear: only an ark will offer protec-
tion against the swirling waves. He instructs the monks, therefore, to
build an ark, a dwelling place of God: "Make Him a temple, make
Him a house, make Him a pavilion. Make Him an ark of the covenant, make Him an ark of the flood, no matter what you call it, it is
all one house of God." He has in mind the *arca sapientiae*, the moral
or tropological meaning of the ark. When the heart becomes an ark
of wisdom, it learns virtue and redirects its love to God.

How should we build this ark of wisdom? Hugh begins outlining a resolution when he makes the following comment:

> When we let our hearts run after earthly things without restraint, a multitude of vain thoughts arises, so that our mind becomes so divided that even the order (*ordo*) of our native discrimination is disturbed. For, since the worldly things that we desire so unrestrainedly are infinite, the thoughts (*cogitationes*) that we conceive when we remember (*memoria*) them cannot be finite. As from moment to moment they arise one after another in so many different ways, even we ourselves cannot understand by which order or how they enter or leave the mind. If, then, we want to have ordered, stable, peaceful thoughts (*cogitationes*), let us make it our business to restrain our hearts from this immoderate distraction.

Again, Hugh laments our desire being directed toward the innumerable multitude of temporal objects. They seem to enter and leave the mind without any discernible pattern or order. Because these thoughts (*cogitationes*) plague us, we need to get rid of the uninhibited distraction of our thoughts, the disorder of our desires, and the instability of our character.

How do we go about this? Hugh centers on redirecting our thoughts, drawing them instead to the ordered structure of Noah's ark. He explains that the three levels of the ark (Gen 6:16) refer to three kinds of thoughts—right, profitable, and necessary thoughts. On the first story, we meditate on the Scriptures and the virtues of the saints. On the second, we copy their virtues in our actions. And on the third, we have the virtues themselves. Hugh doesn't use the term, but he seems to have in mind that when we reach the third story, our actions turn into habits. And in the single cubit at the very top of the ark (Gen 6:16), the virtues combine into the unity of love. Here the multiple distractions and desires are finally reordered into unity. Love, explains Hugh, "unites us to God; and that is why the ark is gathered into one at the top, that even now we should be thinking of the One, desiring the One, even our Lord Jesus Christ." In Christ, all the virtues unite through love.

BUILDING A MYSTIC ARK

THE ARK OF WISDOM (the life of virtue) gets off the ground only if we first learn to change our thoughts. To facilitate this process, Hugh devised a detailed diagram of the ark. The monks at Saint Victor were likely familiar with this so-called *Mystic Ark* as a thirteen-by-fifteen-foot mural, painted on one of the cloister walls. Hugh also gave them a detailed description of the painting in *The Mystic Ark*, a little book that more or less functioned as the fifth part to *Noah's Ark*.

Hugh's diagram (figure 4.1)—reproduced by art historian Conrad Rudolph—is remarkable for its scope and its detail. It delineates most of the central tenets of the faith, which Hugh meant to be learned by heart. He begins by discussing the literal structure of Noah's ark (*arca Noe*). He speaks in detail of this ark—with the lavender rectangle making up the lower level, the cream-colored rectangle the middle level, and the red rectangle the top level. Clearly, though, Hugh is interested in more than just Noah's ark. First, he also has in mind other biblical scenes, for the painting reminds us not only of Noah's ark but also of the ark of the covenant in the holy of holies (Exod 25:10–22) and of Isaiah's vision of the Lord on his heavenly throne,

Figure 4.1: *Hugh's Mystic Ark*

surrounded by seraphim (Isa 6:1–2). Second, Hugh thinks of what surrounds the ark. A map of the world—Europe, Asia, and Africa—makes clear that the church is situated within a larger universe. Hugh also points out that all of history leads to a twofold judgment: Christ's right hand holds a banner that reads, "Come, ye blessed of my Father, possess you the kingdom prepared for you from the foundation of the world" (Matt 25:34), and the scepter in his left hand contains the words "Depart from me, you cursed, into everlasting fire, which was prepared for the devil and his angels" (Matt 25:41). Hugh's diagram is cosmic in scope.

Hugh moves from a basic portrayal of the historical ark to an allegorical description of the church as ark (*arca ecclesiae*). Here he talks of the ark as a Christ-shaped structure. Christ's head and limbs reach beyond the ark, and the torso of his body represents the ark or the church. The two cherubim protecting the ark gaze on Christ, along with the heavenly choirs of angels on each side of his face—representing the nine orders of angels that Dionysius had discussed in his sixth-century work *The Celestial Hierarchy*. Hugh superimposes the entire history of the church on the ark, listing patriarchs, kings, and popes, a genealogy that runs across the length of the ark. He also divides this same history into three periods:

Systems of Periodization

Old Testament/New Testament
> OT   Old Testament
> NT   New Testament

Three periods
> A. Natural law
> B. The written law
> C. Grace

Three types of people (plank system)
> ■ Of nature: green (the earth is also green)
> ▢ Of the law: yellow
> ■ Of grace: red (the third stage is also red)

Six ages
> 1. Adam up to the flood
> 2. The flood up to Abraham
> 3. Abraham up to David
> 4. David up to the captivity
> 5. The captivity up to the coming of Christ
> 6. The coming of Christ until the end of all time
> (7. Perpetual Sabbath)
> (8. Reigning perpetually with Christ)

natural law, written law, and grace. The breadth of the ark, meanwhile, represents Jews and gentiles, as well as men and women. Figure 4.2, along with the key that is shown on this page, shows how the entire biblical narrative finds a place within Hugh's ark: Old and New Testaments; natural law, written law, and grace; as well as the six ages beginning with Adam and moving on to the eternal kingdom itself.

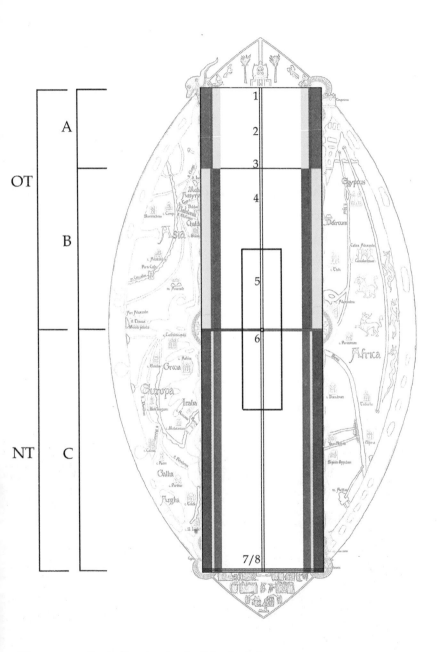

Figure 4.2: *Periodization in the Mystic Ark*

Hugh gives most of his attention to a tropological, or moral, reading of the ark (*arca sapientiae*). He depicts twelve ladders of spiritual progress (each of them with vices and virtues), which connect to rooms through which God's people have progressed throughout salvation history. Of course, the book of Genesis mentions neither ladders nor specific rooms. This doesn't bother Hugh: "Scripture does not tell the number of these compartments. In spite of that I put six little rooms in the Ark." Hugh's purpose is to impress upon his monks the central aspects of the faith and to facilitate their spiritual progress. The various ladders and rooms are teaching tools for the sake of discussion and memorization.

We don't have the space here to look at each and every detail of *The Mystic Ark*. But I want to make an exception for one small excerpt, taken from the center section of the ark (figure 4.3). It will have to do by way of illustration:

Here we see, very middle—right in the fold of this book—a lamb. Christ, the lamb slain from the beginning of the world (Rev 13:8), is the single cubit at the top of the ark. The River Jordan runs through

Figure 4.3: *Central Section of the Ark*

the middle of the ark, dividing Old and New Testaments. The rationale, explains Hugh, is as follows: "I lead the river Jordan through the middle of the Ark, that is, from one wall to the other next to the side of the column above, in the likeness of baptism, which in the Holy Church is the end of law and the beginning of grace, whose holy water flowed from the side of Christ." Ladders detailing the ascent of the saints reach from the corners of the ark to the cubit at the top. On the north side, we find in blue the *Liber vite* (Book of Life), which signifies Christ's humanity. On the south side, Hugh depicts the *Lignum vite* (tree of life), which signifies Christ's divinity. The rooms on the north are named *Fides, Spes*, and *Caritas* (Faith, Hope, and Love), while those on the south represent *Scientia, Disciplina*, and *Bonitas* (Knowledge, Discipline, and Goodness). By the time the believers come to the rooms of Love and of Goodness, they have entered the third level (in red). Clearly, they have achieved the desired stability in their moral lives and have arrived at the "ark of mother grace" (*arca matris gratiae*). Put differently, they have come to Jerusalem, the City of the Great King (*Civitas regis magna*) or the Promised Land (*Terra promissionis*). Saint Peter is there, along with the

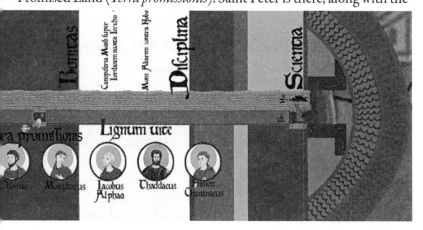

other apostles. "I put Peter first," writes Hugh, "and around him, on his right and left the other apostles with their icons, six on the right and five on the left." The ark centers the church's life in Christ.

CONCLUSION

IN BOTH HIS lectures on Noah's ark and his mural of the mystic ark, Hugh addresses the monks' perennial problem of distraction, confusion, instability, and disorder. It is important for Hugh that he focus their attention. They may well have appreciated his talks, but they must have been particularly engaged once Hugh gathered them around the painting of *The Mystic Ark*. Hugh's pedagogical strategy, it seems, was to use a combination of words and images—both indispensable for Hugh, as he recognized the inescapably visual character of memory.

We know lectio divina as a four-step exercise: reading, meditation, prayer, and contemplation. But there's nothing sacred about these four steps. Hugh sometimes omits prayer from the list (without, of course, in any way denying that the upward journey is prayerful throughout), and he refers to the three remaining stages as thought (*cogitatio*), meditation (*meditatio*), and contemplation (*contemplatio*). He does so also in *The Mystic Ark*, talking about three levels, with ladders connecting them as an ascent from thought, via meditation, to contemplation.

As we can see in figure 4.4, a ladder goes up from the ark's bottom left corner. Someone (in red) crawls out of a cave, his face covered; he is blind. He falls down, strikes a rock, and breaks the jar that he is carrying. This person, explains Hugh, stands for *Ignorantia*. On the other side of the same ladder (also in figure 4.4) stands someone (in purple) who looks at the pieces and reads the scroll that is hanging down: "In the beginning God created heaven, and earth" (Gen 1:1).

Figure 4.4: *Ignorantia and Cogitatio*

Figure 4.5: *Meditatio*

Figure 4.6: *Contemplatio*

This is *Cogitatio*, whose thought is about God's presence in the created order. Next, in the second story of the ark, sits *Meditatio* (in blue), putting the broken pieces of the jar back together (figure 4.5). Finally, *Contemplatio*, the smith (in green) at the third level of the ark, melts the pieces into liquid, which flows up through a pipe alongside the ladder into the central cubit at the top (figure 4.6). In case we didn't get the point, Hugh makes the figurative meaning explicit. It is "the integrity of the soul, which ignorance breaks to pieces, thought finds again, meditation collects, and contemplation, by melting it with the fire of divine love, pours ... back into the mint of divine likeness to be formed anew."

Hugh's pictorial allegory refers to our problem as ignorance. But he obviously has in mind much more than mere lack of factual knowledge. He worries instead about our spiritual blindness, which mistakes this-worldly goods for ultimate goods and, as a result, aimlessly gropes about, confused and distracted by the numerous images that flit through the mind. Hugh recognizes that these "swirling thoughts" render us incapable of prudently, and with deliberation, turning to the future. Swirling thoughts cause something like dementia. By fragmenting our attention, they make us confused, fearful, incapable of foresight.

Hugh's lectures and his mural offer a kind of lectio divina. His words and painting allow the monks to refocus their attention. The steps of *cogitatio*, *meditatio*, and *contemplatio* constitute a healing exercise. The first step, for the Parisian teacher, is the healing of memory through *cogitatio*. His writings offer new thoughts to replace the unsettling and disorienting images and memories swirling about in our minds. In this way, Hugh wants to reorient our desires. And in all this, the goal is nothing less than contemplation of the lamb at the center of the ark.

V

Chewing and Belching

COSMIC CULINARY SCHOOL

I

S OUR CULTURE obsessed with food? The psychologist Abraham Maslow once commented, "To a man with a hammer, everything looks like a nail." The master chef of a fine-dining restaurant may be tempted to relate everything in the universe to his Saturday-night haute cuisine menu. And the dean of a culinary academy may include in the curriculum not just cooking but also courses on business, history, culture, aesthetics, perhaps even philosophy. Needless to say, a culture that looks at all of life through the grid of food is one that takes the Epicurean pleasure principle to the extreme.

I don't think we've quite fallen victim to Maslow's fallacy when it comes to food. Yes, we live in an Epicurean world in which eating (and the enjoyment thereof) plays an outsized role. But I suspect that most chefs can look beyond their dinner menus, and I doubt that culinary schools view gastronomy as the queen of the sciences.

More importantly, the master chef and culinary dean have a point. Everything *is* part of a cosmic culinary program. Christ is, after all, our food and drink—the heavenly manna and the tree of life. Augustine, reflecting on the eucharistic body and blood, makes this comment: "If you receive them well, you are yourselves what you receive." By eating Christ, we become Christ. To live is to eat, and this process of eating changes (or transfigures) us into the food we eat. The nineteenth-century materialist philosopher Ludwig Feuerbach had a point: "Man is what he eats" (*Der Mensch ist was er ißt*). Christ is all and in all (Col 3:11; cf. 1 Cor 15:28).

Lectio divina—reading the Bible as the Word of God—isn't just *like* eating; it *is* eating. Our everyday eating and drinking are symbols or types that hint at the real or prototypical eating and drinking that unite us to Christ. If Christ is Alpha and Omega (first and last), then the ordinary world of experience is modeled on him. If he is the food that gives life to the world, then having a full belly at a cookout tells us something of the archetypal Cookout on which our summer get-togethers are patterned. Divine reading and the eucharistic meal offer true life through union with Christ. We eat more truly, therefore, when we embark on lectio divina than when we have a backyard barbecue. Food on the grill gives us a shadowy glimmer of the eating and drinking we do when we feast on God's Word.

The language of *eating God's Word* is prevalent in the lectio divina tradition. In this chapter, we'll deal with topics that may seem banal and even coarse: beekeeping, chewing the cud, belching. Again, though, I'm not treating these activities as the model or prototype on which to base the practice of lectio divina. The prototype, rather, is eating Christ. To give us some clue as to what it means to eat Christ, he stoops down and gives us pictures of bees and burps: symbols or types that give us some basic notions of what true life in union with God's Word is like.

EATING THE SCROLL

FEW BIBLICAL PASSAGES are as suggestive for exploring the metaphor of eating as God's instruction to the prophet Ezekiel: "Son of man, thy belly shall eat, and thy bowels shall be filled with this book, which I give thee, and I did eat it: and it was sweet as honey in my mouth" (Ezek 3:3). This passage gained prominence and depth through John the Seer's evoking it in Revelation 10:9–10. The language of eating a scroll identifies God's words as food, while the reference to honey invites exploration of the sweet character of the Scriptures. Saint Gregory the Great goes out of his way in his homily on this text from Ezekiel to explore every aspect of God's injunction to the prophet. No aspect of the biblical text may be lost, for "the crumbs of it compose the simple life and large pieces build a keen understanding." The twelfth-century image below, taken from a Bible kept in the National Library of France in Paris, depicts Ezekiel seated inside the letter *E*. God's hand feeds him the scroll, which in Latin reads, "Eat this book, and go speak to the children of Israel" (Ezek 3:1).

Saint Gregory begins his homily, which he preached around 592 or 593, by establishing that Scripture is our food and drink. He appeals to Amos 8:11, "I will send forth a famine into the land: not a famine of bread, nor a thirst of water, but of hearing the word of the Lord." Noting that Scripture is both food and drink, the pope distinguishes them by suggesting that we can simply drink the "plainer sayings," whereas more obscure passages must be chewed (studied) and swallowed (understood).

The biblical text comments straightforwardly, "And I opened my mouth, and he caused me to eat that book" (Ezek 3:2). Gregory, however, recognizes that he cannot possibly take this literally, and so he

Figure 5.1: *Ezekiel eating the scroll (Ezek 3:3)*

explains that the mouth is actually a reference to the heart—in line
with Psalm 12:2, which Gregory translates, "Deceitful lips are in his
heart, and in his heart hath he spoken evils." So, when God opens
the mouth of our hearts, he opens our understanding and fills our
thoughts with the sweetness of the Scriptures. When Ezekiel goes on

to state, "Thy belly shall eat, and thy bowels shall be filled with this book," Gregory explains that both belly and bowels speak of the heart. His evidence is Jeremiah's cry of lament, "My bowels, my bowels are in pain" (Jer 4:19), and, especially, Jesus's own comment that from the believer's "belly" rivers of living water shall flow (John 7:38). In both cases, explains Gregory, the Scriptures allude to the understanding of the heart or of the mind.

Gregory ends his reflections on eating God's words with a warning in two directions. First, his listeners must realize that God's food will satisfy and his drink inebriate only if our minds are transformed and we no longer seek the earthly things we used to love: "For it is said of the elect through the Psalmist: 'They shall be inebriated with the plenty of Thy house' [Ps 36:8]." Second, preachers must recognize that they can edify others only if their own lives are in line with the Scriptures they preach. Gregory takes Ezekiel's comment that the scroll was "sweet as honey in my mouth" (Ezek 3:3) as meaning that the preacher, having learned to love God in the bowels of his heart, now knows "how to speak sweetly about Him." God's words, explains Gregory, have served as sweet honey in his own mouth first, so that he now truly "dyes the pen of his tongue in his heart."

EATING IN STEPS

IF WE ARE meant to *eat* the Scriptures, can we link the various steps of lectio divina to stages of the eating process? This is exactly what Guigo II, whom we met in chapter 2, does in the *Ladder of Monks*: "Reading, as it were, puts food whole into the mouth, meditation chews it and breaks it up, prayer extracts its flavor, contemplation is the sweetness (*dulcedo*) itself which gladdens and refreshes." Guigo is not content simply to assert that the Scriptures are our food. He wants to look at the details, constructing an outline in which each of the steps of lectio divina corresponds to a stage within the eating process.

Guigo next introduces the verse on which he wants to meditate: "Blessed are the clean of heart: for they shall see God" (Matt 5:8). Guigo compares this beatitude to a grape. We begin by biting and chewing the grape (reading and meditation). Here, we compare the Lord's beatitude with numerous other texts, so that lots of juice can be pressed out of this one little grape. It is actually smell, not taste, that gives us a first intimation of the sweetness of the grape, explains Guigo. When we chew the grape, we smell the sweetness, but we don't yet experience the sweetness itself. Prayer is the means through which we first experience the sweetness. We call out to the Lord that we long to see him "no more from without, in the rind of the letter, but within, in the letter's hidden meaning."

When the Lord responds to our prayer and restores our soul, "He slakes its thirst and He feeds its hunger." The taste of the grape's sweetness inebriates the soul. Here Guigo elaborates on the goal of divine reading—namely, contemplation. We experience the sweetness of the Lord, which is like getting drunk: we are no longer in control but are taken out of ourselves. (Guigo doesn't use the term, but we could describe it as *ecstasy*, a word that derives from *ek-stasis*, literally "standing outside of oneself.") But this is no ordinary drunkenness. It's a *sober* inebriation. Guigo here borrows an ancient paradox, which can be traced all the way to Philo of Alexandria in the first century, and of which the fourth-century mystical theologian Gregory of Nyssa was particularly fond. For Guigo, sober inebriation is not just a state that puts us outside our regular mental faculties; it also is an experience that escapes ordinary description.

Guigo refers to Jesus's beatitude as a grape (*uva*) because this imagery evokes several important aspects of lectio divina: the grape has an outward rind and flesh inside, which calls to mind the distinction between the historical and spiritual meanings. The grape's sweetness points to the sweetness of the Lord, as noted in a biblical text to which Guigo (as well as numerous other patristic and medieval authors) alludes, Psalm 34:8: "O taste, and see that the Lord is sweet (*suavis*)." It is the sweet taste of God that lectio divina is after. And, as we just saw, the grape imagery also allows Guigo to allude to the experiential character of contemplation: like sober drunkenness, it lies utterly beyond our reach and descriptive power.

The grape imagery reminds us that reading is like harvesting—though Guigo doesn't mention this connection. The first stage of lectio divina—the simple act of reading—is similar to harvesting grapes. The Latin term for reading (*legere*) can also mean "gathering," "gleaning," or "picking." The first-century Roman author Pliny describes the layout of vineyards in his *Natural History*, explaining that four rows of vines form a square (*pagina*). The vines grow onto trellises, which are like lines that give cohesion to these squares, or *paginae*. When we read a text, we are like grape harvesters, gleaning or reading the grapes (letters) off the trellises. The link between reading and harvesting is clearer in German than it is in English. In German, a grape harvest is a *Traubenlese*—literally, a "grape reading." Harvesters read the words (grapes) off the lines (trellises) that form the pages (*paginae*) where the grapes grow.

Hugh of Saint Victor makes explicit use of the harvesting metaphor when he likens Scripture to a forest, through which we wander while picking fruit off the trees: Scripture's "thoughts, like so many sweetest fruits, we pick as we read (*legendo carpimus*) and chew as we consider them." For Hugh, gleaning the words from the Scriptures is like picking fruits off the trees in the forest. The important point is that when medieval authors such as Guigo and Hugh reflected on what they were doing when engaged in reading, agricultural and viticultural images would quickly come to mind—hence the felicitous title of Ivan Illich's book on Hugh of Saint Victor, *In the Vineyard of the Text*.

Bernard of Clairvaux offers numerous examples of the link between eating and reading. He begins his first sermon on the Song of Songs by making clear to his readers that they should be ready for hard work. Drawing on the Pauline distinction—made in 1 Corinthians 3:1–2 and Hebrews 5:12–14—between teaching as milk (for infants) and solid food (for the mature), Bernard explains he will provide solid food. He compares the three books of Solomon—Proverbs, Ecclesiastes, and Song of Songs—to three loaves of bread (cf. Luke 11:5). He invites his listeners to start eating the Song of Songs as the third loaf: "You have already tasted these two, loaves you have accepted as being provided by a friend from his store (Lk 11:5). Come for the third loaf, too, so that perhaps you may recognize what is best." Whereas the first two books have cured his listeners' self-love (Proverbs) and love of the world (Ecclesiastes), they may now turn to the third, which offers holy, contemplative discourse.

The Cistercian abbot draws on eucharistic language to explain who will break this third loaf: it must be the master of the household himself. "Know the Lord in the breaking of bread," insists Bernard with a reference to the experience of Cleopas and his friend, to whom Jesus revealed himself "in the breaking of the bread" (Luke 24:35). Bernard considers himself inadequate to explain the Song of Songs: "I should not dare to do it myself. Look upon me as someone from whom you expect nothing." Bernard presents himself alongside his congregation as needing God's help to understand the mystery of the Song: "'The eyes of us all are turned upon you in hope, Lord' (Ps 145:15). 'The little children beg for bread; no one gives it to them' (Lam 4:4). They trust that they will receive it from your merciful love. O most Kind, break your bread for those who are hungering for it; by my hands, if you will allow, but by your own power." Of course, Bernard is the one explaining the Song to his listeners. But only the Lord Jesus himself can give the power necessary to do this well, for this particular loaf of bread—much like the Eucharist—offers us Christ himself. For Bernard, there is a certain order in eating: we first drink milk and next eat solids; and Solomon's third loaf is best of all, for here the Lord offers himself in the contemplative discourse of the Song of Songs.

Anselm, too, captures the process of lectio divina through the metaphor of eating. He encourages the reader of his *Meditation on Human Redemption* to reflect on the salvation that Christ has procured:

Consider again the strength of your salvation and where it is found. Meditate upon it, delight in the contemplation of it. Shake off your lethargy and set your mind to thinking over these things. Taste (*gusta*) the goodness of your Redeemer, be on fire with love for your Saviour. Chew (*mande*) the honeycomb of his words, suck (*suge*) their flavour which is sweeter than sap, swallow (*gluti*) their wholesome sweetness. Chew by thinking, suck by understanding, swallow by loving and rejoicing. Be glad to chew, be thankful to suck, rejoice to swallow.

Saint Anselm uses four imperatives related to eating: taste, chew, suck, and swallow. The first, taken from Psalm 34:8 ("O taste, and see that the Lord is sweet"), likely covers the entire process. Each of the other three focuses on one aspect of eating from the honeycomb: chewing, sucking, and swallowing. Figure 5.2 summarizes Anselm's uses of the honeycomb metaphor.

Eating Metaphor	Meaning	Response
Chew	Think	Be glad
Suck	Understand	Be thankful
Swallow	Love	Rejoice

Figure 5.2: *Anselm on tasting the goodness of the Lord*

Chewing the text is hard work. The rational mind is at work, thinking about what the text is saying, trying to figure out how the words function in the context of the passage, the book as a whole, and the entire canon; trying to understand the genre, the structure of the passage, and so forth. For Anselm, lectio divina involves hard work. We must take our time chewing the text itself. What is more, we should be glad to engage in this laborious activity of thinking about what the text might mean.

Anselm moves from chewing to sucking, and with that, from thinking to understanding. He does not specify how he wants us to distinguish between thinking (*cogitare*) and understanding (*intelligere*), but he likely has in mind that whereas in thinking we rationally analyze the literal meaning, in understanding we arrive at the reality of the spiritual meaning. Understanding gives us spiritual insight, which reaches beyond mere discursive analysis or argumentation.

Anselm must have found the language of sucking attractive as a metaphor for spiritual understanding. The waxy hexagonal cells of the honeycomb would need to be chewed, but the honey inside could be sucked out of the comb. The sucking imagery implies a more ready flow from text to reader than the language of chewing. The reader is now able directly to drink in the spiritual reality that had been hidden within the text. Just as God had made the Israelites suck (*sugeret*) honey from the rock (Deut 32:13; cf. Ps 81:16), so too he makes the biblical reader suck the honey as he arrives at a spiritual understanding of the text.

Anselm completes the triad of images by asking his reader to swallow the honey through loving and rejoicing. Just as swallowing completes the eating process, so loving completes the reading process. Any monk who had internalized Saint Augustine's famous book on reading (*De doctrina Christiana*) would have regarded love as the telos or end of interpretation. Anselm was no exception. The purpose of reading was to move from thinking via understanding to love itself—that is to say, to the climax of contemplative union with the God of love. By moving directly from understanding (*intelligere*) to love (*amare*), Anselm may seem to skip prayer in the process of divine reading. In reality, however, for Anselm the entire meditative process is suffused with prayer. Anselm's prayers, comments R. W. Southern, "have some element of meditation in them, and vice versa." In other words, it is prayerful meditation that leads to understanding and love.

READING AS BEES

HONEY IS AN evocative metaphor. If Christ is the rock (1 Cor 10:4), and if God's people sucked honey from the rock, then—so a mind trained by the practice of lectio divina would conclude—to suck honey must mean to internalize the teachings of Christ. The identification of Scripture as a honeycomb was irresistible also because the Psalms explicitly link the two. David praises God's ordinances, saying they are "sweeter than honey and the honeycomb" (Ps 19:10). Likewise, Psalm 119 exclaims, "How sweet are thy words to my palate! more than honey to my mouth" (Ps 119:103). For Christian readers, the theme of Scripture as honey was grounded directly in the biblical text. To be sure, it was not only the Scriptures that explored the theme. Classical Roman philosophers such as Seneca and Quintilian had earlier compared writing and speaking to the bees' activity of producing honey. Spiritual writers took the honey metaphor both from classical writers and from the divine Scriptures.

Throughout the lectio divina tradition, biblical readers have been interested in honey and bees. Monastic writers, especially those within the Cistercian tradition, delighted in sweetness of honey as the aim of divine reading. Saint Bernard of Clairvaux has aptly been named the Mellifluous Doctor. The name sticks not just because his own words flowed (*fluere*) like honey (*mel*) but also because he suckled his readers with the sweetness of the words from Scripture. The spiritual gift of honey from the rock provided every reason for Anselm's injunction to be thankful in response.

Once Scripture is understood as a honeycomb, numerous other aspects of the world of beekeeping also offer typological potential. Henri de Lubac and Fiona Griffiths both offer discussions of the various associations that beekeeping evoked for monastic readers. They point to at least four areas of significance:

- *Spiritual reading.* Bees produce honey inside the wax of the honeycomb. Just so, medieval authors explained, the outward letter of the Scriptures contains a hidden, spiritual meaning. The popular twelfth-century theologian Honorius of Autun draws this comparison: "The honeycomb is honey in the wax; honey in the wax is the spiritual understanding lying hidden in the letter, but the honeycomb is dripping, while sweet allegory is flowing from the letter." The practice of lectio divina involved a search for spiritual or allegorical truths by means of meditation; the process was a search for the sweet taste of biblical honey. Beekeeping was akin to monastic reading.

- *Organization.* Bees' communal life in a hive made them a cherished symbol of the monastic community. Bees seemed to live together peaceably within a hierarchical structure, much like monks are wont to do. Figure 5.3 is a picture from *The Aberdeen Bestiary* (ca. 1200) that depicts the orderly life of the bees: looking perfectly identical, they descend in military-style formation on their hives.

  The Aberdeen Bestiary highlights the bees' organized life together: "Expert in the task of making honey, they occupy the places assigned to them; they construct their dwelling-places with indescribable skill, and store away honey from a variety of flowers. They fill their fortress, made from a network of wax, with countless offspring. Bees have an army and kings; they fight battles." Saint Ambrose, who would become the patron saint of bees, heaps similar praise on them. He commends them for having the same abode, for living within one native land, for sharing the same food and activities, for electing a king and serving him while remaining free, for their architectural skills, and for their division of labor. Ambrose even substitutes the bee for the ant of Proverbs 6:8: "Scripture rightly commends the bee as a good worker: 'Behold the bee, see how busy she is, how admirable in her industry, the results of whose labors are serviceable to kings and commoners and are sought after by all men.'" Beehives were model monasteries.

- *Learning and wisdom.* Bees take nectar from flowers and store it in the cells of the hive, which functions akin to a memory palace in which monks store the biblical information gathered in meditation. The notion of the hive as a memory palace of sorts goes back to Seneca, who in the first century suggested we should imitate bees, "taking the things we have gathered from our diverse reading, first separate them (for things are better preserved when they are kept distinct), then, applying the care and ability of our own talent, conjoin those various samples into one savor."

Not surprisingly, considering the medieval interest in both memorization and beekeeping, monks similarly connected memorizing to the beehive as storage facility.

Figure 5.3: *"Of Bees," from The Aberdeen Bestiary*

To monks, murmuring lips resembled the buzzing of bees. The repetitive murmuring would eventually give each biblical verse its secure place within the mental beehive. Bees, therefore, functioned as symbols of wisdom and learning, both in classical culture and in later Christian tradition. The ninth-century Benedictine theologian Rabanus Maurus, for instance, comments, "Divine Scripture is a

honeycomb filled with the honey of spiritual wisdom."
Bees instilled wisdom in monks.

+ *Virginity*. Since bees were thought to reproduce without
  sexual intercourse, they were models for monastic purity
  and celibacy. Ambrose, relying on Virgil, offers the following description of the asexual reproduction of bees:
  "The act of generation is common to all. Their bodies
  are uncontaminated in the common act of parturition,
  since they have no part in conjugal embraces. They do
  not unnerve their bodies in love nor are they torn by the
  travail of childbirth. A mighty swarm of young suddenly
  appears. They gather their offspring in their mouths from
  the surface of leaves and from sweet herbs." The notion
  that bees procreate asexually was commonplace in the
  Middle Ages. The twelfth-century French theologian
  Hildebert of Lavardin, for example, writes, "The virgin is
  a little bee, who makes wax and procreates without coitus."
  Bees taught monks about virginity.

The world of bees sheds much light on the monastic life. Spiritual
reading, cooperation within hierarchical structure, memorization of
Scripture, and chastity were all realities that the monks could appreciate by observing the bees.

CHEWING THE CUD

MEDITATIVE READING IS repetitive. We keep going back to the
same passage, time and again. As we saw in chapter 4, meditation and
memorization go hand in hand. The food does not, therefore, simply

disappear in the stomach once we have swallowed it. Human beings turn out to be ruminant animals: they chew the cud. Ruminant animals—cattle, sheep, camels, giraffes, deer—only partially break down their food before bringing it back up. This repeated chewing or ruminating of half-digested food that has been in the *rumen* (the stomach's first chamber) eases the food's digestion. Practitioners of lectio divina engage in this same practice. As the Cistercian abbot William of Saint-Thierry puts it, "Some part of your daily reading should also each day be committed to memory, taken in as it were into the stomach, to be more carefully digested and brought up again for frequent rumination." No matter how often the path has been taken from thinking to understanding to love, we keep going back to the same Scriptures, chewing the cud. We ruminate to digest the Scriptures more thoroughly.

Talk of chewing the cud in connection with reading was common both in classical and in Christian thought. The first-century Spanish rhetorician Quintilian writes in *The Orator's Education*, "Students of any age who are concerned to improve their memory by study should be willing to swallow the initially wearisome business of repeating over and over again what they have written or read, and as it were chewing over the same old food." Saint Augustine, in his *Confessions*, speaks of the "stomach of the mind" (*venter animi*), where gladness and sadness are stored like sweet and bitter food. Similarly, in his book *On the Trinity*, he explains that the mind can snatch something from a beautiful piece of music and "deposit it in the memory as though swallowing it down into its stomach, and by recollection it will be able somehow to chew (*ruminare*) this in the cud and transfer what it has learnt into its stock of learning."

In Scripture, chewing the cud is a good thing. Animals that chew the cud and have split hooves are considered clean (Lev 11:3; Deut 14:4–6). Camels, though they chew the cud, do not have split hooves. Old Testament law, therefore, declares them unclean (Lev 11:4; Deut 14:7). Pope Gregory the Great reflects on this ambiguity in camels in an allegorical interpretation of Job 1:3, which tells us that Job had seven thousand sheep and three thousand camels. Saint Gregory explains that the (clean) sheep are the Hebrews and that the (unclean) camels may well refer to gentiles. At the same time, it may also be that the camels are a reference to the Samaritans. Why? He explains as follows: "For camels indeed chew the cud, but their hooves are not cloven. Samaritans also chew the cud in a way, since they obey a part of the law, and they are without cloven hooves in a way, since they hold part of the law in scorn." The Samaritans considered only the five books of Moses as authoritative. And, though Gregory doesn't explicitly mention it, the Samaritans were thought to be the mixed offspring of northern Israelites and people from other nations exiled to the same area by the Assyrians (2 Kgs 17). We could also say: Samaritans chewed the cud (they had the Law and were partially Hebrew in ethnic background), but they did not have split hooves (they were without the Prophets and the Writings and were ethnically mixed).

When he interprets the same reference to camels in Job 1:3 tropologically (or morally), Saint Gregory notes a similar ambiguity. The way we deal with earthly matters is never perfect. The mind inevitably experiences some kind of distraction. It often is not properly dedicated to heavenly things. The mind, explains Gregory, "is not cloven footed, because it does not separate itself completely from all worldly occupations; nevertheless, it chews the cud, for it arranges worldly affairs wisely and hopes for heaven with a confidence bordering on certainty." As camels in this life, we lack the purity we long for by faith. Though meditating on heaven as we chew the cud, we don't have split hooves, for we are still distracted by worldly concerns.

Chewing the cud is linked, then, with purity. Pure animals chew the cud. (And cud-chewing camels are impure for a different reason: they don't have split hooves.) The moral lesson is straightforward: it is incongruous to engage in lectio divina while being morally ship-wrecked. *By definition*, to meditate is to be clean, for only clean animals can chew the cud. William of Saint-Thierry reflects in one of his meditations on being permeated with the sweet fragrance of the Lord in the Eucharist: "As your clean beasts, we there regurgitate the sweet things stored within our memory, and chew them in our mouths like cud for the renewed and ceaseless work of our salvation. That done, we put away again in that same memory what you have done, what you have suffered for our sake." William links the physical chewing of the host to the spiritual chewing of Christ's work of salvation. Both require purity, since only clean animals can properly ruminate.

Chewing the cud inevitably involves belching. Also here, the monastic authors had biblical precedent. Psalm 45, a famous wedding song, addresses the king, the groom of the psalm (vv. 2–9), before turning to the bride (vv. 10–17). The psalm begins with the words "My heart hath uttered (*eructavit*) a good word: I speak my works to the king: My tongue is the pen of a scrivener that writeth swiftly" (v. 1). The verb *eructare* can both mean "to utter" and "to belch," and theological interpreters were often tempted to combine the two meanings. Thus, the image from the early twelfth-century St. Albans Psalter (figure 5.4) depicts the psalm's author seated within the letter *E*—since the word *eructavit* is the first word of the psalm in Latin—with a pen in his right hand and with his left hand reaching his tongue as a pen. The tongue both belches and writes.

Saint Bernard of Clairvaux reflects on this theme of belching in Sermon 67 of his series on the Song of Songs, preaching from 2:16, "My beloved is mine and I am his." The Mellifluous Doctor observes that the bride's words lack a verb; they don't make for a complete sentence. Literally, she says, "My beloved to me, and I to him." Bernard notes that we cannot understand this incomplete sentence. "Why would you seek in such a spontaneous outburst for the grammatical arrangement and sequence of words, or for the rules and ornaments of rhetoric?" Love has so inebriated the bride that she "belches forth rather than utters whatever rises to her lips." The bride, when she belches, acts in line with Psalm 145:7, since she is "belching (*eructabunt*) the memory of the abundance of Thy sweetness." The bride only has her memories left: the groom has already left her. And Bernard himself is even further removed from the original experience: he has to be satisfied with a report—just a belch, really—from the bride. He merely catches a whiff of her belch, but even this whiff is enough to recognize the scent of the Savior and to rekindle the longing for union with the heavenly Groom.

CONCLUSION

THE EATING METAPHOR is pervasive in the lectio divina tradition. Every one of the monastic writers we have looked at compares reading to eating, spurred on by the Scriptures' own use of this comparison. These writers all loved to explore and elaborate on the comparison, turning to themes adjacent to eating such as harvesting, chewing the

Figure 5.4: *The psalmist "belching" a goodly theme (Ps 45:1); St. Albans Psalter*

cud, belching, and beekeeping. Mostly the Bible itself goaded their minds. After all, that's where the monks would read of clean animals chewing the cud, of belching a goodly theme, and of God's words being sweet drippings from the honeycomb. The Bible was the key source shaping the monastic imagination, and it provided monks with a set of mental pictures that explained what divine reading is all about.

No matter how much Christians through the centuries may have loved the Scriptures, however, lectio divina aims beyond the words of the Bible. The sweetness that these words convey is the sweetness of the Lord himself. *Gustate et videte quoniam suavis est Dominus* ("O taste, and see that the Lord is sweet"); thus runs the Vulgate of what we know in our English Bibles as Psalm 34:8. The Lord is sweet. Or, to put it in the language of Anselm's triad of thinking, understanding, and love: the Lord is love. To taste sweetness in and through the practice of lectio divina is to taste the sweetness (or love) of God himself. It is to be united to God.

Lectio divina, therefore, is most fundamentally the search for God. We do lectio because we want to taste his sweetness or experience his love. The reason Bernard, William, and others linked lectio divina with the Eucharist is that the two offer one and the same thing—or, rather, one and the same person: Jesus. To meditate on Scripture is to eat Jesus, just as to partake of the host is to eat Jesus. There is no difference in terms of the identity of the one we ingest.

When we listen to the words "O taste, and see that the Lord is sweet," what we hear is "O taste, and see that Jesus is sweet." Jesus is the Lord himself. When Honorius suggests that "honey in the wax is the spiritual understanding lying hidden in the letter," he directs us to look for Jesus, the Lord himself, hiding within the letter of the text. The reality at which divine reading aims, therefore, is Jesus. He incarnates the sweetness and love of God.

When we eat Christ, we become Christ. This simple but profound insight, derived from the teaching of Saint Augustine, grounds the practice of lectio divina. When we experience the sweetness and love of God, we become the sweetness and love of God. Man is what he eats.

Why do lectio divina? Because by *enjoying* God's sweetness in Christ, we *become* God's sweetness in Christ.

VI

Trees

UBIQUITOUS TREES

JESUS IS THE POINT of reading the Bible. We are meant to conform to him. In particular, we are meant to conform to his cross. Cruciformity is the heart of biblical teaching, for it is on the cross that we come to know the love of God. Lectio divina, therefore, must be centered on Christ and the cross. Many of the lectio divina examples that we have looked at focus on the Psalms. And indeed, we encounter Christ in them. But longing for cruciformity also draws us to the Gospels. Nowhere is the love of God spelled out in clearer terms than in the Gospels. They too, therefore, have been the focus of Christian devotion, and in lectio divina, people have especially felt themselves drawn to the Gospels' narration of the passion of Christ on the cross.

One clear example of meditation on Jesus (a very human Jesus), his suffering (a very brutal suffering), and cruciformity (a very painful cruciformity) is found in Saint Bonaventure's *The Tree of Life* (*Lignum vitae*), which he wrote sometime between 1257 and 1267. The title of the book unmistakably points to the cross as the heart of its teaching. And although Bonaventure's cross is life-giving—the tree yields twelve distinct fruits—we experience its life only by being nailed with Christ to the cross. In this chapter, we will reflect on Bonaventure's link between trees and union with Christ. I will place the discussion within a broader framework of trees in general, for medieval spiritual writers recognized a variety of ways in which trees can betoken our union with Christ. They saw the cross as one of a number of trees (albeit the most important one) that unites us with Christ. And, as will become clear, lectio divina shaped the way Bonaventure and others used the tree metaphor to speak of this union with Christ.

Bonaventure was not the first theologian to reflect on trees. Starting around 1100, writings about trees (we might call them arboreal texts) began to turn up everywhere in the theological landscape. "Trees," explains Sara Ritchey, "appear ubiquitously in the art and letters attesting to Christocentric devotion, primarily because twelfth-century exegesis dictated that a tree was responsible for both the incarnation and the crucifixion of Christ." The twelfth and thirteenth centuries abound with meditations on and representations of trees that connect them somehow with salvation in Christ.

The link between Christ and trees did not originate in the Middle Ages, though. Christians throughout the centuries have reflected on the connection. Within the Scriptures themselves, trees play a significant role, and already here we can see christological links. We first read about trees in Genesis 2:9, which tells us that God planted "the tree of life ... in the midst of paradise: and the tree of knowledge of good and evil." Eating from the first gives eternal life (Gen 3:22). This tree of life resurfaces in several key eschatological passages. The description of the tree of life in Revelation 22:2 is quite embellished compared to the minimalism of the creation story. In the new Jerusalem, the tree straddles both sides of the river, has different kinds of fruit each month, and heals the nations with its leaves. The embellishments are taken from the prophetic passage of Ezekiel 47:12 (though this text doesn't mention a tree of life but "all trees that bear fruit"). John the Seer has a vision of the eschaton that calls to mind the paradisal tree of life through the lens of Ezekiel's prophetic promise.

But why identify the cross (or Christ) as this tree of life? The reason lies in various other biblical references. Most significant is Proverbs 3:18, which personifies wisdom: "She is a tree of life to them that lay hold on her: and he that shall retain her is blessed." When Christians see Proverbs personifying *wisdom* as a tree of life, they can hardly avoid the conclusion that this tree of life is *Christ*. The New Testament, after all, is unambiguous about Christ being the wisdom of God (1 Cor 1:24; Col 2:3). Just as eating from the tree of life would give eternal life, according to the book of Genesis, so the gaining of wisdom offers blessedness in Proverbs. What is more, when Saint Paul refers to Christ as God's wisdom, he has the cross in mind first and foremost. Christ crucified, the apostle asserts, while folly to gentiles, is the wisdom of God. It is specifically the tree of the cross that shows God's wisdom.

Isaiah 11 looks forward to a ruler from the line of Jesse, David's father, who will justly rule the nations, and whose reign will put an end to violence, even in the animal kingdom. The messianic king is described with the metaphor of a tree: "And there shall come forth a rod out of the root of Jesse, and a flower shall rise up out of his root" (Isa 11:1). Christians, following Saint Paul (Rom 15:12), have long recognized Christ as the Davidic descendant mentioned in Isaiah. Christ, therefore, was the branch that grew from the exilic stump of Jesse's tree.

Another tree passage is Deuteronomy 21:22–23, which insists that someone hanged on a tree is accursed by God. Saint Paul applies this reference to the cross of Christ: "Christ hath redeemed us from the curse of the law, being made a curse for us (for it is written: Cursed is every one that hangeth on a tree)" (Gal 3:13). And the apostle immediately adds that this curse means blessing—in line with the promises of eternal life (Gen 3:22) and blessedness (Prov 3:18)—for those who by faith are Abraham's seed (Gal 3:29). No biblical passage directly identifies the cross as the tree of life. But to Christians, the constellation of passages is irresistibly suggestive. Once we've linked Christ, wisdom, and tree in Proverbs 3:18, we would have to be ardent literalists not to link the various other tree passages also to the cross of Christ.

The result is a rich tradition of meditation on arboreal texts. Ritchey explains that three major tree-types dotted the medieval theological landscape: the Jesse Tree; the Trees of Vices and of Virtues; and the Tree of the Cross. The Jesse Tree had its origin in Isaiah 11. Many held that Mary was the shoot (*virga*) that came from Jesse's root (*radix*), while Christ himself was the branch or the flower (*flos*). Jesse Trees, which were depicted in stained-glass windows, manuscripts, paintings, carvings, and the like, depicted the genealogy of Jesus, beginning with David's father Jesse at the bottom and leading to Mary and Jesus at the top.

Trees of Vices and of Virtues depicted morality as a bunch of fruits hanging from trees. Figures 6.1 and 6.2 are among the most well-known examples. These two trees are found in at least some copies of the *Speculum virginum* (Mirror of Virgins), which was probably written by Conrad of Hirsau at the Abbey of Andernach, Germany, in the mid-twelfth century. The book takes the form of a dialogue between spiritual director Peregrinus (Pilgrim) and his female disciple

Theodora. It became a popular guide among communities of religious women in Germany and France over the next several centuries. The two tree images hail from the early thirteenth century, from the Cistercian Himmerod Abbey in Germany.

Part of the dialogue between Peregrinus and Theodora centers on her desire to enter the garden of delights with the flowers and fruits of the Tree of Virtue. She wants to leave the vices behind and adopt the virtues instead. Peregrinus explains to Theodora the aim of the exercise: "Leaving the left side, let us return to the right, let us transform the trunk of transgression into the tree of life, let us enter Paradise, in its delight and by its flowing abundance beyond all the rewards of the world." By moving from the image on the left to the one on the right, Theodora can change her life of vices into a life of virtues. Careful meditation on the two images is the first step of this transformative process.

On the left, Theodora will have seen the Tree of Vices, which has pride as its root. Pride is identified as Babylon and holds the golden cup, which makes all the earth drunk (Jer 51:7). Pride yields the fruits of anger, vanity, sloth, envy, gluttony, greed, and—at the very top, identified with the first Adam—lust. Each of these vices has seven sub-vices, with the exception of lust, which has no fewer than twelve. The serpent twists himself around the tree of knowledge of good and evil (Gen 2:9). Dragons look to devour the Adamic figure; and the fruits of the vices, which hang down, drag people down toward hell.

By contrast, on the right Theodora would have recognized humility as the root of the Tree of Virtues. On both sides of the tree, cherubim protect the life of virtue. The tree, which grows in Jerusalem, has seven main flowers: justice, prudence, temperance, and fortitude

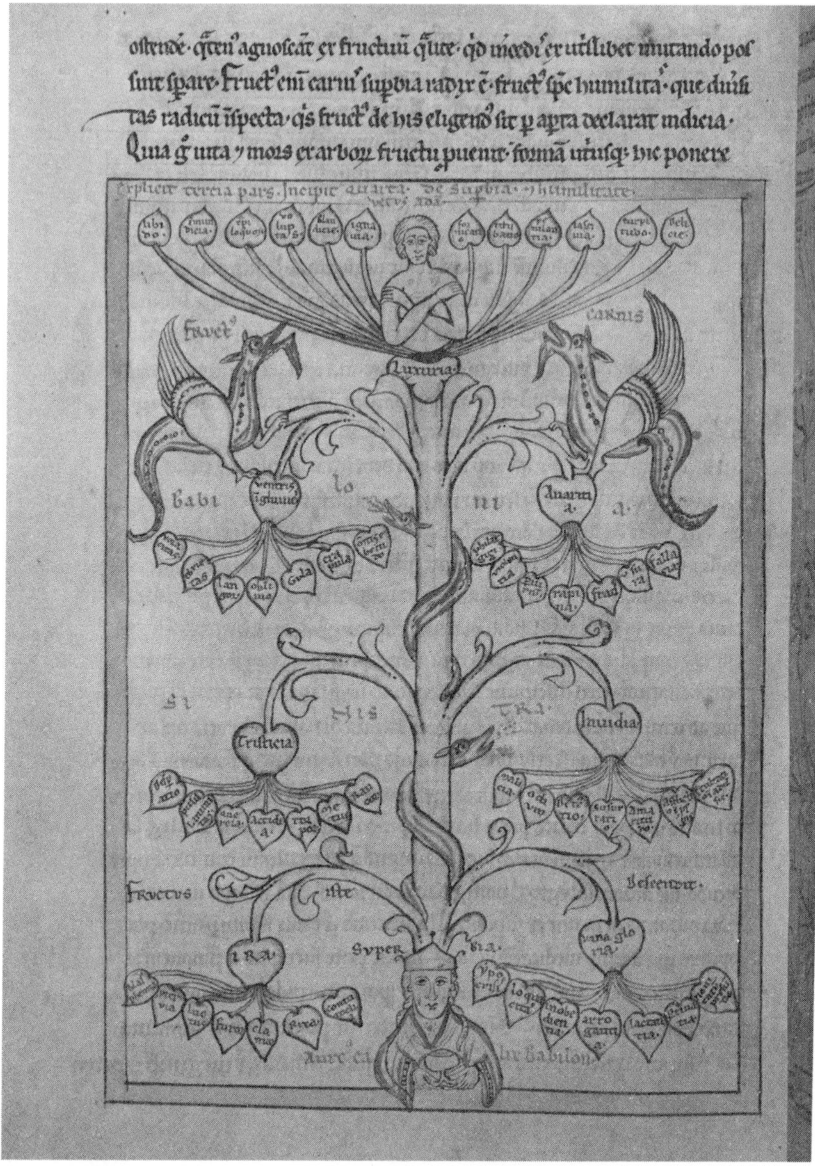

Figure 6.1: *"Tree of Vices" from the Speculum virginum*

placuir·ur er aſſiðariðe peiors·grã indeat melious·veem g adã atten
de in arce uirriose arbonis poſiru·nouu adã obrine puenr ſpalus pneupa
ru·Deniq· ſi pſtanti derion·id e ſi bonu malo coiunxeris·qð in his emi
near uatenr intelligis·Collanis enum qiurario ofrioir·luce clari pacebir
eſtimatio meliorum·

Figure 6.2: *"Tree of Virtues" from the Speculum virginum*

(traditionally known as the cardinal virtues), along with faith and hope, as well as charity at the very top (the so-called theological virtues). Each of the virtues is subdivided into seven additional virtues, though charity, identified with Christ himself as the new Adam, is made up of ten rather than seven distinct virtues. The branches and fruits of the tree of life (Gen 2:9) all move up toward heaven, where Christ is.

The third type of tree frequently depicted in the twelfth and thirteenth centuries is the Tree of the Cross. This is the tree Bonaventure speaks of in *The Tree of Life*. This tree identifies the cross (or Christ on the cross) with the tree of life in Paradise. It is not surprising that Bonaventure was attracted to this third type of tree. It allowed him to meditate on the cross and to reflect in detail on the various aspects of Christ's suffering. Since identification with Christ in his suffering—cruciformity—was the focus of Bonaventure's spirituality, he readily turned to the common imagery of the cross as a tree. In so doing, Bonaventure joined many of his contemporaries, who also used various kinds of trees to reflect on Christ and on union with him. The biblical stock of tree metaphors was widely in use, and Bonaventure's first readers would quickly have recognized the genre of writing they had in front of them.

BONAVENTURE'S MEMORY TREE

BONAVENTURE MENTIONS IN his prologue to *The Tree of Life* that he hopes to arrive at his aim—getting us to conform to the Tree of the Cross—by taking into account each of the mind's three faculties: understanding (*intellectus*), memory (*memoria*), and will (*voluntas*). The first concerns the *what* of learning: the understanding intellectually appropriates the content of the Gospel scenes. And since Bonaventure recounts, each time fairly straightforwardly, the content of numerous biblical episodes, he obviously aims at the intellect. Still, the Seraphic Doctor not only addresses the intellect but also aims at both memory and will (or affections) directly and extensively.

Let's discuss both in turn. Bonaventure explains that he wants the memory of the Gospel scenes to be "imprinted" (*imprimatur*) on the mind. Since the bride in the Song of Songs speaks of her groom as a bundle of myrrh between her breasts (Song 1:13), Bonaventure treats the Gospel stories as this bundle of myrrh. Deliberately employing arboreal prose, he writes,

> I have endeavored to gather this bundle of myrrh from the forest of the holy Gospel, which treats at length the life, passion and glorification of Jesus Christ. I have bound it together with a few ordered (*ordinatis*) and parallel words to aid the memory (*memoriae*). I have used simple, familiar and unsophisticated terms to avoid idle curiosity, to cultivate devotion and to foster the piety of faith. Since imagination aids understanding, I have arranged in the form of an imaginary tree (*imaginaria ... arbore*) the few items I have collected from among many, and have ordered (*ordinavi*) and disposed them in such a way that in the first or lower branches the Savior's origin and life are described; in the middle, his passion; and in the top, his glorification.

Bonaventure has ambled through the Gospel forest and has collected a number of branches. He has bound them together and arranged them as an imaginary tree.

Much like Hugh used the ark's rooms to store all of salvation history, so Bonaventure uses the tree's branches with its leaves, flowers, and fruit to itemize details of the Gospel story of Christ. And much like Hugh, Bonaventure does this at least in part out of concern for proper organization; twice, he uses the verb *ordinare*. When we order the Gospel scenes and place each one in its proper location, it is easy to remember them all. This ordering is important for Bonaventure, considering the large number of events in Jesus's life, passion, and glorification that he discusses. By giving each of them a place on the tree, Bonaventure makes it easy to remember the various items in their sequential order. The tree, in other words, serves as a kind of memory tree: it is a repository in which to store the items that we want to keep in our minds. The memory tree helps us select individual items for special meditation.

Bonaventure devises various additional techniques, which are also meant to facilitate memorization. He divides the book into three main parts in which to store the Gospel content, dealing with the mysteries of Jesus's origin, passion, and glorification. He then divides each of these three mysteries into four fruits or branches, so that there are twelve fruits in total. Finally, he divides each of the fruits into four Gospel details, which artwork usually superimposes on top of leaves that hang from the branches. The result is a tree with twelve fruits or branches and forty-eight leaves, every one of them representing a distinct scene of Jesus's origin, passion, and glorification. Bonaventure's book likely contained an actual picture of the tree, though his comment in the block quote above—"I have arranged in the form of an imaginary tree the few items I have collected"—is a bit ambiguous. But even if the original manuscript did not carry an image, the detailed description of the tree certainly inspired illustrators and painters over the next several centuries.

Figure 6.3: *Bonaguida's Tree of Life*

The Seraphic Doctor would no doubt have approved of us analyzing his book with the help of one of these later paintings, by Pacino di Bonaguida (figure 6.3). It dates from around 1310–1315. Bonaguida painted his *Tree of Life* for the Convent of Monticelli, a convent of Poor Clares—an order of Franciscan nuns—in Florence.

Bonaguida's painting follows Bonaventure's book fairly closely. The main exception is the Christ figure hanging on the tree, which is absent from Bonaventure's book. Still, the figure is quite appropriate: Jesus's physical suffering on the cross was central to the spirituality of Bonaventure and of the subsequent Franciscan tradition. Jesus's passion may take up only one-third of *The Tree of Life*, but it is the central part. The descriptions of Jesus's pain and suffering that Bonaventure offers here are, very deliberately, heart-wrenching. Section 28—the leaf closest to Jesus's loincloth, hanging from the fourth branch—is titled "Jesus Given Gall to Drink" (figure 6.4).

Figure 6.4: *Detail from Bonaguida's Tree of Life*

Bonaventure draws our attention to the blessed Virgin, who watches the scene, and he addresses her directly:

You were present at all these events,
standing close by and participating (*particeps*) in them
in every way.
This blessed and most holy flesh (*carnem*)—
which you so chastely conceived,
so sweetly nourished
and fed with your milk,
which you so often held on your lap,
and kissed with your lips—
you actually gazed upon
with your bodily eyes
now torn by the blows of the scourges,
now pierced (*perforari*) by the points of the thorns,
now struck by the reed,
now beaten by hands and fists,
now pierced (*perfodi*) by nails and fixed (*affixam*)
to the wood of the cross,
and torn by its own weight as it hung there,
now mocked in every way,
finally made to drink gall and vinegar.

The descriptions are earthy and physical. We picture Mary feeding baby Jesus with her milk, holding him on her lap, gazing at him, and kissing him. Bonaventure then drastically juxtaposes these sweet images with his body being torn, pierced, struck, beaten, and fixed on the cross. The contrast that Bonaventure depicts between Jesus's infancy and his passion makes the latter stand out all the more. But the infancy and crucifixion scenes are both centered on the flesh (*carnem*) of Jesus. Bonaventure's Jesus is, for the most part, a this-worldly, human, and physical Jesus. In the Bonaventurean vision, this is what makes it possible for the Virgin, as well as for us, to stand close by and even to participate (*particeps*) in the events.

As we would expect, each of the twelve branches of Bonaguida's painting has four scenes, closely patterned on Bonaventure's descriptions in *The Tree of Life*, except that the top right branch only has three. Bonaguida has moved the last scene—our eternal happiness in Jesus as the Alpha and the Omega—to Jesus's footrest, or *suppedaneum*, with the words "ALPHA ET Ω" (Alpha and Omega). Bonaguida has also added various details to the bottom and the top of the Tree of the Cross. At the very bottom, he depicts various scenes from Genesis 2 and 3: the creation of Adam and Eve, their fall into sin, and their expulsion from Paradise. This reminds us that the crucified Christ is the second Adam and that Christ's death on the Tree of the Cross undoes the effects of Adam and Eve's eating from the tree of knowledge of good and evil.

Bonaventure seems to be reading his own book, *The Tree of Life*, in the cave underneath the cross. And immediately above the scenes from Paradise, we have the four figures of Moses, Francis, Clare, and John the Evangelist. Moses, appropriately, holds up Genesis 2:9 (about the tree of knowledge of good and evil), and John reads Revelation 22:2 (about the tree of life). Meanwhile, Saint Francis reflects on Paul's insistence in Galatians 6:14 that he boasts only in the cross, and Saint Clare is contemplating the bundle of myrrh from Song 1:13.

Above the cross, a pelican feeds her offspring with her own blood, a common patristic and medieval trope representing Jesus's death on the cross. To the left of the pelican, Ezekiel reads from 47:12 ("the fruits thereof shall be for food, and the leaves thereof for medicine"), and to the right Daniel reads from 4:9 ("Its leaves were most beautiful, and its fruit exceeding much: and in it was food for all"). Angels and saints occupy the heavenly choir stalls, overlooked by Mary and Jesus.

Perhaps the main difference between Bonaventure's book and Bonaguida's painting is that Bonaventure didn't put pictures inside the roundels. Instead, he wrote a lengthy poem, one stanza for each of the twelve fruits, one line for every biblical scene—in other words, twelve stanzas with four lines each. Bonaventure mentions the poem in the prologue. Unfortunately, he has not left us a copy of the poem; but it seems that *The Tree of Life*'s forty-eight section headings strung together make up most of the original poem. For example, the first of the twelve fruits ("His Distinguished Origin") has the following four sections:

Iesus, ex Deo genitus	Jesus Begotten of God
Iesus, Praefiguratus	Jesus Prefigured
Iesus, emissus caelitus	Jesus Sent from Heaven
Iesus, Maria natus	Jesus Born of Mary

These four section headings of this first fruit probably combined into one stanza of Bonaventure's poem, depicted on the lowest branch at the bottom left of the tree. Each of the lines was likely given a separate leaf hanging from this branch. It is not hard to match Bonaventure's four leaves (figure 6.5) with Bonaguida's four roundels at the bottom left of his tree (figure 6.6).

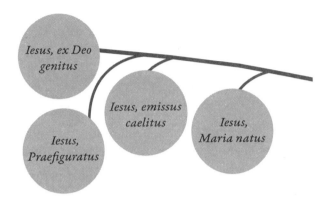

Figure 6.5: *The Four Leaves of Bonaventure's First Fruit*

Figure 6.6: *The Four Leaves of Bonaguida's First Fruit*

The top left roundel in figure 6.6 depicts the Father begetting the Son ("Iesus, ex Deo genitus"). The one underneath it shows Daniel's description of a stone "cut out of a mountain without hands" (Dan 2:34), smiting the image that Nebuchadnezzar saw in his dream—a messianic prophecy ("Iesus, Praefiguratus"). The third roundel presents the Annunciation on the left and the Visitation on the right ("Iesus, emissus caelitus"). And the last roundel gives us Jesus's birth in a manger ("Iesus, Maria natus").

Besides the twelve stanzas hanging as leaves from the branches, Bonaventure probably wrote three additional stanzas, making for a total of fifteen. He may have placed one of the three underneath the tree, which allowed it to serve as a kind of refrain, and as a result the monks may well have chanted the poem responsively. The refrain ran as follows:

O crux, frutex salvificus,	O cross, salvation-bearing tree,
Vivo fonte rigatus	Watered by a living fountain,
Cuius flos aromaticus	Your flower is spice-scented,
Fructus desideratus	Your fruit an object of desire.

An additional two stanzas, perhaps placed above the Tree of the Cross, prayed for the gifting of the Holy Spirit:

His nos ciba fructibus,	Feed us with these fruits,
Illustra cogitatus,	Shed light upon our thoughts,
Rectis duc itineribus,	Lead us along straight paths,
Hostis frange conatus	Crush the attacks of the enemy.
Sacris reple fulgoribus,	Fill us with your sacred light,
Spira pios afflatus,	Breathe holy inspiration,
Sisque Christum timentibus,	Be a peaceful way of life
Tranquillus vitae status. Amen.	For those who fear Christ. Amen.

These last two stanzas, which Bonaventure included at the end of
the prologue of *The Tree of Life*, make clear that the success of meditation depends, not on our intellectual abilities, but on the grace
of God. It is impossible to avoid Adam's example of eating from the
tree of knowledge of good and evil, suggests Bonaventure, unless
we prefer "faith to reason, devotion to investigation, simplicity
to curiosity and finally the sacred cross of Christ to all carnal feeling or wisdom of the flesh." The early Franciscan spiritual master,
though himself by no means averse to intricate theological discussion, sensed a tension between spirituality and theology (or feeling
and intellect), which, sadly, in the late Middle Ages would turn into
an unbridgeable gap.

Bonaventure was a skilled teacher. He carefully ordered the structure of his book: three main sections, twelve fruits, four leaves for
each fruit. He used the pictorial image of the tree of life as a frame in
which to situate the various Gospel scenes. He even used poetic chant
to assist the process of memorization. Once his monks had memorized
the poem—which is to say, each heading of the forty-eight sections
of the book—they would have had a handle on the Seraphic Doctor's
entire book. Reciting the poem while visualizing the tree, one by one
the Gospel scenes would flash before their eyes. Bonaventure's tree
was a memory tree.

PIERCED ON THE TREE

Let's move from the memory (*memoria*) to the will (*voluntas*).
Though not an anti-intellectualist, Bonaventure did focus on the will—
and, with that, on affections, experience, and feeling. Shaped by earlier

medieval masters of spiritual reading, Bonaventure was convinced that our affections, more so than our intellectual apprehension, unite us to Christ. Therefore, he turned to lectio divina to shape the affective life of his readers. Richard Martignetti, who has written the definitive book on Bonaventure's *The Tree of Life*, remarks, "We can best understand the *Lignum vitae* if we see it as the fruit of Bonaventure's own *lectio divina*, of his own prayer and reflection on the Scriptures and on other Scriptural meditations that were available to him." Lectio divina forms the backdrop against which we can best understand what it is that Bonaventure tried to do in *The Tree of Life*.

Through repeated *lectio*—which is to say, through memorization—Bonaventure made the stories of the Gospels his own. He meditated deeply on his own relationship to his Lord and Savior, and in *The Tree of Life* he offered the fruit of this meditation. His goal with the book was that his readers might go through the same process. Bonaventure's desire, writes Martignetti, was that "we use the *Lignum vitae* to allow ourselves to enter more deeply into the Scriptures and allow our imaginations to foster for us a deeper experience of Christ and his love. Such is the way of reading and meditating in lectio divina, a way that leads the *viator* into true prayer of the heart." In short, the book's purpose is for the *viator* or traveler to experience Christ more deeply—to be nailed to the cross with Christ.

Being crucified with Christ had been the heart also of Saint Francis's spirituality. In the year 1224, two years before his death, Francis saw the risen Lord Jesus in a vision at Mount Alverna. Bonaventure, in *The Life of St. Francis* (1263), famously describes the vision—and its effects—as follows:

On a certain morning about the feast of the Exaltation of the Cross, while Francis was praying on the mountainside, he saw a Seraph with six fiery and shining wings descend from the height of heaven. And when in swift flight the Seraph had reached a spot in the air near the man of God, there appeared between the wings the figure of a man crucified, with his hands and feet extended in the form of a cross and fastened to a cross. ... As the vision disappeared, it left in his heart a marvelous ardor and imprinted on his body markings that were no less marvelous. Immediately the marks of nails began to appear in his hands and feet just as he had seen a little before in the figure of the man crucified.

God's burning love came to Francis in the vision of a fiery seraph, who showed him the crucified Lord. The experience imprinted the stigmata of Jesus's hands, feet, and right side on Francis's body. Bonaventure relates that in the last few years of his life, blood would often flow from the side of Francis's body.

Understandably, then, no biblical text was more important to Bonaventure than Galatians 2:20, "with Christ I am nailed to the cross." After recounting the story of Francis's vision, Bonaventure opens the next chapter of *The Life of Saint Francis* with the comment, "Now fixed with Christ to the cross [Gal 2:20], in both body and spirit, Francis not only burned with a Seraphic love of God but also thirsted [John 19:28] with Christ crucified for the salvation of men." The Pauline line again features in the prologue of *The Soul's Journey into God*. After mentioning the burning love of the crucified Lord with a reference to Galatians 2:20, Bonaventure adds, "This love also so absorbed the soul of Francis that his spirit shone through his flesh when for two years before his death he carried in his body the sacred stigmata of the passion." Finally, the Seraphic Doctor also uses Paul's text as the opening line of *The Tree of Life*: "With Christ I am nailed to the cross, from Galatians, chapter two." He goes on to say that disciples of Christ must carry both in the soul and in the flesh the cross of Christ—obviously thinking back to the experience that Francis had toward the end of his life.

Bonaventure's Latin Bible rendered the line from Galatians more graphically than do most contemporary English versions: *Christo confixus sum cruci*. The word *confixus*—"pierced through"—reminded Bonaventure of the horrible, bodily suffering that Jesus endured on the cross. He was nailed to the cross; or, as Bonaventure puts it in *The Tree of Life*, "Thrown roughly upon the wood of the cross, spread out, pulled forward and stretched back and forth like a hide, he was pierced (*perforatur*) by pointed nails, fixed (*affixus*) to the cross by his sacred hands and feet and most roughly torn with wounds." Francis, for Bonaventure, was the model of real cruciformity. Francis, in some sense, *was* the tree of life to whom Bonaventure wished to conform himself. Identification with Jesus's bodily torture forms the heart of Bonaventure's spirituality.

Bonaventure, then, wished for his meditation on the Tree of the Cross to serve as a means for the readers to be conformed to Jesus's suffering. Bonaventure wanted them to recognize Francis, Paul, and Jesus in the tree that he described in his book, so that, by meditating on Galatians 2:20, his reader too might share in the suffering of Christ, this time "not by the martyrdom of his flesh, but by the fire of his love consuming his soul." Through *lectio* and *meditatio* of *The Tree of Life*, the suffering of Christ (as well as of Paul and Francis) would be impressed upon the reader's mind; it would be inflamed with love and so would enter mystically into contemplative union with Christ.

Contemplative union with Christ, then, is something experiential. Bonaventure mentions in the prologue that he wants his reader to truly feel that he is nailed to the cross. The affection and feeling can be experienced only by an intense contemplation—using every one of our faculties—of the crucified Jesus. The vocabulary is striking. Bonaventure is not content with simply passing on the contents of the Gospel stories. Today, we would say he aimed at the heart, not just the head. The very structure of *The Tree of Life* served to facilitate this experiential participation in Christ. The forty-eight sections are all divided in two. Each time, Bonaventure first gives a rather straightforward description of the episode that he offers for meditation. Here, he aims at the intellect (*intellectus*). Next, however, he directly speaks to his own soul or to the reader, appealing at length to the emotional life, using every possible rhetorical ploy he can find to draw the reader into an emotional encounter with the narrative. Here, he obviously aims at the will (*voluntas*).

Bonaventure is perhaps most explicit about the centrality of the will and the affections when he deals with the last fruit, "Jesus, Fountain-Ray of Light." Here he digs deep into the tradition to speak of Jesus as the "superessential Ray" of light. He urges his soul to "run with living desire" to the fountain. He addresses the "sweet stream" that comes from this fountain, knowing that the guests at the banquet may "drink to joyful inebriation" from this "powerful fiery torrent." He wishes for its "longed-for waters" to refresh the "thirsting throat of our parched hearts," so that we may sing to Jesus a song of praise, "proving by experience that *with you is the fountain of life, and in your light we will see light.*" This entire section takes the shape of an extended reflection on Psalm 36:9, which Bonaventure finally quotes at the end. Throughout, he makes clear that the *lectio* and *meditatio* of his book are meant to lead to an ecstatic, experiential union with Jesus.

Bonaventure often tells his readers to imagine themselves as part of the story, in the presence of the characters, perhaps even as one of them. Bonaventure does this, for instance, in connection with Jesus's presentation in the temple:

> Rejoice, then,
> with that blessed old man and the aged Anna;
> walk forth
> to meet the mother and Child.
> Let love overcome your bashfulness;
> let affection dispel your fear.
> Receive the Infant
> in your arms
> and say with the bride:
> I took hold of him
> and would not let him go [Song 3:4].
>
> Dance with the holy old man
> and sing with him:
> Now dismiss your servant, Lord,
> according to your word in peace [Luke 2:29].

Bonaventure asks us to identify with Anna and Simeon so as to meet Mary, take Jesus in our arms, and make the *Nunc Dimittis* our own. The Seraphic Doctor's rhetoric, repeatedly, takes the form of what in later Ignatian spirituality would be called *composition of place*. Bonaventure composes an imaginative place, in which we can encounter the narrative's characters. This encounter shapes our imagination, encouraging us to be conformed to Jesus himself.

CONCLUSION

I DO NOT mean to hold up Bonaventure as the best possible, let alone the only model for reading the Gospels. Bonaventure, too, had his shortcomings. Picking up on the physical sufferings of the human Jesus, he foregrounded the will—affections, emotions, and feelings—in reflecting on the nature of true discipleship. In retrospect, it is easy to see how later spirituality might take these early Franciscan discoveries and run with them, misconstruing the unity of divinity and humanity, of intellect and will. But wisdom would dictate that we hold back on some of this criticism. Bonaventure confessed "Jesus Begotten of God" as the first item of the first fruit. Bonaventure was an eminently Trinitarian theologian. He also recognized the invaluable worth of the human intellect (*intellectus*), indispensable for the soul's journey into God; even lectio divina relied, for Bonaventure, not just on the will but also on the intellect.

Most importantly, Bonaventure's *The Tree of Life* offers a key contribution to the practice of lectio divina. I do not simply mean that he gives us the fruit of his own meditations or that he aims to draw us into spiritual reading by means of his book, though that is all true. Rather, Bonaventure reminds us that cruciformity—being pierced by the love of God—is the heart of biblical teaching. Only if we feel the nails of the cross will we also join Christ in his resurrection life. When we embark on divine reading with honesty and integrity, it will yield suffering. But surely, we rejoice when we remind ourselves that cruci-formity means suffering along with Bonaventure, with Francis, with Paul, and ultimately with Christ himself.

VII

Bread of Tears

LECTIO DIVINA AND SPIRITUALITY

I DON'T PARTICULARLY CARE for the word "spirituality." I use it, both because of its obvious biblical resonance—of God as Spirit as well as the human spirit—and because conforming to common usage allows me to converse more easily with others. But what makes me uneasy about the term is the comfy, fluffy, soporific connotation that it typically carries. Many people today think of themselves as spiritual, not religious. If we have a vague sense of peace, connection, and meaning that permeates our lives and the cosmos as a whole, we're spiritual. But we've become wary of identifying with particular religious beliefs, let alone organized institutions, practices, and rituals; we don't like thinking of ourselves as religious.

Lectio divina may seem like just the thing for people who think of themselves as spiritual but not religious. You don't need to go to church to do it. You can practice it all alone or in a group of close friends. It doesn't seem to impose inordinate demands on its practitioners. All it takes is to set aside some quiet time with the Psalms, the Gospels, or some other biblical book. What is more, meditative reading gives us the feeling of peace and joy that we often miss in the hustle and bustle of our daily lives. Lectio divina may seem like a spiritual practice designed for precisely a time and place like ours.

This chapter is designed to shatter any such comfortable link between lectio divina and spirituality. Lectio divina is not easy; it's hard. Lectio divina is not fluffy or sleep-inducing; it's rough and disruptive. Lectio divina—and especially the third step of prayer (*oratio*)—is about the difficult work of repentance. It's about turning around (*conversio*), which is hard when you've moved a long time in the same direction and enjoy the pleasures it gives. As we move from cruciformity to compunction, we recognize that lectio divina forces us to face hard truths about our own life.

COMPUNCTION: JOYFUL SORROW

WRITING USED TO be a physical, even violent activity. Mary Carruthers's description of how writing functioned in the premodern world may be somewhat unnerving:

> We should keep in mind the vigorous, if not violent, activity involved in making a mark upon such a physical surface as an animal's skin. One must break it, rough it up, "wound" it in some way with a sharply pointed instrument. Erasure involved roughing up the physical surface even more: medieval scribes, trying to erase parchment, had to use pumice stones and other scrapers. In other words, writing was always hard, physical labor, very hard as well on the surface on which it was being done; this vigorous physical aspect, I believe, was always part of that master-model of memory as a written surface.

In our age of computers, we tend to forget the harsh and laborious character of writing throughout most of history. Carruthers's phrase "memory as a written surface" makes the point that not only was writing a rough, physical activity but meditation or memorization was too. Technology may have made writing easier, but meditation hasn't lost its demanding character.

The "wounding" of the parchment Carruthers mentions is matched by a "wounding" of the mind in meditation. The word "compunction" gives us a sense of just how painful lectio divina can be. The Latin term *compunctio*—which marks the discourse on lectio divina from the time of John Cassian in the fifth century onward—speaks of the reader being painfully "pierced" in confrontation with the text. The language of compunction comes from the Latin *pungere*—to pierce or puncture. What divine reading does—if we do it as it is meant to be done—is to violently pierce the core of our being. The monastic writers took the term *compunctio* from the book of Acts. When Peter finished his Pentecost sermon, the people who heard it "had compunction in their heart"—*compuncti sunt corde* in the Vulgate (Acts 2:37). Contemporary versions often translate that they were "cut to the heart." Compunction takes us far from any comfy, fluffy, soporific notions that we may entertain about lectio divina. This is not to say that compunction is simply about morbid introspection. Contemplation, joy, and peace are the result. And it is not always sin but sometimes joy that pierces the heart. Either way, the heart must be pierced for the process of lectio divina to reach its desired end.

Having traveled from Palestine to Lower Egypt in the late fourth century, John Cassian and his friend Germanus sat down at Abba Isaac's feet to learn from him about prayer and compunction. Abba

Isaac explained to the two young pilgrims the various types of prayer, paying special attention to "living pure prayer," which combines each of the types of prayer into one and which "the Spirit lifts up to God in unspeakable groanings." The state of mind that results is shaped "by the contemplation of God alone and by the fire of love." Abba Isaac then elaborated on the petitions of the Lord's Prayer, since this prayer contains the "fullness of perfection" and carries us to the ineffable "prayer of fire," which rises "beyond all human consciousness."

The transition to this ineffable prayer of fire—which is the state of contemplation itself—is marked by compunction. In other words, for Abba Isaac, compunction is the moment we move from meditation and the various types of prayers to contemplation in ineffable prayer. He explains that different activities can bring on this prayer of fire: singing the Psalms or listening to one of the brothers sing them; the spiritual discourse of a perfect man; the death of a brother or friend; or even the memory of one's own lack of warmth and carelessness. Each of these is an occasion that the Spirit may use to induce compunction in the soul.

For John Climacus, the seventh-century monk from the monastery on Mount Sinai, compunction (*katanyxis*) is pretty much the same thing as mourning (*penthos*). He discusses them together in step seven of *The Ladder of Divine Ascent*. Saint John defines compunction as "an eternal torment of the conscience which brings about the cooling of the fire of the heart through silent confession." It is sin that causes the conscience to be in pain. "True compunction," writes John, "is pain of soul without any distraction." This pain over sin has to do with confession and repentance, for only they cause the sorrow we need. In such pain, we cannot but mourn our sin. Mourning, explains Climacus, "is a melancholy of the soul, a disposition of an anguished heart that passionately seeks what it thirsts for." If he does see a difference between compunction and mourning, Climacus doesn't bother to explain. He treats the two as interchangeable.

Both expressions are closely linked also with what Climacus calls the "gift of tears." The pain of mourning leads to tears. He calls it a gift, for the tears often come unexpectedly, and the Lord comes uninvited, without our striving for it. But this gift is not one for which we should passively wait. Saint John counsels us, "Do not cease laboring for it," and he tells us to "hold fast to it." We should recall both our sins and the judgment of God, so that the tears will come: "Never stop imagining and examining the abyss of dark fire, its cruel minions, the merciless inexorable judge, the limitless chaos of subterranean flame, the narrow descents down to underground chambers and yawning gulfs, and other such images." Mourning is the result both of God graciously entering the soul and of us reflecting on our sin. Climacus regards both perspectives as equally valid.

But why mourn if it involves detesting our lives, keeping the fires of hell before our eyes, and experiencing agonizing pain? Climacus explains that compunction leads to joy and consolation. As soon as we experience the pain of compunction, comfort mixes in and takes over. "Inward joy and gladness mingle with what we call mourning and grief, like honey in a comb," says Climacus. "God secretly brings consolation," and when it arrives, we are just like children, laughing and crying at the same time. Climacus even invents a new word to describe this mingling of joy and grief in compunction. He calls it *charmalypē*, a term made up from the Greek words for "joy" (*charma*) and "grief" (*lypē*). In "joyful grief," joy enters into the grief. Or, as Climacus also puts it, the fear lifts and "joy comes dawning." Compunction, while driven by sorrow for sin and fear of hell, invariably gives way to comfort and joy, a foretaste of eternal life.

TEARS AND NO TEARS

FOR CASSIAN AND CLIMACUS, compunction entails great inward turmoil. Lectio divina, therefore, can be an emotional roller coaster. Its very purpose is to transform us, and the only way to get there is by allowing the Scriptures to speak into our lives. In lectio divina, Scripture interprets the reader as much as the reader interprets Scripture. Indeed, we read two books at the same time: the book of Scripture and the book of experience.

The great Cistercian writer Bernard of Clairvaux begins the third of his *Sermons on the Song of Songs* (ca. 1135) with the comment,

> Today we read the book of experience (*libro experientiae*). Let us turn to ourselves and let each of us search his own conscience about what is said. I want to investigate whether it has been given to any of you to say, "Let him kiss me with the kiss of his mouth" (Sg 1:1). Few can say this wholeheartedly. But if anyone receives the spiritual kiss of Christ's mouth he seeks eagerly to have it again and again. I think no one can know what it is except he who has received it.

The bride's bold request, "Let him kiss me with the kiss of his mouth," confronts us with our own experience. Our own life is a book that is opened to us as we open the book of Scripture.

Just as the book of Scripture opens to us the book of experience, so it is our personal experiences that give us access to the inward sense of

Scripture. After speaking at some length about the "blessed tears" that come to us through the prayerful meditation on Scripture, Guigo II, the twelfth-century prior of the Grande Chartreuse, questions why he even bothers with this talk about the sweetness of tears:

> Why do we try to express in everyday language affections that no language can describe? Those who have not known such things do not understand them, for they could learn more clearly of them only from the book of experience (*libro experientiae*) where God's grace itself is the teacher. Otherwise it is of no use for the reader to search in earthly books: there is little sweetness in the study of the literal sense, unless there be a commentary (*glossam*), which is found in the heart, to reveal the inward sense.

According to Guigo, it is useless to try and explain the ineffable realities that the reading of Scripture makes present to us. Instead, it is the book of experience that functions like a gloss or commentary; experience reveals the spiritual or inward sense of Scripture.

The flip side of these observations is that whenever we lack experience, this becomes a pressing issue in trying to search the spiritual depth of Scripture: How can we reach the inward sense if we don't have the *liber experientiae* that allows us to read the Scriptures well? Bernard, for his part, clearly worried about this. A person who has already experienced Christ's spiritual kiss mentioned at the beginning of the Song of Songs can legitimately pray with David, "Restore unto me the joy of thy salvation" (Ps 51:12). But Bernard isn't convinced he can put this prayer on his lips. "A soul like mine," he comments, "burdened with sins, cannot dare say that, while it is still crippled by fleshly passions (1 Tim 3:6), and while it does not feel the sweetness of the Spirit, and is almost wholly unfamiliar with and inexperienced (*inexperta*) in inner joys." The requirement of feeling or emotion means that lack of experience precludes one from understanding Scripture, which in turn would serve to keep the desired experience beyond reach.

Bernard's worry is one that has troubled many spiritual writers. Precisely because Scripture confronts our lives—including our sins and shortcomings—monastic authors often worried that their lack of experience exposed them as hypocrites. Germanus, John Cassian's fellow pilgrim to the Egyptian desert, knew of a sorrow and grief that sometimes melted him into tears—which in turn gave him great joy. But he also worried that sometimes the tears stayed away:

> Sometimes it has happened to me that wishing once more for these tears of compunction to flow I have spent all my efforts on this. I recall to mind all my mistakes and all my sins, and still I cannot recover that rich abundance of tears. My eyes stay dry, like the hardest stone, and not even the tiniest drop is shed. And just as I rejoice in that outflowing of tears, so I grieve when I cannot recover it at will.

The grave implications of dry eyes deeply concerned Germanus. Sometimes he grieved, but the grief wasn't matched by tears.

Nowhere perhaps is anxiety over a lack of tears expressed more poignantly than in Anselm's *Prayers and Meditations*, most of which he initially sent in 1072 to Adelaide, daughter of William the Conqueror. Ladies at court such as Princess Adelaide and Countess Mathilda of Tuscany used Anselm's prayers and meditations for their personal devotions. The Benedictine abbot tells them in his preface that the purpose of the prayers and meditations is "to stir up the mind of the reader to the love or fear of God, or to self-examination. They are not to be read in a turmoil, but quietly, not skimmed or hurried through, but taken a little at a time, with deep and thoughtful meditation." Anselm cautions his readers to read only as much as is "useful in stirring up his spirit to pray," and that the reader "can begin and leave off whatever he chooses." In short, Anselm's prayers and meditations were meant to function much like the biblical text itself: their purpose was meditation, prayer, and contemplation. Anselm—and in this he would be followed by many other monastic writers over the next few centuries—offered his own writing as material for lectio divina.

Anselm ratchets up the emotional tension to an unprecedented level. He consistently abases and chastises himself—no matter who it is that he addresses in prayer, whether Christ, Mary, John the Baptist, Peter, Paul, Stephen, or Benedict. Anselm is deeply troubled by his lack of emotion and lack of tears. In his prayer to Saint Paul, Anselm appears to see no way out, since he fails to "dissolve entirely in tears." And without these tears, what hope does he have? "When truly, because of my wretchedness, feeling and grief are not in me, how can I hope? Without hope, how can I pray? And without prayer, what can I obtain?" Anselm is convinced that his sins condemn him before God. He calls out in his prayer to Saint John the Evangelist: "Grief, sorrow, groans, sighs, where are you present if here you are absent? Where are you fervent if here you are tepid?"

Anselm considers his dilemma well-nigh insuperable. In the first of his three prayers to Saint Mary, he confesses this about his sins: "If they are concealed they cannot be healed, if they are seen they are detestable." Praying to Saint John the Baptist, Anselm acknowledges,

If I look within myself, I cannot bear myself;

if I do not look within myself, I do not know myself.

if I consider myself, what I see terrifies me;

if I do not consider myself, I fall to my damnation.

If I look at myself, it is an intolerable horror;

if I do not look at myself, death is unavoidable.

> Evil here, worse there, ill on every side;
>
> but there is too much evil here,
>
> too much that is worse there,
>
> too much ill on every side.

Eileen Sweeney captures the double bind of Anselm's dilemma quite well: he "cannot reveal his sins because they are 'detestable' and would make him detested, but, on the other hand, sins cannot be forgiven unless they are confessed."

How to overcome this double bind? To begin, we should look to the practices of prayer and meditation. The way I see it is that Anselm intended the prayers and meditations—that is to say, *the very practice of praying and meditating*—as the means to overcome the dilemma. Anselm may say that he is incapable of confessing his sins, but of course his prayers do exactly that. And it was surely his hope that when Adelaide, Mathilda, and others would use them in lectio divina, they would be so pierced by compunction and so haunted by desire as to make these prayers experientially their own. By using these prayers and meditations for the purpose of lectio divina, his readers could deal with their sinfulness and so bridge the gap between heaven and earth. The result was an introspective spirituality—with an emphasis on self-abasement—hitherto unknown in Christian tradition. The so-called Anselmian transformation (R. W.

Southern) placed the individual naked before God, agonizing over his unworthiness with an unparalleled exuberance of expression.

Theologies of tears invariably have a shadow side, and each of the three monastic writers that we have looked at—Bernard, Cassian, and Anselm—struggled with it: Sometimes the tears don't come. Sometimes the much-vaunted experience is simply absent. None of the three authors, however, ends in despair. Even Anselm must have experienced enough of the presence of God that he turned back again and again to the Scriptures in order, yet again, to seek the face of God.

SCRIPTURAL TEARS

IT TOOK AUGUSTINE a long time to turn decisively to the Christian faith. All sorts of obstacles stood in the way, but nothing was as much of a hindrance as his unwillingness to let go of sinful habits—especially sexual ones: "Ingrained evil had more hold over me than unaccustomed good. The nearer approached the moment of time when I would become different, the greater the horror of it struck me." When Augustine describes the moment of conversion, its experiential character stands out. Dredging up all his misery "from a hidden depth of profound self-examination," Augustine finally broke down in a "massive downpour of tears (*imbrem lacrimarum*)," which made him quickly leave the presence of his friend Alypius:

> To pour it all out with the accompanying groans, I got up from beside Alypius (solitude seemed to me more appropriate for the business of weeping [*flendi*]), and I moved further away to ensure that even his presence put no inhibition upon me. He sensed that this was my condition at that moment. I think I may have said

something which made it clear that the sound of my voice was already choking with tears (*fletu*). So I stood up while in profound astonishment he remained where we were sitting. I threw myself down somehow under a certain figtree, and let my tears (*lacrimis*) flow freely. Rivers (*flumina*) streamed from my eyes, a sacrifice acceptable to you (Ps. 51:17), and (though not in these words, yet in this sense) I repeatedly said to you: "How long, O Lord? How long, Lord, will you be angry to the uttermost? Do not be mindful of our old iniquities" (Ps. 6:4). For I felt my past to have a grip on me. I uttered wretched cries (*voces miserabiles*): "How long, how long is it to be?" "Tomorrow, tomorrow." Why not now? Why not now? Why not an end to my impure life in this very hour?

As he was "weeping in the bitter agony" of his heart, Augustine heard a child's voice chant the words "Pick up and read, pick up and read." Hurrying back to his friend, he did exactly that, reading the passage that first struck him as he opened his Bible: "Not in rioting and drunkenness, not in chambering and impurities, not in contention and envy. But put ye on the Lord Jesus Christ: and make not provision for the flesh in its concupiscences" (Rom 13:13–14). A light of relief flooded Augustine's heart: he had broken with his past and in repentance turned decisively to his God.

Tears are central to Augustine's account. Only the use of multiple different terms allows him to get close to an adequate description: "downpour" (*imber*), "weeping" (*fletus*), "tears" (*lacrimae*), "rivers" (*flumina*), "cries" (*voces*). The narrative is deliberately dramatic. It is not as though he is faking the account, for he is obviously recounting great emotional upheaval. Still, there is something deliberate about Augustine's tears: his voice choking, he gets up from beside Alypius because "solitude seemed to me more appropriate for the business of weeping." Augustine *knows* he is about to weep, and so he finds a place where he doesn't need to restrain himself. At that point, Augustine writes, I "let my tears (*lacrimis*) flow freely."

The open display of emotion in this conversion account is remarkable. Augustine's introspection, both here and elsewhere, has been the topic of much debate. Here I want to draw attention to one aspect of it: the link between his personal experience and Scripture. Augustine intentionally points out that his tears are in line with biblical precedent. He appeals to David's prayer of Psalm 51, after his sin with Bathsheba. In this well-known penitential psalm, David laments his sexual transgression and recognizes it as a sin against God himself (Ps 51:4). David does not mention tears. But that does not deter Augustine. David does, after all, plead with God to fill him with "joy and gladness" (51:8), speaks of his bones as being "humbled" (51:8), and prays, "Restore unto me the joy of thy salvation" (51:12). Most importantly, David comes clean with the words "A sacrifice to God is an afflicted spirit: a contrite and humbled heart, O God, thou wilt not despise" (51:17). It does not take much to imagine David weeping before God. Which is exactly what Augustine does when he cries out, "Rivers (*flumina*) streamed from my eyes, a sacrifice acceptable to you." Augustine senses an affinity with David in repentance from sexual sin and concludes that David's emotional descriptions of grief imply rivers streaming from his eyes. And so, Augustine interprets David's sacrifice (51:17) as referring to tears, no matter their absence from the biblical text.

Scripture offers the (surmised) precedent for Augustine's tears. In this case, it is Psalm 51. But those practicing lectio divina over the centuries have recognized their experience of weeping also in other biblical passages. Abba Isaac explains to Cassian and Germanus the different types of tears through a biblically construed taxonomy. The first tears are those caused by the thorn of our sins. Scripture gives examples of this in Psalm 6:6 ("I have laboured in my groanings, every night I will wash my bed: I will water my couch with my tears") and in Lamentations 2:18 ("Let tears run down like a torrent day and night: give thyself no rest, and let not the apple of thy eye cease"). Then there are tears that flow from the contemplation and longing of eternity, such as Psalm 42:2–3 ("When shall I come and appear before the face of God? My tears have been my bread day and night"). A third type of tears is caused by fear of hell and judgment, as expressed in Psalm 143:2 ("Enter not into judgment with thy servant: for in thy sight no man living shall be justified"). Yet another kind of tears is caused by the sinfulness of others, as when Samuel wept over Saul (1 Sam 15:35) or the Lord wept for Jerusalem (Luke 19:41). And finally, sometimes believers simply express their worries and anxieties with tears to the Lord. Jeremiah did so when he cried, "Who will give water to my head, and a fountain of tears to my eyes? and I will weep day and night for the slain of the daughter of my people" (Jer 9:1); as did the poor, worried man who poured out his complaint to the Lord in Psalm 102: "I did eat ashes like bread, and mingled my drink with weeping" (Ps 102:9). Abba Isaac explains that each of these five types of tears has biblical precedent.

BIBLE, IMAGINATION, AND TEARS

SCRIPTURE IS PROMINENT also when the English Cistercian abbot Aelred of Rievaulx talks about tears. Aelred, however, does not simply point to biblical precedent (as do John Cassian and, more or less, Saint Augustine). Instead, he employs the rhetorical strategy of composition of place, which we discussed in the previous chapter. Aelred asks his readers to imaginatively enter into the weeping of biblical characters. He does this, for example, in *Jesus at the Age of Twelve*. Here the abbot traces Jesus's birth in Bethlehem, his upbringing in Nazareth, and his first journey to Jerusalem as a twelve-year-old. Aelred wrote the book sometime between 1153 and 1157 for Yvo, a monk of Warden Abbey in Bedfordshire, a daughter house of Rievaulx. Aelred divides the small treatise into three sections, dealing in turn with the historical, the allegorical, and the moral sense. He pays attention especially to Jesus's journey to Jerusalem (Luke 2:41–52).

Aelred treats the allegorical sense as an imaginative entry of the reader into the life of Jesus: "His bodily progress is our spiritual progress, and what we are told he did at each stage of his life is reproduced in us spiritually according to the various degrees of progress—as is experienced by those who advance in virtue." As he turns to the meaning of the name Bethlehem ("house of bread"), he distinguishes between bread made from fine wheat flour and bread cooked in ashes. The former refers to the eternal Word; the latter to the Word made flesh. The eternal Word—bread made from fine wheat flour—is the Bread of Angels, which is the psalmist's designation for the manna that God gave the Israelites in the desert (Ps 78:24–25). Only angels can eat this bread, for only they "taste and see fully and perfectly" that the Lord is sweet (Ps 34:8). When a hungry prodigal son visits the House of Bread (Bethlehem), instead of seeing there this bread made from fine wheat flour, he finds bread cooked in ashes—the Word become flesh. And Aelred adds the encouragement: "so that he may eat ashes with his bread and mix his drink with tears" (Ps 102:9).

Yvo should follow the pattern of the incarnation, adopting the humility of the Word become flesh, giving up wealth, thereby foregoing a place at the inn. "Then," comments Aelred, "will you eat bread with ashes when the Lord feeds you with the bread of tears and gives you tears in abundance to drink. So you are born in Christ and so is Christ born in you." With these words, the abbot of Rievaulx explicitly turns to Psalm 80:6: "How long wilt thou feed us with the bread of tears: and give us for our drink tears in measure?" The bread of tears (*panis lacrimarum*) of Psalm 80 turns out to be identical to the bread of angels (*panis angelorum*) of Psalm 78, for it is when we visit the house of bread (Bethlehem) and find there the bread of angels, as it is now cooked in ashes, that we weep in repentance, so that our tears produce Christ in our hearts. Christ is the bread of our tears. Aelred intimates that we ourselves become the house of bread. His spiritual interpretation of Jesus's birth in Bethlehem is at the same time an allegorical exegesis of four different psalms—Psalms 34, 78, 80, and 102—all of which, for Aelred, center on Christ as our bread. It is by crying the tears of two of these psalms—Psalms 80 and 102—that we are united to Christ.

Aelred again turns to the theme of tears when, in his section on the moral sense, he tells Yvo to meditate on Christ's goodness by entering the house of Simon the Pharisee and watching how, with mercy, Jesus looks on the sinful woman who washes his feet with "tears of repentance" (Luke 7:36–50). "Kiss, kiss, kiss, blessed sinner, kiss those dearest, sweetest, most beautiful of feet," Aelred exhorts his reader. The Pharisee may not repent, but for the blessed sinner, conversion is possible. Taken up in the emotional frenzy, Aelred addresses his own soul as he identifies with the sinful woman:

> What are you about, my soul, my wretched soul, my sinful soul? There certainly is the place for you safely to shed your tears, to

atone for your impure kisses with holy kisses, to pour out all the ointment of your devotion free from fear, without any touch or movement of vice to tempt you. Why do you hold back? Break forth, sweet tears, break forth, let no one check your flowing. Water the most sacred feet of my Savior, of my Champion. I do not care if some Pharisee mutters, if he thinks I should be kept away from his own feet, if he judges me unworthy to touch the hem of his own garment. Let him mock, let him laugh and jeer, let him turn his eyes away, let him hold his nose; for all that I will cling to your feet, my Jesus, I will hold them fast with my hands, press my lips to them, and I will not stop weeping and kissing them until I am told: "Many sins have been forgiven her, because she has loved much" [Luke 7:47].

The Cistercian abbot draws his readers into the narrative by suggesting that they identify with characters in the narrative who are close to Jesus. Time and again, this allows for tears of repentance to flow, so that his readers can experience the love of Jesus.

Aelred does something similar when he tells his sister in *A Rule of Life for a Recluse* (ca. 1160–1162) to follow Peter to the high priest's courtyard, reminding her that this is the place where Peter "comes to his right mind and weeps bitterly" (Luke 22:62). Reflecting on the three-hour darkness at the crucifixion, he insists that his sister should weep with the sun over Christ's death: "It is not surprising if when the sun mourns you mourn too, if when the earth trembles you tremble with it, if when rocks are split your heart is torn in pieces, if when the women who are by the Cross weep you add your tears to theirs (*collacrymaris*)." This last verb—a combination of *con* (with) and *lacrimare* (to weep)—articulates precisely what Aelred expects his sister to do: enter the biblical narrative and join the women at the cross in their weeping.

Aelred encourages his sister to keep Mary Magdalene company as she visits the tomb. Referencing John 20:11 ("Mary stood at the sepulchre without, weeping. Now as she was weeping, she stooped down and looked into the sepulchre"), Aelred tells his sister to weep with Mary as Jesus sweetly calls to her, "Mary!"

> At this utterance let all the floods burst forth, let tears stream up from the very bottom of your heart, let sighs and sobs issue from your inmost depths. "Mary." O blessed one, what did you think, what did you feel, when you prostrated yourself at this utterance and answered his greeting with the cry: "Master"? Tears preclude any further utterance as the voice is stifled by emotion and excess of love leaves the soul dumb, the body without feeling.

When Jesus tells her not to touch him, the anchoress does not give up:

> Why may I not touch you? May I not touch, may I not kiss those lovable feet, for my sake pierced with nails and drenched in blood? Are you less gentle than usual because you are more glorious? But I will not let you go, I will not leave you, I will not spare my tears, my breast will burst with sobs and sighs unless I touch you.

Aelred asks his sister (as well as other anchoresses) to take her own place within the passion narrative, to identify personally with key figures such as Peter and Mary, making their tears her own.

CONCLUSION

LECTIO DIVINA IS not for the faint of heart. The compunction or piercing of the soul in divine reading is sharp, it is fierce, and it is agonizing. It is a practice marked by tears, so much so that the absence of tears often caused emotional upheaval in spiritual writers. Reading some of the spiritual masters on lectio divina can easily raise apprehensions and fears of the practice. If Bernard hardly thought he knew the book of experience, and if Anselm struggled to bridge the gap between his sin and God's face, aren't our rudimentary attempts at lectio divina cavalier and presumptuous?

Perhaps. But if anything stands out in this chapter, it is that compunction is biblical. Scripture itself models for us the grief of compunction. This, at least, was the conviction of the medieval authors we have studied. When they scoured the biblical text, they saw their own pangs of conscience and their own tears reflected all over the place. When reading Augustine's conversion narrative, don't we empathize with him as he speaks of his tears as a sacrifice offered to God (Ps 51:17)? And when we follow along with Aelred's imaginative entries into the biblical text, doesn't it strike us as right that, with the sinful woman, we kiss the feet of Jesus, shedding tears of repentance (Luke 7:36–50)? Both authors turned to Scripture as the source for their teaching on tears.

We have too long ignored the language of sin. Insisting on starting with grace, at times we hardly discuss sin at all. But lectio divina works on the conviction that the Bible pries open our lives and exposes the secrets of our hearts. We need a retrieval of compunction and tears, for the joy of salvation rests on experiential repentance from sin. Patristic and medieval authors, Eastern and Western theologians, they all engaged in introspection. They looked within, and it made them weep—for grace, for forgiveness, for renewal, for change.

An introspective conscience isn't the same as morbid despair. True, Bernard takes a dim view of his own experiences. But he also bashfully notes his brief moments of contemplation. Preaching on Song 3:1 ("In my bed by night I sought him whom my soul loveth"), the Mellifluous Doctor writes, "Even though I also had been privileged sometimes to enjoy that favour, do you suppose it would be possible for me to describe the ineffable?" His introspection eventually brought him through compunction to the joy of seeing the face of God.

Saint Anselm, I would say, is no different. True, his *Prayers and Meditations* may make us apprehensive of lapsing into frightful anguish. But his introspective spirituality does not leave him or his readers without hope. Anselm asks us to read him as we would Scripture itself: with confidence that through a meditative reading of his prayers and meditations, we may be pierced and be changed. Anselm's introspection aims for the experience of a divine inbreaking of grace.

Too easily, we confuse introspection with morbid despair. It's a deadly confusion. John Climacus's notion of "joyful grief" (*charma-lypē*) should remind us that looking within allows the joy of eternity to enter our hearts. The bread of tears is indispensable food, for it is none other than the real presence of Christ.

VIII

The Better Part

"I SOUGHT HIM WHOM MY SOUL LOVETH"

THE LAST STEP in lectio divina is contemplation. It is the final purpose of the entire exercise. When done well, divine reading is a search for God. Bernard of Clairvaux reflected on this search in the sermon we encountered at the end of the previous chapter. It was his last sermon on the Song of Songs, preached just before his death in 1153. Bernard's text was Song 3:1—"In my bed by night I sought him whom my soul loveth: I sought him, and found him not." The sermon discusses seven reasons for the soul's search. Bernard considers the last one the most important: "to feel the delight which is found in his caresses."

Bernard's sermon offers a lucid description of the purpose of the search for God that characterizes lectio divina. The aim, for Bernard, is not any particular earthly good. Nor is it any kind of activity: "I sought him whom my soul loveth." The soul searches for the Groom—namely, the Word. Bernard describes the delight of his caresses as follows:

The soul is sometimes rapt in ecstasy, and withdrawn from the
bodily senses, and so completely absorbed in admiration of the
Word that she loses even consciousness of self. This happens
when, under the attraction of the Word's ineffable sweetness,
she in a manner steals herself from herself, or rather is ravished
away and escapes from herself, in order that she may enjoy the
Word.

In contemplation, the soul feels the delight of the Word's caresses. The
experience is a mystical one: the soul is withdrawn from the bodily
senses and even escapes from herself, so completely lost is she in the
Word. Bernard cautions that this experience of contemplation is "as
rare as it is delightful, and as short-lived as rare." And despite offering
a description, Bernard acknowledges that words cannot capture the
experience: contemplation is learned not through the ear but through
the heart.

Saint Bernard's single-minded focus on the Groom as the end of
his search raises the question of how the active life (*vita activa*) relates
to the contemplative life (*vita contemplativa*). To explore this question
further, we will first look at how biblical types of action and contemplation function in the Augustinian tradition (Augustine of Hippo,
Gregory the Great, and Aelred of Rievaulx). We will then ask how to
deal with some of the tensions involved in the relationship between
action and contemplation (turning especially to Thomas Aquinas and
William of Saint-Thierry). We will see that, although they recognized
the importance of both, their ultimate focus was invariably the eternal
contemplation of God.

AUGUSTINE

Saint Augustine turns to several biblical tropes to develop his thoughts on the topic. He compares Leah and Rachel (Gen 29–30), the Synoptics and the Gospel of John, Martha and Mary (Luke 10:38–42), as well as Peter and John (John 21:15–25). For Augustine, action and contemplation are linked in the person of Christ. That is to say, we meet Christ both in action and in contemplation.

How does Augustine make this point about Christ? He explains that Leah and Rachel both have their place within the body of Christ. Both the Synoptic Gospels and John's Gospel give us Christ, the former focusing on his temporal actions, the latter on his teachings. Martha and Mary both receive Christ in their home, the one feeding Christ, the other being fed by him. When people care for the hungry and for others in need, they are actually serving Christ, in line with his claim, "As long as you did it to one of these my least brethren, you did it to me" (Matt 25:40). Augustine notes that Jesus loves John more than Peter (John 13:23) even though Peter loves Jesus more than does John (John 21:15). But both the active life (Peter) and the contemplative life (John) are expressions of love for Christ, and Christ loves both types of life. He is the focus of both the active and the contemplative life.

Of course, the two are not identical. Nor does Saint Augustine rank them the same. The key difference between the two is that action concerns temporal life, while contemplation has to do with eternal life. Mary may have chosen the better part (Luke 10:42), but a life of action is indispensable as long as there are needs that must be cared for. Augustine emphatically refuses to accept that all we need is the contemplative life:

If that's really the case, let people all give up ministering to the needy; let them all choose the better part, which shall not be taken away from them. Let them devote their time to the word, let them pant for the sweetness of doctrine, let them busy themselves with [knowledge of salvation]; don't let them bother at all about what stranger there may be in the neighborhood, who may be in need of bread or who of clothing, who needs to be visited, who to be redeemed, who to be buried. Let the works of mercy be laid aside, everything be concentrated on the one science. If it is the better part, why don't we all grab it, when in this case we have the Lord himself as our attorney? After all, we are not afraid of offending against his justice in this matter, when we are indemnified by his judgment.

Augustine unequivocally insists that we dare not neglect the active life. In the hereafter, without any needs left to care for, works of mercy will no longer be relevant. Eternal life will be pure contemplation. But as long as we see needs around us, we are duty bound to care for them. Martha, explains Kimberly Baker, "is a traveler in the world of need, who, because of her attention to the needs of others, will find rest and welcome in the homeland. There, in eternity, there will be no one to serve ... not because service is unimportant but because there will be no more need in eternity." Here and now, Christians engage in the active life because of the hardships people face. Then and there, all that will be left is the rest of the contemplative life, with God himself satisfying our every need.

Augustine may seem to separate action and contemplation: action now, contemplation in the hereafter. And it is true that Augustine links contemplation closely to the eschaton, when we will see God face-to-face. But he makes clear that even here and now we already get glimpses of the contemplative life. We identify with Mary sitting at Jesus's feet when we feed on him, enjoying his justice and his truth. The future life of contemplation already shows up in such momentary experiences of contemplation. It is as if they are small sacraments of eternal enjoyment. The active life and contemplative life, therefore, exist side by side in the Christian life. It is by definition a mixed life.

Augustine goes further by insisting that action and contemplation are in a cyclical relationship. On the one hand, action is geared toward contemplation because the life of virtue yields contemplation. The hard work of preaching bears fruit, just as Leah gives birth to many children. Meanwhile, Rachel's otherworldly life is barren because it engages in leisure. So, we must first marry Leah, or else we will never be united with Rachel. On the other hand, contemplation in turn gives way to action, because the contemplative wants to share the experience with others. This activity of sharing follows contemplation, while also being intimately connected to it. For Augustine, it is impossible to conceive of a contemplative life (here on earth) that does not generate action. He is at pains to affirm both action and contemplation; they belong together in and through our incarnate Lord.

Still, if asked which one has priority—action or contemplation—Saint Augustine would not hesitate: contemplation, not action, is the goal of the Christian life. Since it is the final end of the Christian life, contemplation is the better part that will never be taken away from Mary (Luke 10:42). Just as Augustine famously insists that earthly things must be used for the sake of the enjoyment of God, so too, he considers the active life as instrumental for the sake of the ultimate end of the vision of God. Now we are still pilgrims on the road; then we will be residents at home. The active life finds its fulfillment in the eternal contemplation of God. All Christians, even Martha, will arrive at the contemplative rest in which Mary already shares today.

GREGORY THE GREAT

AUGUSTINE'S TROPES—especially that of Martha and Mary—have echoed through the history of the church. One noteworthy example is Saint Gregory the Great, who reflects on the relationship between action and contemplation in his *Homilies on the Book of the Prophet Ezekiel*. In his second sermon on the prophet's vision of the new temple, the pope turns to Ezekiel 40:4–5, where Ezekiel is told,

> And this man said to me: Son of man, see with thy eyes, and hear with thy ears, and set thy heart upon all that I shall shew thee: for thou art brought hither that they may be shewn to thee: declare all that thou seest, to the house of Israel. And behold there was a wall on the outside of the house round about, and in the man's hand a measuring reed of six cubits and a handbreadth: and he measured the breadth of the building one reed, and the height one reed.

Pope Gregory, who preached his sermon on this passage around the year 593 (as the Lombards besieged Rome), insists that the text speaks of eyes and ears of the heart and that therefore it enjoins the prophet to embark on contemplation, the fruit of which he must share with others ("declare all that thou seest, to the house of Israel"). Gregory explains that the wall "on the outside of the house round about" refers to the incarnate Lord protecting us (who are inside, making up the house—which is to say, the temple), and the text assumes that there is also a wall inside the temple, which is God himself.

Gregory identifies the "measuring reed" as Holy Scripture, which Jesus holds in his hand. It contains both the active life and the contemplative life. The reed's six cubits refer to the active life, since God completed his works on the sixth day (Gen 2:2). The reed's handbreadth speaks of the contemplative life. It refers to the seventh day. Yet it falls short of a cubit, indicating that on earth, "we taste the mere beginnings of inward contemplation."

Gregory discusses Martha and Mary as well as Leah and Rachel by way of illustration. His elaboration is thoroughly Augustinian. He turns to Jesus's words to Martha, "Martha, Martha, thou art careful and art troubled about many things: But one thing is necessary. Mary hath chosen the best part, which shall not be taken away from her" (Luke 10:41–42). He comments,

> Behold Martha's part is not censured but Mary's is praised. Nor does He say that Mary has chosen a good part but the best, so that Martha's too was shown to be good. But why Mary's is the best is implied when it says: *"Which shall not be taken away from her."* The active life indeed fails with the body. For who will offer bread to the hungry in the Eternal Kingdom where none goes hungry? Who will give drink to the thirsty where none thirsts? Who will bury the dead where none dies? Therefore the active life is taken away with this present age but the contemplative is begun here.

It seems clear that Gregory spent some time perusing Augustine's reflections on Martha and Mary: Gregory affirms the active life; he insists that Mary's part is best because it won't be taken away from her; he maintains that the active life arises from the needs of the present age; and he insists that the contemplative life starts already today. Each of these observations goes back to Augustine.

Next, Gregory turns to Leah and Rachel. He recognizes why Augustine spoke of Leah's life as "laborious": her name comes from a root that means "to be wearied" or "to labor." Rachel's name means "sheep" or "principle." So, while Leah's eyes are weak (Gen 29:17) so that she is restricted to a life of laborious action, Rachel is able to see the rational principles of things in Christ, who is the beginning or principle of all things. Like Augustine, Gregory insists that those who desire the contemplative life "must first in the night of this present life perform the works which they can, sweat with effort, *i.e.* accept Leah in order that they afterward rest in the arms of Rachel, in order to see the beginning." Also, like Augustine, Gregory explains how it is that Leah is fertile while Rachel is barren: the active life produces sons from preaching, while the contemplative life seeks rest in silence. And like Augustine, Gregory discerns a cyclical relationship between the active and the contemplative: "Just as a good order is to strive from the active to the contemplative, so the spirit frequently reverts from the contemplative to the active."

Saint Gregory concludes with two additional biblical illustrations: Jacob wrestling with the angel (Gen 32:22–32) and Isaiah seeing the Lord sitting on a throne (Isa 6:1). The former speaks of the mental struggle involved in contemplation. Jacob does conquer the angel, though even in his conquest he only "grazes the hem of the uncircumscribed light"; Jacob merely sees an angel, not God himself. When the angel grasps the tendon of Jacob's thigh so that he becomes lame on one foot, Gregory interprets this as meaning that love of the world (the one foot) is weakened, while love of God (the other foot) grows strong. So, in contemplation, God "withers every carnal desire in us" as we scorn earthly cares and "lay hold on God in inward sweetness." Similarly, Isaiah contemplates the glory of God as he is seated on his throne—the human and angelic creatures making up his temple. Isaiah, like Jacob, contemplates merely the "train" that fills the temple: "Whatever is seen of Him momentarily is still not He himself." The contemplative only has a "foretaste of inward peace," unable to sustain it for long.

AELRED OF RIEVAULX

AELRED OF RIEVAULX'S sermon on Martha and Mary—preached for the feast of the Assumption of Mary—offers a final example of Augustinian reflections on the active and contemplative life. According to the Latin text of Luke 10:38, Jesus entered a certain *castellum* (meaning "castle" or "village"). As a result, the twelfth-century Cistercian abbot reflects on what makes a castle strong. This takes his mind to the castle's moat (humility), its wall (chastity), and its tower (charity). The Mother of God had each of these. The east gate of her castle remained shut (cf. Ezek 44:1)—closed with the seal of charity—so that the devil was unable to enter. Jesus did enter this castle, physically, and he will enter us spiritually if we have the spiritual castle inside us.

The blessed Virgin Mary, then, received Jesus both in body and in spirit. On this feast of her Assumption, Aelred celebrates her as the one who lived the mixed life perfectly. Clothing, feeding, and carrying Jesus, as well as fleeing with him to Egypt—"all this pertains to physical activity," or, we could also say, to Martha. But treasuring all these words, meditating on his divinity, contemplating his power, and savoring his sweetness— "all this pertains to Mary." The blessed Virgin lived both the active and the contemplative life.

Like Augustine, then, Aelred makes an appeal for the mixed life. Both Martha and Mary need a place in this castle of ours: "If Mary alone were in this home, there would be no one to feed the Lord; if Martha alone, there would be no one delighting in the words and presence of the Lord." The Cistercian abbot, however, describes the need for Martha's presence in the castle slightly differently than did Augustine and Gregory: Aelred suggests that we must labor for food and drink, and we also have to "subdue the flesh with vigils, fasts, and manual labor." In other words, the active life is not just about the needs of others—whether it be physical hunger or hunger for the gospel—but also about spiritual disciplines. In the face of temptation, the flesh must be subdued so that the active life may properly prepare for the contemplative life.

The mixed life implies that we need to divide our attention, sometimes engaging in the life of Martha, sometimes in that of Mary: "At the time of *lectio* we must stay still and quiet, not yielding to idleness or drowsiness, not departing from Jesus' feet, but sitting there and listening to his word. But when it is time for work we should be alert and ready and on no account should we neglect the ministry of love in order to obtain quiet." When it's time for divine reading, we should get ready for contemplation, and when it's time for work, we should give ourselves wholeheartedly to the task at hand. Meanwhile, Jesus's comment to Martha that "Mary hath chosen the best part, which shall not be taken away from her" (Luke 10:42) is in no way a reprimand. Instead, Aelred reads it as an encouragement to Martha to "put up with these labors and miseries," knowing that they will come to an end. Martha, apparently, will take on the role of Mary in the hereafter.

To be sure, Aelred was not always insistent on Martha and Mary living in the same castle. In his *Rule of Life for a Recluse*, written for his sister around 1160–1162, he insists strongly that the mixed life is not for her. For his sister, who has taken the life of an anchoress upon herself, only "one thing is necessary" (Luke 10:42)—namely, passing into the unity of the One, which is the unity of charity, "as it were the edge and border of the spiritual vesture." Comparing Martha and Mary, Aelred tells his sister to adopt Mary's role:

> She did not walk about to run hither and thither, was not concerned with the reception of guests, not distracted by household worries, not busy with answering cries of the poor. She just sat at Jesus' feet and listened to what he had to say. This is your portion, dearly beloved. Dead and buried to the world and unable to speak of it. You should not be distracted but absorbed, not emptied out but filled up. Let Martha carry out her part; although it is admitted to be good, Mary's is declared better. Did Mary envy Martha? Rather it was the other way about. So let those who seem to make the best out of living in the world envy your life; it is not for you to envy theirs.

Aelred insists that others can do good to their neighbors while his sister should instead pray for them. Mary's role is better than Martha's, and his sister should not pine for the active life. So, whereas Aelred's sermon on Luke 10 takes the Martha-and-Mary trope as referring to the mixed life, his *Rule of Life for a Recluse* separates them into two separate states of life.

TENSIONS

By NO MEANS are the active and the contemplative life always in a harmonious relationship. Jesus's comment to Martha might already seem to imply a tension of sorts. We might well read Jesus's comments to Martha as a mild rebuke. His "Martha, Martha" could easily be taken this way. When he observes that she is "careful," or anxious, and "troubled," Jesus is hardly complimenting her. And when he adds that only "one thing is necessary" and that Mary has chosen the "best part," these remarks might well seem to imply a slight reprimand. Doesn't Jesus gently correct Martha by pointing her to Mary's contemplative attitude?

Perhaps, and I am inclined to think so. But Augustine, Gregory, and Aelred all declined to read Jesus's words this way. They all insisted that Jesus does not correct Martha. The reason, presumably, is that they all wanted to uphold that the active life is good and may not simply be abandoned. Their logic presumably went something like this: if the active life is good, and if Martha is a stand-in for this active life, then we cannot possibly read Jesus's words as a reproach. My hunch is that these medieval theologians got rid of the narrative tension between Martha and Mary for the sake of theological consistency. Not that I would cavil too much: they were right to uphold the active life as indispensable, even if this particular passage doesn't do much to advance it. And it is surely noteworthy that each of these medieval authors came to Martha's defense. Perhaps the common prejudice against the Middle Ages as mired in otherworldliness needs some modification.

An affirmation of the active life comes to the fore also in the common medieval recognition that different people have different callings. The variety in monastic orders arose partly from diverging approaches to the active life. The traditional Benedictines had been contemplative in character—though even Benedict's Rule had included work as part of the daily routine. The motto of *ora et labora* (work and pray) meant that both action and contemplation were part of the daily Benedictine schedule. As the Rule puts it, "Idleness (*otiositas*) is the enemy of the soul." The stricter orders of the Carthusians (founded by Bruno of Cologne in 1084) and the Cistercians (established by Robert of Molesme in 1098) withdrew from the world, but they continued to prize the Benedictine demand of manual labor. Their admiration of solitude and desert spirituality was in no way opposed to the active life.

Other orders deliberately adopted an active missionary calling. Greg Peters, in *The Story of Monasticism*, sketches the rise of some of these orders that flourished after the Gregorian Reform of the eleventh century. The non-cloistered Premonstratensians (founded by Norbert of Xanten in 1120) included both lay and clergy, men and women, all committed to both preaching and pastoral work—a rather active calling. Life at the Abbey of Saint Victor in Paris, founded by William of Champeaux in 1108, included meditation (with a focus on lectio divina), but its leading theologians promoted a broad liberal arts education. Hugh of Saint Victor's *Didascalicon* (published in the late 1130s) offered a remarkably wide-ranging liberal arts curriculum to the residential as well as non-residential students of Saint Victor. While lectio divina traditionally consisted of four steps (*lectio, meditatio, oratio*, and *contemplatio*), Hugh added an additional one between the third and fourth steps: *operatio*, or performance. And Peters points out that the active life was affirmed nowhere more unabashedly than in military orders such as the Hospitallers and the Knights Templar in the eleventh century. It now became possible to be a monk even in the military.

When in the thirteenth century Saint Thomas Aquinas reflected on action and contemplation in the *Summa theologiae,* he too affirmed diverse callings. He begins by insisting that the queen—his term for theology—is "surrounded with variety," using the wording of Psalm 45:9 about the queen who is married off to her king. Religious orders vary, both in terms of purpose and of practices, maintains Aquinas. He specifies by arguing that religious orders may be established specifically for the active life: "Religion clean and undefiled before God and the Father is this: to visit the fatherless and widows in their tribulation and to keep one's self unspotted from this world" (Jas 1:27). Although the active life is geared directly toward love of neighbor, its ultimate aim is identical to that of the contemplative life—namely, love of God. And here Aquinas quotes the same text to which Augustine often appealed: "As long as you did it to one of these my least brethren, you did it to me" (Matt 25:40). Aquinas, too, believed that the active life both aims at and results from contemplation, so that it would be wrong to disavow religious orders that focus on the active life. (We should not forget that the Dominicans' focus on preaching and the Franciscans' care for the poor put both of these thirteenth-century mendicant orders in active service to the world around them.) As examples of orders that committed themselves to the active life, Aquinas mentions military religious orders, orders for preaching and hearing confessions, and orders for the purpose of study.

Still, if theologians of the Great Tradition affirmed the role of the active life, they also unanimously agreed that Mary's part is better than Martha's. Rachel is more delightful than Leah (and has sharper vision). John, not Peter, is the mystical theologian who lay close to the breast of Jesus. Every one of the spiritual writers we have looked at in this chapter affirmed this priority of the contemplative life. None, however, teased out their relationship with as much theological precision and detail as did Thomas Aquinas. With an appeal to the traditional Martha-and-Mary trope, Aquinas explains, in line with his predecessors, that the contemplative life is greater than the active life. The reason is simply that only the contemplative life aims directly at God as its end.

Ever attentive to the complexity of the relationship between action and contemplation, however, Aquinas then fine-tunes his ranking in the following way:

	Typology (Luke 10)	Content	Rationale
Active life #1		Teaching and preaching	Proceeds from contemplation
Contemplative life	Mary	Prayer and study	Seeks the end for its own sake
Active life #2	Martha	Outward occupations (almsgiving, hospitality, etc.)	Restricts itself to external actions

Figure 8.1: *Aquinas on the Active and Contemplative Life*

What stands out in this chart—and is truly remarkable—is that Aquinas regards the active life of teaching and preaching as higher than the contemplative life. He makes the reason sound obvious: teaching and preaching complete contemplation and so must be higher. As Aquinas puts it, "It is better to enlighten than merely to shine." Or, as the Dominican adage has it, this kind of action is a matter of *contemplata aliis tradere*—passing on the contemplated realities to others. The highest type of life, then, is an active life that shares the fruits of contemplation (active life #1).

We can summarize Aquinas's position like this: the contemplative life is greatest because it aims at the end for its own sake. Mary has chosen the better part. But even Mary can be bested, for when she shares the fruits of her contemplation with others, she fully completes her role. I must confess I'm not quite persuaded of Aquinas's innovative claim that the active life (of teaching and preaching) is greater than the contemplative life. He was right to highlight the great need for active life #1, but in the hereafter, the *vita activa* simply gives way to the *vita contemplativa*.

Still, Aquinas agrees that only contemplation aims directly at God. And this recognition of Mary's superiority over Martha, which was widespread, introduces a tension in the Christian life. We aren't home until we get to heaven, leaving behind both active life #1 (teaching and preaching) and active life #2 (caring for those in need). No matter how committed we may (rightly) be to the active life, the desire to eternally see God face-to-face haunts any authentic Christian spirituality. Even when one's life is rightly ordered to teaching and preaching—sharing the fruits of one's contemplation with others—the desire will still be for more of God:

As the hart panteth
> after the fountains of water;

so my soul panteth
> after thee, O God.

My soul hath thirsted
> after the strong living God;

when shall I come and appear
> before the face of God? (Ps 42:1)

The psalmist is convinced that only in the temple, in God's presence, will his desire be satisfied. Only when in eternity we arrive at God's "holy hill," his "tabernacles," or his "altar" (Ps 43:3–4) will we have attained the perfection of contemplation.

CONCLUSION

THE LONGING FOR contemplation makes us restless, perhaps impatient. Saint Augustine felt this when he was called to the active life of a bishop while he would have much preferred the life of a contemplative. Augustine linked action with the present, temporal life, and contemplation with heavenly rest and vision of God. Still, the bishop of Hippo followed what he saw as God's call and committed himself to the hustle and bustle of his episcopal task. With similar reluctance, Saint Gregory the Great turned from monk to pope. He often wrote of his desire to devote more time to a life of contemplation. In a letter to Theoctista, the emperor's sister, he complained, "I have lost the profound joys of my peace and quiet, and I seem to have risen externally, while falling internally. Wherefore, I deplore my expulsion far from the face of my Creator." Typically, the saints' desire is for more contemplation of God.

The Cistercian abbot William of Saint-Thierry also displays an aversion to the duties of the active life and expresses his longing to spend more time in leisure with God. In his book *On Contemplating God* (1121–1124), he allegorically reflects on the binding of Isaac in Genesis 22. Abraham is traveling with Isaac to one of the mountains of Moriah and then tells his young men, "Stay you here with the ass; I and the boy will go with speed as far as yonder, and after we have worshipped, will return to you" (Gen 22:5). After the angel of the Lord appears to Abraham and stops him from sacrificing his son, Abraham recognizes that the Lord has seen him and that he has seen the Lord on the mountain (Gen 22:14).

At the outset of his treatise, William encourages his readers to go up to the mountain of the Lord: "Yearnings, strivings, longings, thoughts and affections, and all that is within me, come and let us go up to the mountain or place where the Lord both sees and is seen!" Clearly, the abbot is embarking on a discourse on contemplation. He insists, therefore, on leaving behind the life of action: "Worries and anxieties, concerns and toils, and all the sufferings involved in my enslaved condition, all of you must stay here with the ass—I mean my body—while I and the lad—my intellectual faculties—hasten up the mountain; so that, when we have worshipped, we may come back to you." William associates the active life with the body (the ass, which must be left behind) and the contemplative life with the intellect (the lad, who may come along to see God on the mountain). William acknowledges that he will have to come back from the mountain, "and that unfortunately, all too soon." He nonetheless will do so, "for the brethren's sake."

The body of the treatise takes the form of a prayer. Here, William struggles to reach up to God. He insists, "I do have in me the desire to desire you and the love of loving you." But the brief moments in which he experiences the sweet savoring of God's presence are fleeting, and his desire easily wanes. As he comes to the conclusion of the book, he writes with a sense of self-deprecating humor, "But now the ass is braying again, and the lads are clamoring!" Bodily requirements call him away from the mountain of contemplation and back to the active life.

William of Saint-Thierry speaks, I think, for the entire tradition that precedes him. He laments the ass braying again and the lads clamoring for his attention. Why? *Not* because he despised the active life. Christian spirituality cannot possibly repudiate the *vita activa*. The needs in the world around us require it, and by trying to skip it, we risk missing the aim of contemplation itself. Besides, how could one who has seen the face of God not want to share this joy with others? Neither is the reason for William's lament that he was lazy. As we have seen, monastic writers such as William saw great value in work and had little use for laziness. Rather, William—and here he summarizes the entire lectio divina tradition—regrets the braying ass and the clamoring lads for the simple reason that the top of the mountain is by far the better place to be.

IX

Into Great Silence

A SIXTEEN-YEAR WAIT

IT TOOK THE monks rather a long time to respond. It was 1984 when Philip Gröning first approached the Carthusian monks of the Grande Chartreuse in southeastern France. He wanted to film the life of the monastery and turn it into a documentary. After a sixteen-year waiting period, the positive response finally came in the year 2000, resulting another five years later in the documentary film *Into Great Silence*.

Carthusians are known for their strict observance of silence as a spiritual practice. *Into Great Silence* faithfully and impressively reflects this: pregnant silence marks the entire film. To be sure, sounds are not absent: rain and thunder engulf the charterhouse; knives, scissors, razor, spade, and hammer intrude on the silence. Monks walk up and down the stairs, stand up and sit down in choir stalls, clang with pots and pans, and ring the bells. The numerous sounds are impossible to miss; the silence of the documentary makes them stand out that much more.

We also hear the voices of the monks. One of them repeatedly calls out for a cat, trying to lure it to its feeding bowl. Two novices make their solemn vow of conversion. A monk reads from the Carthusian Statutes over dinner. One Sunday afternoon, as the monks enjoy their weekly four-hour walk, they discuss the meaning of handwashing. A blind monk gives an interview, expressing thankfulness to God for happiness, to which he believes his blindness has contributed. Frequently, human voices sound the regular chanting of the Psalms. Most noteworthy perhaps, considering monastic strictures on laughter, a small group of monks slide (or fall) down a snow hill, precipitating hooting and hilarity.

For the most part, though, the monks keep silent. This lack of talk is connected to at least two other lacks in the film. The first is the lack of a plot. Human interaction is often key to narrative plot development. In this film, the only development is cyclical: meals, offices, day and night, annual seasons. The repetitious character of the cycles reinforces the weightiness of the silence. The second lack is the lack of company. The monks are mostly solitary, on their own. They receive their meals through the window of their cells. They do lectio divina and pray the minor hours (Terce, Sext, None, and Compline) in the solitude of their cells, joining together as a community only three times a day, for the major hours (Matins, Lauds, and Vespers). Bruno of Cologne founded the order in 1084 as a mixture of eremitic (solitary, secluded) and cenobitic (communal) monasticism, though it is the former that stands out in Carthusian spirituality. *Into Great Silence* is marked by a distinct lack of talk, lack of plot, and lack of company.

The film's original German title is simply *Die große Stille*—*The Great Silence*. It obviously refers to the predominance of silence in the Grande Chartreuse, but I suspect the director also had in mind the period between evening Compline and morning Matins, which monks refer to as the "Great Silence." This regular nocturnal silence is the lengthiest recurring silence in Carthusian spirituality. Both senses of "great silence" come through in the German title. The English version of the film has altered the title slightly: *Into Great Silence*. I'm not sure why, but I think that it makes a deliberate, theological point: the monks are moving *into* the life of God. He himself is the Great Silence they move toward. The film may be more cyclical than narrative, but the monks know that their lives are marked by movement all the same: their silence takes them into the life of God, into Great Silence itself.

SILENCE AND SOLITUDE

SILENCE GOES HAND in hand with solitude—lack of company. It does so for obvious reasons: in the company of others, we talk; on our own, we are silent. Solitude, we might say, is a precondition for silence. Without solitude, the silence of contemplation eludes us. It makes sense, therefore, that the lectio divina tradition would hold out solitude and silence as ideals. Hermits, taking their cue from the fourth-century desert monk Saint Anthony, live in caves or huts, alone—or, at most, in relative isolation scattered through a desert area. In the Middle Ages, anchorites would build their cells up against the church walls and so would isolate themselves from the rest of the townsfolk. (The term "hermit" stems from *erēmos*, the Greek word for "desert," while the word "anchorite" comes from the Greek verb *anachōreō*, "to withdraw.") Eremitic and anchoritic spirituality are the most solitary forms of monasticism.

By contrast, Benedictine monasticism is cenobitic (from *koinos bios*, "common life"), and as such is basically communal. But even Benedictine spirituality knows solitude. Benedict himself lived for three years in isolation in a cave near Subiaco just east of Rome before agreeing to serve as abbot in a nearby monastery. When the monks ended up resenting his leadership and poisoned his wine, Benedict "returned to his beloved place of solitude (*solitudinis*), where he lived alone with himself (*secum*)."

Gregory the Great, in recounting Benedict's story, elaborates at some length on the expression "to live with oneself" (*secum*). Saint Gregory observes that it is the opposite of wandering "here and there" because of mental agitation. He provides two instances from Scripture of someone who "came to himself." The first is the prodigal son who, "returning to himself" (*in se ... reversus*), decided to go back home (Luke 15:17). The second is the apostle Peter who, "coming to himself" (*ad se reversus*) after the angel had freed him from prison, recognized that this was God's doing (Acts 12:11). Gregory explains that these two stories of returning to oneself imply that we can be led "out of ourselves" (*extra nos*) in two different ways:

> Either we sink beneath ourselves (*sub nosmetipsos*) by a mental lapse, or we rise above ourselves (*super nosmetipsos*) by the grace of contemplation. So he who fed the pigs fell beneath himself (*sub semetipsum*) by unclean wandering of the mind. But he whom the angel freed and swept his mind away in ecstasy was out of himself (*extra se*), yes. But he was above himself (*super semetipsum*). Both returned to themselves (*ad se*): the one returned to his heart from erroneous work; the other returned from contemplative heights to his previous state of mind.

Therefore, venerable Benedict dwelt with himself (*secum*) in that solitude (*solitudine*) when he guarded himself in a mental cloister. For every time the ardor of contemplation wrapt him on high, he left himself behind (*sub se*).

The prodigal may have been alone in a distant land, but he did not experience true solitude: he was not "with himself" (*secum*). By contrast, Peter, after the angel led him out of prison, experienced true solitude. Having returned from ecstatic contemplation, he was now "with himself" (*secum*) in a state of solitude.

We can visualize Saint Gregory's play with prepositions using figure 9.1, which rehearses the narrative development of Luke 15 and Acts 12:

	Outside (*extra*) himself	Return	Solitude
The Prodigal	Under (*sub*) himself	to (*ad*) himself	With (*cum*) himself
Peter	Above (*super*) himself	to (*ad*) himself	With (*cum*) himself

Figure 9.1: *The Prodigal and Peter*

The prodigal son was outside (*extra*) himself because he had sunk beneath (*sub*) himself, so that he first had to return to (*ad*) himself in order to be with (*cum*) himself. Peter also was outside (*extra*) himself, but in his case, this is because he was above (*super*) himself; returning to (*ad*) himself meant, in his case, the end of his ecstasy.

Gregory applies his play with prepositions to the situation of Saint Benedict because Benedict lived in solitude with (*cum*) himself; he was always ready for God to take him outside (*extra*) himself in ecstatic contemplation. Benedict recognized that he needed solitude (being *secum*, or "with himself") to experience this contemplation.

Solitude is an integral aspect of every form of monasticism—even cenobitic monasticism. The reason is simple: all monks aim at contemplation of God. Nor should solitude be an exclusively monkish preoccupation. When in the 1120s Guigo I wrote his rule—known as the *Consuetudines*, or *Customs*—he used it for the formation of the monks of the Grande Chartreuse. But because he traced, in detail, biblical precedents for solitude, his comments also benefit people beyond the confines of Carthusian charterhouses. The eulogy on the solitary life, which concludes the *Consuetudines*, points out that Isaac went out "to meditate in the field" (Gen 24:63). When Jacob was left all alone by the Jabbok River (Gen 32:24), he saw God face-to-face. Moses, Elijah, and Elisha all loved solitude and in those situations were visited by God (Exod 24:18; 1 Kgs 19:8–9; 2 Kgs 2:25; 4:25). Jeremiah "sat alone" (Jer 15:17), filled with sorrow for his people, calling for a "solitary place" (9:2), so that he might weep for his people. The same prophet suggests that it is good "to wait with silence for the salvation of God" (Lam 3:26) and to sit "solitary and be silent," so that he might rise above (*super*) himself (3:28)—"thus indicating almost everything that is best in our vocation: the stillness and solitude, the silence and the desire for celestial gifts." John the Baptist, despite being the greatest born among women (Matt 11:11), "chose the safe solitude of the desert." Even Jesus, though solitude could not possibly increase his virtue, left us an example by fasting in the wilderness (4:2). He fled not only other people but even his own apostles by going up into the hills alone (14:23). Guigo may have intended his eulogy for the sake of his monks, but it holds universal and perennial import.

One is never less alone than when alone, according to a common monastic trope. The solitary may lack company in the sense that no friends are present physically. But both meditation on the Scriptures and prayer to God put the true solitary in the company of other saints—if not physically, then at least spiritually. Solitude is not meant to isolate us from our friends or from the church. This is the reason the prodigal was lonely instead of solitary (*secum*) in the distant country. Of course, solitude carries dangers, not least the danger of isolation. The solitary life should not be undertaken lightly. Still, it is in solitude that we may experience the contemplation that is a foretaste of the Great Silence of eternity. The reason we need not be alone when we are alone is that in solitude, we experience the presence of God. I already noted in chapter 1 that friendship and solitude are not each other's opposites. Friendship, Aelred of Rievaulx explains, makes one out of many. Human friendships find their destiny when in solitude friendship unites us eternally with God.

SILENCE AND GOD

SOLITUDE SERVES SILENCE. Silence is the aim of lectio divina, for God is the Great Silence. The fourth and final step of lectio divina, contemplation, yields rest in God himself. Cardinal Robert Sarah repeatedly reflects on lectio divina in his 2016 book *The Power of Silence*. Inspired by conversations at the Grande Chartreuse with the prior general of the Carthusian order, Dom Dysmas de Lassus, Sarah often alludes to the link between lectio divina and silence. Describing the move from the third step (*oratio* or prayer) to the last (*contemplatio*), Sarah writes,

> The silence of eternity is the consequence of God's infinite love.
> In heaven, we will be with Jesus, totally possessed by God and

under the influence of the Holy Spirit. Man will no longer be capable of saying a single word. Prayer itself will have become impossible. It will become contemplation, a look of love and adoration. The Holy Spirit will inflame the souls who go to heaven. They will be completely given over to the Spirit.

Cardinal Sarah explains that in heaven, prayer gives way to contemplation. But those familiar with lectio divina will know that the transition from time to eternity—and so from prayer to silence—takes place not only after death. This transition is anticipated in the spiritual practice of lectio divina. When we are finished reading, meditating, and praying over the Scriptures, we are silent. In this silence, we move from time to eternity. Contemplation takes us into the silence of God.

Dysmas de Lassus notes that the heart-to-heart conversation with God in prayer and meditation blossoms into contemplation. Dom Dysmas then writes, "When we are face to face with a God who has become man, how can we not remain silent? Reading, study, and reflection, these initial stages finally lead to silence." The Carthusian prior here mentions the incarnation, just as Cardinal Sarah in the quote above speaks of being with Jesus in heaven. Both mention God's love in Christ. It is a love so deep that it is inexpressible in words. Lectio divina and the Christian life both end in silence because the love of God is too great to capture adequately in words.

John Cassian's *Conferences*, which date from around the year 420, mention the same move from prayer to contemplation. In Conference 9, Abba Isaac discusses four types of prayer: supplications, prayers, pleas, and thanksgivings. All four are valuable, and everyone needs all of them. Still, Abba Isaac discerns a certain progression. Especially beginners use supplications to seek pardon for sin. As we progress, we offer prayers (or vows), in which we renounce sin and undertake the life of virtue. Having grown in charity, we next make pleas for others. Finally, we offer thanksgiving. Overwhelmed with God's kindnesses in the past and his promises for the future, we fall silent: "Looking with purest gaze at the rewards promised to the saints, our spirit is moved by measureless joy to pour out wordless thanksgiving (*ineffabiles gratias*) to God." Abba Isaac explains that this thanksgiving sometimes takes on an ecstatic intensity:

> Aflame with all this their hearts are rapt (*raptantur*) in the burning prayer which human words can neither grasp nor utter (*nec comprehendi nec exprimi*). Sometimes the soul which has come to be rooted in this state of real purity takes on all the forms of prayer at the same time. It flies from one to the other, like an uncontrollable grasping fire. It becomes an outpouring of living pure prayer (*ineffabiles ... preces purissimi*) which the Holy Spirit, without our knowing it, lifts up to God in unspeakable groanings (*gemitibus inenarrabilibus*). It conceives so much within itself at that instant, unspeakably pours forth so much in supplication, that it could not tell you of it at another time nor even remember it.

The notion of ineffability or indescribability pervades Abba Isaac's description. He reminds Cassian and his friend Germanus of Saint Paul's talk in Romans 8:26 of the Spirit praying for us with "unspeakable groanings" (*gemitibus inenarrabilibus*) and of the apostle being rapt up (*raptus*) in Paradise, where he heard "secret words which it is not granted to man to utter" (2 Cor 12:4).

The lectio divina tradition talks about ineffable thanksgiving and unspeakable groanings since words cannot properly express the experience. Saint Augustine famously articulates the incomprehensibility of God in Sermon 117, in a discussion of John 1:1 ("In the beginning was the Word: and the Word was with God: and the Word was God"). This is a truth we cannot possibly comprehend, insists Augustine. His Latin expression famously states, *Si enim comprehendis, non est Deus* (If you comprehend, it is not God). God is silence because he is beyond comprehension. It is fitting to contemplate God in silence because words do not do him justice. We must fall silent in the presence of God.

The point is not that God is emptiness or nothingness. In that case, we might conclude that by saying nothing at all, we comprehend God. The opposite is the case: it is God's fullness or plenitude that prevents our words from properly grasping him. Rowan Williams, explaining why human words do not adequately grasp God, comments, "Theological negation does not grow out of a fastidiousness about commitment to the practices of faith, but out of a different kind of anxiety, the proper fear of closing our selfhood to the immeasurable plenitude of that which is worshipped." Negative theology—the negation of whatever positive statements we make about God—stems from the recognition that our words are merely sacraments that hint at the overflowing fullness of the reality of God.

To say that God is love is not to lie. After all, we don't want to fall prey to what Williams calls "fastidiousness"—an excessively delicate approach—when it comes to our faith commitments. Saying that God is love is to make a true statement. It is just that these words hardly begin to capture what God has done for us in Jesus Christ. Joseph Cardinal Ratzinger puts the point beautifully: "Wherever God's word is translated into human words there remains a surplus of the unspoken and unspeakable which calls us to silence." We cannot but fall silent when faced with the reality of the love of God.

We speak most fully and daringly of God's love when we talk about the Trinity. God's speech in the human history of Jesus Christ reflects divine speech in eternity: the incarnation reflects the eternal generation of the Son. The Father eternally speaks his Word, expressing his love by begetting his Son. He speaks this Word in utter silence, for it is an ineffable mystery. Thomas Merton makes the point that whereas Babylon—the city of hatred and division—is scattered by its many languages, the City of God knows only one language, that of charity:

> There is only one language spoken in the City of God. That language is charity. Those who speak it best, speak it in silence. For the eternal Word of Truth is uttered in silence. If He is uttered in silence, He must be heard in deepest silence. And His Spirit, the Spirit of Love, is also poured out into our hearts, proceeding from the Father and the Son, in an everlasting silence.

For Merton, silence, contemplation, and charity are one and the same. The reason is that God utters his eternal Word in the silence of his love. To share in the mystery of the Trinity, we must adopt the silence of the love that flows from the Father to the Son. The silence of contemplation allows us to be reborn into the silence of the eternal charity of God.

SILENCE AND NOISE

THE OPPOSITE OF silence is not sound but noise. Noise is self-produced; it doesn't have a divine source. We might define "noise" as any sound that interferes with listening. Noise comes to the fore most obviously, perhaps, in compulsive and incessant chattering and babbling. The early thirteenth-century rule for anchoresses, *Ancrene Wisse*, offers vivid warnings against needless chatter. Eve, we are told, held a long discussion with the serpent about the apple; by contrast, Our Lady did not debate the angel but obediently consented. The lesson is clear: "You, my beloved sisters, follow our Lady, and not the cackling Eve." Mary spoke only four times: responding to the angel (Luke 1:38), greeting Elizabeth (1:40), at the wedding of Cana (John 2:3), and after finding her son (Luke 2:48).

Such restraint is in line with numerous biblical passages. *Ancrene Wisse* appeals to Psalm 140:11 ("A man full of tongue shall not be established in the earth"); Psalm 39:1 ("I said: I will take heed to my ways: that I sin not with my tongue"); Isaiah 32:17 ("The service of justice [is] silence"); and Isaiah 30:15 ("In silence and in hope shall your strength be"). *Ancrene Wisse*, reflecting on this last verse, suggests that when a nun "opens her mouth with much chattering, and breaks silence, she spits out hope and its sweetness entirely with worldly words, and loses spiritual virtue to the enemy."

In a later passage, *Ancrene Wisse* depicts the anchoress as the lone sparrow on the housetop from Psalm 102:7. It may seem odd that the sparrow, "a chattering bird" that "chatters and chirps the whole time," is said to be solitary. But we should note that sparrows chatter with each other only during mating season: "Because many anchoresses have this same vice, David compares her not to a sparrow who has a mate but to a sparrow by itself: *Sicut passer solitarius*—'I am,' he says as an anchorite, 'like a sparrow that is alone.' For so should an anchoress always chirp and chatter her prayers on her own in the lonely place she is in." *Ancrene Wisse* warns against any chirping and chattering that does not take the form of reading Scripture or offering prayer.

We use noise to drown out the words that God wants us to hear. This is an age-old spiritual problem, but modernity is particularly noisy. What Cardinal Sarah calls the "dictatorship of noise" is in some ways a uniquely modern problem. Modernity is exceptionally noisy: traffic, construction, lawn mowers, radios, and TVs. Increasingly people are concerned about noise pollution. Noise is ubiquitous and often inescapable. And smartphones have perilously amplified the problem— music, videos, news, and social media all produce noise, for they all interfere with genuine listening. True, smartphones also *enable* listening. We can listen to an illuminating lecture or a Bach cantata on our phone. But for the most part, that's not what smartphones do. They give us the illusion of being in control, while in reality they enslave us to our noisy distractions.

Cardinal Sarah makes the point that the noise of modernity goes hand in hand with pride: "Words often bring with them the illusion of transparency, as though they allowed us to understand everything, control everything, put everything in order. Modernity is talkative because it is proud, unless the converse is true. Is our incessant talking perhaps what makes us proud?" Sarah seems to suggest that noise and pride mutually reinforce each other, and that modernity gives rise to both. His suggestion is perceptive, in line with Ecclesiastes 9:17: "The words of the wise are heard in silence, more than the cry of a prince among fools." Noise and pride go together, as do silence and humility. Lectio divina ends in silence because it aims at humility. Or, we could also say, lectio divina is an instrument in putting to death the primal sin of pride. Silence is the first prerequisite for getting rid of pride, for only in silence can we join Elijah in hearing the still small voice of God (1 Kgs 19:12).

SILENCE AND OBEDIENCE

SILENCE STANDS OPPOSED to noise, not to the spoken word. We have already seen that speech and silence are identical in God, eternally generating the Son. In us, they are not the same, though even with us they go hand in hand. The silence of contemplation follows reading, meditation, and prayer. Lots of words precede our silence. The point of lectio divina is not to rid ourselves of speech but to be shaped by divine speech. Lectio divina, therefore, is a training exercise in listening to someone else's words—God's. To listen well, we need silence. The key Deuteronomic confession of the unity of God implores us to listen to God: "Hear, O Israel (*shema yisrael*), the Lord our God is one Lord" (Deut 6:4). The Shema asks us to listen to the God of Israel, something that requires silence. The Shema's listening is nearly identical to obeying. Deuteronomy 6 is packed with verbs such as "command," "serve," "keep," "do" and nouns such as "commandments," "testimonies," "statutes." The "listening" that the Shema demands implies obedience to God's will.

The purpose of lectio divina, therefore, is not merely internal. We long for biblical meditation and prayer to transfigure us externally, in the way we live. Eugene Peterson goes so far as to insist that contemplation actually *means* to live out the Christian life in the ordinary, active, everyday life. Now, I think this overstates the case. Contemplation means to rest in the joy of being united with God, and therefore contemplation and action are not one and the same. Still, Peterson makes an important point: our character and behaviors need to change and conform to God's character and will. The contemplative purpose of silence depends on us having listened first, in our meditation on the Scriptures. Being transformed in virtue through obedient listening is tied directly to the aim of contemplation. It is listening (and obeying) in our everyday lives that makes us more like God and hence more fitted for contemplation. The more we listen and obey, the more we are at ease with silence.

We are made for listening. The Trappist monk and spiritual writer Basil Pennington makes this point in his book *Lectio Divina*. He titles one of his chapters "The Listening That We Are." What he means is that listening is our mode of being; it is the way we exist. Listening is part of our definition. Pennington points to Christ as the reason for this listening shape of human beings:

> The Word was made flesh. Jesus is the most complete expression of the Word in our creation. God is Word. God is communication. And we therefore are especially a *listening*, a listening for that Word. To the extent we truly "hear" that Word, receive that Word into our being and into our lives, we participate in the Divine Being, Life, Love, Joy. Made in the image of God, we have an unlimited, an infinite potential to be like unto him.

We are made to listen because we are made for the Word. The theological point is quite traditional. But by speaking, unconventionally, of the listening that we *are*, Pennington makes clear that by listening (and obeying) we act in line with who we *are*. When we disobey, we go against the way God made us in the Word.

Maurus, Saint Benedict's first disciple, recognized this importance of listening. The son of a Roman nobleman, he had received his training from Benedict in Subiaco and served him in various capacities. Later tradition tells us that Saint Benedict sent him to Gaul in the year 543, where according to tradition he founded Glanfeuil Abbey. The first historical account of Saint Maurus is that of Gregory the Great, in *The Life of Saint Benedict*. In figure 9.2, we witness Benedict giving his Rule to his disciple Maurus along with two other monks.

The first words Maurus would have read in the Rule's prologue were meant to instill obedience in the new monk:

> Listen carefully, my son, to the master's instructions, and attend to them with the ear of your heart. This is advice from a father who loves you; welcome it, and faithfully put it into practice. The labor of obedience will bring you back to him from whom you had drifted through the sloth of disobedience. This message of mine is for you, then, if you are ready to give up your own will, once and for all, and armed with the strong and noble weapons of obedience to do battle for the true King, Christ the Lord.

The Latin under the picture of Benedict and Maurus contains the first words of this same quotation: *Avsculta, o fili, praecepta magistri*—"Listen carefully, my son, to the master's instructions." Nothing was more important for Maurus than to learn to listen to his abbot and his rule.

As Maurus kept reading the Rule, he would have noted this emphasis on obedience and listening throughout. Benedict devotes the entire fifth chapter to obedience. He describes it here as the "first step of humility" (*primus humilitatis gradis*). Twice quoting Luke 10:16, Benedict makes clear that the abbot stands in the position of God or of Christ: "Whoever listens to you listens to me." Monks should obey immediately, quickly, and gladly. Elsewhere, too, Benedict insists that

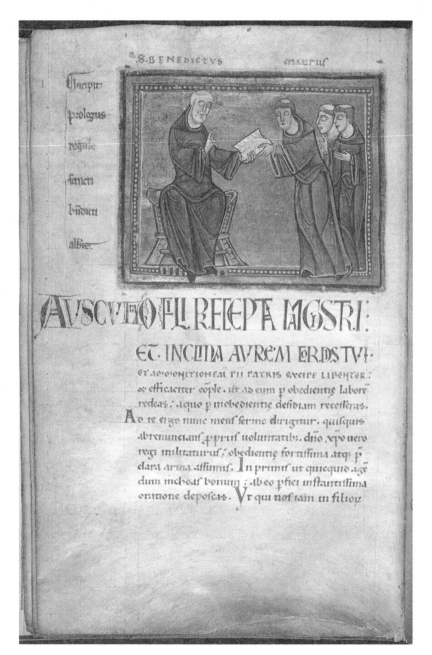

Figure 9.2: *Saint Benedict delivers his Rule to Maurus*

the abbot speaks with the authority of Christ. The abbot, he explains, represents Christ, for the abbot has the name of Christ, which we acknowledge in crying, "Abba, Father!" (cf. Rom 8:15).

Fittingly, the next two chapters deal with silence (chapter 6) and humility (chapter 7). For Benedict, these two topics are directly linked to obedience. He begins chapter 6 with the observation that our words should always be few: "I will guard my ways so as not to sin with my tongue. I placed a guard at my mouth. I was speechless and humiliated, refraining even from good speech" (Ps 39:1–2). Even when our speech is wholesome, we should beware of being garrulous. But Benedict regards silence as important especially with a view to fostering a humble, receptive, and obedient attitude toward those in authority: "Speaking and teaching are the master's task; the disciple is to be silent and listen. Therefore, any requests to a superior should be made with all humility and respectful submission." Note the linking between silence and listening. For Benedict, obedience begins with silence.

The chapter on humility continues similarly. Outlining twelve steps on the ladder of humility, Benedict insists that we reach the top only by means of humility. Every step is a deepening of humility. Many of these steps of humility return to the theme of obedience. Like Jesus, the monk should do the will of him who sends us (John 6:38) (step 2). And like Jesus, who became obedient to the point of death (Phil 2:8), the monk must "submit to the superior in all obedience" (step 3). This obedience even accepts injustice and suffering if need be (step 4). The monk confesses evil thoughts to the abbot (step 5), puts up with low and dishonorable treatment (step 6), and regards himself as lower than all the rest (step 7). The monk does only what the Rule and his superiors endorse (step 8). He keeps silent, except when asked a question (step 9), cognizant of biblical warnings: "In the multitude of words there shall not want sin" (Prov 10:19), and "A man full of tongue shall not be established in the earth" (Ps 140:11). The monk ought not be quick to laugh (step 10), for "a fool lifteth up his voice in laughter" (Sir 21:20). When speaking at all, the monk should do so "gently and without laughter, humbly, and seriously," with "few and careful words," not being given to shouting (step 11). The monk's humility is evident not only in his heart but even in his bodily posture, bowed and gazing on the earth (step 12). Five of the steps of humility obviously link it with obedience (steps 2, 3, 4, 5, and 8), and three of them tie humility to silence (steps 9, 10, and 11). Saint Benedict deliberately links the themes of obedience, silence, and humility.

It is hardly surprising that Gregory the Great depicts Maurus as an obedient disciple of Saint Benedict. Pope Gregory tells the story of how one of the young monks, Placidus, fell in a river and was taken along by the current. Though far away in his cell, a long distance from the scene of the accident, Benedict realized what just happened and told Maurus to go and rescue Placidus. Maurus hurried to the river, ran (like Peter) over the water (cf. Matt 14:29), grabbed Placidus by the hair, and ran back to shore. He then (also like Peter) "came to himself (*ad se*)" (cf. Acts 12:11). Realizing what had just happened, Maurus was terrified (cf. Matt 14:30).

Saint Gregory displays great caution and skill in attributing credit for Placidus's rescue. He points out that Maurus acted out of obedience: "When he had asked and received the blessing, Maurus obeyed the order of his father and ran to the place where the boy was being carried by the current." Maurus first obtained the abbot's blessing and only then ran to the river. Benedict, therefore, heaps praise on Maurus, insisting "that the thing was not due to his [i.e., Benedict's] merits but to Maurus's obedience." Maurus himself, though, attributes the miracle to the authority of Saint Benedict, who had told him to go. And Placidus confirms that it is Benedict who saved him: "When I was being hauled from the water, I saw the abbot's cape above my head and thought he was dragging me out of the water." Pope Gregory's account safeguards Benedict's priority over Maurus. At the same time, he portrays Maurus as a second Peter, whose obedience makes him a model for every future monk.

CONCLUSION

SILENCE AND HUMILITY defeat noise and pride. But how? The dictatorship of noise often seems to triumph, both in our personal lives and in the culture of modernity. What is it that has given monks throughout the centuries confidence to dedicate their lives to solitude and silence? Do we today have proper warrant to take them as our guides? Are we sure that time spent on lectio divina is not a waste? Do silence and humility pay off? Or do we, by turning to silence and humility, simply allow noise and pride to stake out additional turf?

Here I want to turn once more to Robert Sarah's *The Power of Silence*. The title holds out remarkable confidence in silence and humility over noise and pride. Why? I think because the cardinal knows that appearances deceive: noise and pride do not hold final sway; rather, silence and humility save the world. Of course they do, seeing as God himself is silence and humility. Cardinal Sarah points to Saint Paul's famous words in Philippians 2 that connect the incarnation with the humility of God:

For let this mind be in you, which was also in Christ Jesus: Who being in the form of God, thought it not robbery to be equal with God: But emptied himself, taking the form of a servant, being made in the likeness of men, and in habit found as a man. He humbled himself, becoming obedient unto death, even to the death of the cross. For which cause, God also hath exalted him and hath given him a name which is above all names: That in the name of Jesus every knee should bow, of those that are in heaven, on earth, and under the earth: And that every tongue should confess that the Lord Jesus Christ is in the glory of God the Father. (Phil 2:5–11)

Saint Paul insists that humility and obedience constitute the path toward exaltation and power. God's love is self-emptying or sacrificial love. We see this on Holy Thursday, with Jesus on his knees, washing his disciples' feet. "The washing of their feet," explains Sarah, "is a revelation, an unveiling of what God is. He is love: humble, priestly, sacrificial love; and God's humility is the very depth of God."

Jesus deliberately enacts the silence and humility of God, not only when he sets out for the solitude of the desert or the mountain, but also when he holds his peace when the high priest questions him: "Answerest thou nothing to the things which these witness against thee?" (Matt 26:62). Jesus's silence is that of the sacrificial lamb: "He was offered because it was his own will, and he opened not his mouth: he shall be led as a sheep to the slaughter, and shall be dumb as a lamb before his shearer, and he shall not open his mouth" (Isa 53:7). In Jesus's silence we recognize the self-emptying, sacrificial humility of God.

The silence of Jesus's humility leads, inexorably, to the silence of his death: "Greater love than this no man hath, that a man lay down his life for his friends" (John 15:13). After uttering seven words on the cross, Jesus dies and silence reigns. His self-emptying silence yields its ineluctable consequence, the silence of death. But the apostle claims it is precisely this obedience unto death that gives Jesus the name that is above all names (Phil 2:8–9). Or, to use Paul's words of Romans 6, "Knowing that Christ rising again from the dead, dieth now no more, death shall no more have dominion over him" (Rom 6:9).

Noise and pride do not have the final say—not over Christ, not over our lives, and not over our world. In fact, noise and pride have no say at all: they are fake, counterfeit, simulacra, poor imitations of the Word of God. Lacking truth, goodness, beauty—even being itself—noise and pride are powerless. Silence and humility have revealed themselves in Christ as the true face of being. And so, we dare let this mind be in us, which was also in Christ Jesus (Phil 2:5). We dare confess, "If we be dead with Christ, we believe that we shall live also together with Christ" (Rom 6:8).

Lectio divina is dangerous. It predisposes us to the silence and humility that marked the life of Christ. We'd better be prepared, then, because the silence of the fourth step of lectio may serve as a prelude to the silence of death. Still, we are summoned to embrace fearlessly the path to contemplation, for if Saint Paul is to be believed, the silence of death marks the beginning of the silence of eternal contemplation.

Conclusion

I T IS ADVENT, and I am putting the last touches on this book. Longing for Christ's coming inspires the practice of lectio divina. We read, meditate, and pray in the hope that he will come and pierce our hearts. Lectio divina, therefore, is a type of advent reading.

My working assumption here is that of Saint Bernard of Clairvaux. Christ, explains Bernard, comes not just on Christmas Eve (past) or on Judgment Day (future). A third advent is the "intermediate coming" of Christ today, in the conversion of our hearts. The three comings are analogous—both like and unlike one another. His past and future comings are visible. In his coming as an infant and in his coming as judge, Christ is physically present and seen by human eyes. His coming today is different. It is, observes Bernard, a hidden coming. It is this intermediate coming, invisible to the eye, that is the aim of lectio divina.

If Christ's intermediate coming is a hidden one, how do we discern it? This dilemma has become pressing in our modern age, since philosophers such as Hobbes, Hume, and Kant have questioned our ability to move beyond the senses. If sense perception is the only means of knowledge, *contemplatio* of God in Christ would seem impossible.

Prayer (*oratio*), however, repudiates such modern restraints. The truth is, we long for advent. We pray for Christ to come. The book of experience (*liber experientiae*) that we read about in the monastic tradition reaches beyond the limitations of mere sense perception. Christ's hidden coming in his second advent offers a way out of the modern dilemma. The reality of advent teaches us to reckon with the intermediate, hidden coming of Christ.

The spiritual masters of the lectio divina tradition, therefore, offer a way out of the modern epistemological conundrum. There *is* a way to turn from visible to hidden things. It is to open ourselves up to divine piercing. Throughout this book, we have noticed spiritual masters express their longing for Christ's coming in the language of "piercing." This theme comes to the fore especially in patristic commentaries on the Song of Songs. You remember the erotic back-and-forth between bride and groom. At one point, the bride admits to her bystanders (the "daughters of Jerusalem") that her lover has conquered her heart: "I am wounded with love," she exclaims—*vulnerata caritate ego sum* (Song 2:5).

We hardly need to ask what has wounded her heart. The context makes perfectly clear that it is the groom's love. Less obvious from the surface of the text is the lover's means of wounding the heart of his bride. Careful reading, meditation, and prayer, however, have allowed many readers to discover the lover's instrument of wounding. Though it isn't mentioned in the text, readers have often identified the source of wounding as an arrow. One patristic preacher after the other expounds on the theme of archery in connection with verse 5— Cyril of Alexandria, Origen, Gregory of Nyssa, Ambrose, Augustine, Theodoret of Cyrus, Gregory the Great, and I am sure with a bit of searching I'd find more.

Let's just trace a few examples. In the East, Gregory of Nyssa waxes eloquent about archery as he comments on the Song. The bride, he claims, "praises the accurate archer because he has directed his arrow straight at her, for she says, *I have been wounded by love.* By these words she signifies the arrow that lies deep in her heart." The medieval pope Saint Gregory the Great is no different. In his *Morals on the Book of Job*, he asks, "What do we understand by 'arrows' but the words of preachers? ... They transfix the hearts of the hearers. With these arrows Holy Church had been struck, who was saying, *I am wounded with love.*"

So, where is this arrow if we cannot empirically find it in the text? What gives Gregory of Nyssa, Gregory the Great, and other ancient luminaries the confidence to assert that an arrow has wounded the beloved's heart? The answer is quite simple. Seeing as lectio divina is divine or holy reading, it is animated, from start to finish, by a longing search for the presence of the heavenly Groom. The bride, intimately familiar with this Groom, knows that archery is the skill he invariably employs in piercing her heart.

Augustine's familiarity with the Groom shows in his scouring of the Scriptures in search for the Groom's wounding instrument. He links the Song's wounding with love (Song 2:5) to Psalm 45, Scripture's next-most-famous epithalamium after the Song of Songs. The psalmist identifies the Groom's means of wounding his bride with the words, "Thy arrows are sharp: under thee shall people fall" (Ps 45:5). Saul's conversion, explains Augustine, is the most obvious example of this wounding love: "From heaven the arrow was aimed, and Saul was struck in his heart. It was in Saul that it found its mark, for he was not Paul yet, but still Saul, still upright, not yet fallen flat. But the arrow struck him and he fell low in his heart."

Further evidence comes from Isaiah 49:2: the Lord "hath made me as a chosen arrow: in his quiver he hath hidden me." Theodoret directly identifies this arrow as Christ when he comments on the meaning of being wounded with love: "For [Christ] is after all the chosen arrow (Isa. 49:2) that wounds the souls it strikes."

The logic is impeccable: if Christ is the Groom who wounds our heart, then with holy desire we search the Scriptures for *how* he does this. That's what the fathers do by turning to biblical texts such as Psalm 45:5 and Isaiah 49:2. As we saw in chapter 4, the practice of lectio divina turns readers into "living concordances" (Jean Leclercq). Intimate familiarity with the Scriptures enables us to identify the Groom's instrument for wounding his beloved's heart. Archery is his means: biblical words turn into the Spirit's arrow, and it is meditation on these words that gives the Logos entry in the human heart.

Scholars talk about "intertextuality" or "verbal association" to explain what's happening here. I won't object. But really, we should call it *advent reading*. It is a form of reading that reaches beyond the empirical, a reading driven by a longing for Christ to pierce us with the arrows of his love. Lectio divina, animated by desire, recognizes the Archer in the painful piercing of the heart.

Lectio divina is grounded in an advent posture. The most important things are not the ones we see. Meditation on a word (*arrow*) that is absent from the text yields a reality that is hidden from the eye (Christ's piercing of the heart). We need divine reading, for it opens up the heart to the arrow's wounding love.

Eight Theses on Lectio Divina

L ECTIO DIVINA IS a means of grace. God uses our prayerful meditation upon the Scriptures to draw us into his divine life. Below, I highlight key elements in the process, those that I think we should take special note of. You may find these theses helpful, therefore, as you try to get a sense of my approach to lectio divina in this book. I purposely offer *eight* theses. Saints throughout the tradition have spoken of the eschaton as the Eighth Day. The final step of lectio divina—contemplation—gives us a foretaste of the Eighth Day.

1. Christian spirituality is biblical spirituality.

2. Lectio divina is nothing out of the ordinary.

3. Lectio divina and spiritual interpretation are two sides of the same coin.

4. Sermon preparation is an extended type of lectio divina.

5. Lectio divina is not a purely subjective enterprise.

6. If you want lectio divina, be prepared for suffering.

7. Introspection is of the essence of the Christian faith.

8. Lectio divina reminds us that God is our ultimate aim.

EIGHT THESES ON LECTIO
DIVINA EXPLAINED

I. CHRISTIAN SPIRITUALITY IS BIBLICAL SPIRITUALITY.

The most obvious things are often the most overlooked. The most obvious presupposition behind divine reading is that it is biblically centered. The Scriptures are central to the Christian life. They must shape our belief and our spirituality, for they are our indispensable guide into eternal life. Lectio divina is an ancient practice, which has shaped many centuries of Christian devotion, both in East and West, both before and after the sixteenth-century Reformation. Sadly, biblical illiteracy is a threat both in East and West, both in Catholic and in Protestant circles. Lectio divina—with its emphasis on chewing and ruminating on biblical words, so they may shape us—reminds us that you cannot have Christianity without repetitive biblical reading and deep meditation upon the words of the divine Scriptures.

2. LECTIO DIVINA IS NOTHING OUT OF THE ORDINARY.

My book talks a lot about meditative practices of church fathers and medieval monks. That approach comes with a risk: my readers may get the impression that lectio divina is not for them; it's something from centuries past, and only for monks. Nothing could be further from the truth. What animates me in this book is the conviction that—for the most part, at least—biblical reading should be meditative, prayerful, and aimed at the contemplation of God himself. The Scriptures are a means of grace. God intends to use them to bring us to him. This is not to deny the value of all kinds of subordinate goals. But we should resist the modern preoccupation with a purely rational grasp of the one true meaning of the text. The words of the divine Scriptures cannot be mastered; they want to master us. God's purpose with them—that which sets them apart as holy or divine—is that they would change or transfigure us. Divine things aim to divinize.

3. LECTIO DIVINA AND SPIRITUAL INTERPRETATION ARE TWO SIDES OF THE SAME COIN.

If spiritual reading is what the Bible is for, then our exegesis of the Bible should be in sync with spiritual reading. Put somewhat more sharply, once you take lectio divina seriously, you cannot but treat exegesis as a spiritual discipline. The past few decades have witnessed a revival of theological exegesis—which I take to mean a type of exegesis that takes in account (rather than brackets off) theological presuppositions. I'm a great fan of theological exegesis. But my preferred term for it is *spiritual interpretation*. The reason is the word *spiritual* reminds us that in exegesis we move from the letter (or the flesh) to the spirit. We read the Bible in order to find there Christ himself, revealed to us through the Spirit. Meditative reading digs into the words of Scripture so as to find in them the treasure of Christ himself (Matt 13:44). The digging is a Spirit-guided process—spiritual exegesis. So closely linked are lectio divina and spiritual interpretation that the twelfth-century Carthusian monk Guigo II mapped the four steps of lectio (reading, meditation, prayer, and contemplation) onto the four meanings sought in interpretation (literal, allegorical, moral, and eschatological). Much like lectio divina, exegesis aims at the contemplation of God.

4. SERMON PREPARATION IS AN EXTENDED TYPE OF LECTIO DIVINA.

A sermon is the product of the preacher's own meditative reading. A sermon is not a doctrinal treatise; neither does it offer an inductive study of the biblical text per se. A sermon is the outcome of an encounter. The preacher has met with God in and through the biblical text. After reading the biblical text numerous times, after meditating deeply upon its words, and after a prayerful and often painful encounter with the God of the Scriptures, the preacher shares his meditation with the congregation. And by sharing the fruit of meditation, the preacher invites the congregation in turn to meditate upon the biblical text. Many of the writings that I look at in this book function in exactly this way. Anselm, Aelred, Bonaventure, and many others offered their readers the fruit of their own meditation. Their purpose was to draw their readers into a similar prayerful encounter with God. The purpose of the sermon is the same as that of Scripture: it invites listeners to attend to human words so that they may encounter the eternal Word himself.

5. LECTIO DIVINA IS NOT A PURELY SUBJECTIVE ENTERPRISE.

One of the most common misconceptions about spiritual reading is that it is driven by emotion, so that it gives us license to impose our own preconceived notions upon the biblical text. This understanding of lectio divina commonly determines people's evaluation of it: some applaud, while others decry the subjectivism and emotionalism of spiritual reading. I have gone out of my way in this book to debunk the notion that lectio divina is a purely subjective enterprise.

Sure, experience is a big thing in divine reading. There is no escaping this, and the title *Pierced by Love* speaks to the significance of human experience in lectio divina. The reason is obvious: meaning is not a static object that is ours to figure out; rather, meaning occurs within an encounter. And encounters are inherently subjective and experiential. But the experience that we bring to the biblical text is one that is always shaped by the church's prior reading of it throughout the centuries. And it is the church that, through the centuries, has safeguarded the truth of the biblical witness to the living God. The human subject, therefore, is not autonomous in relation to the Scriptures but will—or, at least, should—approach them with humility, always willing to be corrected and transformed by them. Nor is lectio divina a free-for-all, as if genre, grammar, context, and the like were irrelevant. Lectio divina does not preclude the use of word studies, commentaries, and the like. In short, we dare not use lectio divina to excuse our laziness.

6. IF YOU WANT LECTIO DIVINA, BE PREPARED FOR SUFFERING.

Lectio divina aims at God himself. There is no greater joy or happiness than God. We therefore connect spiritual reading with the sweetness of meditating on God's words. And we are right to do so. God's words are "sweeter than honey and the honeycomb" (Ps 19:10). But we should guard against the trap of sentimentalism, reading the Scriptures with the aim of arriving at a certain feeling and avoiding whatever may get in the way of the warm fuzzies that we pursue. The Scriptures, however, do not aim at warm fuzzies or feelings for their own sake. God wants to transfigure us. To be *pierced* by love is a painful process. Perhaps no one knew this better than Bonaventure. When he meditated on

the Gospel accounts of Jesus's suffering, he read them in the light
of Galatians 2:20: *Christo confixus sum cruci*—"I have been pierced
through with Christ." To be pierced through by God's love is a painful thing, for to identify with Christ in his suffering is to undergo the
excruciating process of transformation. Does meditation offer sweetness? Does divine reading aim at happiness? Most definitely. But the
love of God is like a piercing arrow that renders us cruciform, for we
recognize the authenticity of resurrection life in the stigmata that crucifixion has brought about in us.

7. INTROSPECTION IS OF THE ESSENCE OF THE CHRISTIAN FAITH.

With this thesis I look at one chapter in particular: chapter 7, "Bread
of Tears." I want to draw special attention to it because it is counter-
cultural and yet central to the Christian faith. North Americans are
outgoing, even brash perhaps; other cultures generally do not mis-
take us for inward-looking (introspective) people. Nor do we want to
be considered introspective. We believe that what matters is engagement with the external, material world. This Baconian outlook has
also affected the way we treat Scripture: salvation history and sci-
entific exegesis have taken center stage. As a result, we feel ill at ease
when we read earlier theologians: they focused upon the state of their
soul before God and saw their inward struggles reflected in the biblical text. From a modern perspective, we cannot but denounce this
"introspective conscience of the West," to use New Testament scholar
Krister Stendahl's expression (though I try to show in chapter 7 that
it is not just the West, but the entire Christian tradition that used to

be introspective). I won't here make a case for introspection, except to say this: it is only by scraping the rust of sinful accretions from our souls that their beauty begins to shine somewhat like the transfigured Lord Christ himself. It is this transfiguration, I believe, that is central to the Christian pilgrimage and that forms the aim of divine reading.

8. LECTIO DIVINA REMINDS US THAT GOD IS OUR ULTIMATE AIM.

The final step of lectio divina is contemplation. Introspection and contemplation typically go hand in hand, and so it is hardly surprising that along with introspection, also contemplation has taken a back seat in contemporary theological reflection. The very thought that in the hereafter we would eternally contemplate God—typically referred to as the beatific vision—makes us uneasy. Our discomfort has a variety of causes, but I think it is idolatry that is the root cause. Adam and Eve ate of the tree because they saw it was "good to eat, and fair to the eyes, and delightful to behold" (Gen. 3:6). Their idolizing of created objects of the external world made them hide from God when they heard him "walking in paradise at the afternoon air" (3:8). They sensed—rightly, I think—the incompatibility between the worship of things and the worship of God, and they were ashamed of having abandoned the contemplation of God. The modern discomfort with contemplation results necessarily from our myopic, idolatrous focus on this-worldly things. Lectio divina trains our longing for God, for he wants us to find our ultimate joy and happiness only in him.

Sources

M OST OF THE CHARTS I have drawn up myself (figures 2.2, 3.1, 5.2, 8.1, 9.1), while my daughter Meghan kindly assisted me with figures 1.1, 1.2, and 6.5.

The other images are readily available online. Note the following details and acknowledgments:

+ Figure 2.1 is held at Saint Catherine's Monastery in Egypt and is in the public domain.

+ Figures 4.1–4.6 can be found at mysticark.ucr.edu. I reproduce them here with the kind permission of Prof. Conrad Rudolph.

+ Figure 5.1 is held by the Bibliothèque nationale de France, Département des manuscrits (Latin 16744, fol. 81r) and is in the public domain. See https://gallica.bnf.fr/ark:/12148/btv1b85100225/f169.item.

+ Figure 5.3 is held by the University of Aberdeen (MS 24, fol. 63r) and reproduced with permission. See https://www.abdn.ac.uk/bestiary/ms24/f63r.

+ Figure 5.4 is held by the Dombibliothek Hildesheim (MS St Godehard 1, p. 160/fol. 80v) and reproduced with permission. See https://www.albani-psalter.de/stalbanspsalter/english/translation/trans160.shtml.

- ◆ Figures 6.1 and 6.2 are held by the Walters Art Museum (Walters MS W.72, fol. 25v and 26r) and are in the public domain. See https://www.thedigitalwalters.org/Data/WaltersManuscripts/html/W72/description.html.

- ◆ Figures 6.3, 6.4, and 6.6 are held by the Galleria dell'Accademia in Florence. The images reproduced in 6.3 and 6.4 are in the public domain and reproduced here under a Creative Commons license; the image reproduced in 6.6 is © akg-images/ Rabatti & Domingie. Used by permission.

- ◆ Figure 9.2 is taken from the Necrology from the Benedictine abbey of St Gilles (diocese of Nîmes), held by the British Library (MS 16979, fol. 21v) and is in the public domain. See https://www.bl.uk/collection-items/rule-of-st-benedict-with-a-necrology-of-st-gilles-abbey.

Notes

PRAYER FOR LECTIO DIVINA

Psalms and verses are from Douay-Rheims but with standard versification. The collect is "Collect for the Second Sunday in Advent," *Book of Common Prayer* (1662).

INTRODUCTION: DIVINE READING OF DIVINE SCRIPTURE

"Devote yourself (*proseche*) first and foremost..." Origen, "Letter of Origen to Gregory" 4, in Gregory Thaumaturgus, *Life and Works*, trans. Michael Slusser, ed. Thomas P. Halton, FC 98 (Washington, DC: Catholic University of America Press, 1998), 192. See the discussion in Raymond Studzinski, *Reading to Live: The Evolving Practice of Lectio Divina* (Trappist, KY: Cistercian Publications, 2009), 28–58. In what follows, I refer to Gregory as the addressee of Origen's letter, though scholars are divided on whether he actually was.

When monastic authors of the third and fourth centuries spoke of attention... I am relying on the helpful scholarly discussion of Inbar Graiver, *Asceticism of the Mind: Forms of Attention and Self-Transformation in Late Antique Monasticism*, ST 213 (Toronto, ON: Pontifical Institute of Mediaeval Studies, 2018), 88–92.

"For Origen everything in the Scriptures..." Studzinski, *Reading to Live*, 35.

read Guigo II's *The Ladder of Monks*... See Guigo II, *The Ladder of Monks: A Letter on the Contemplative Life and Twelve Meditations*, trans. Edmund Colledge and James Walsh, CSS 48 (Kalamazoo, MI: Cistercian Publications, 1981).

CHAPTER 1: TRANSFIGURATION

The thirteenth-century hymn *Stabat Mater* ... Most attribute the hymn to the Italian Franciscan monk Jacopone da Todi (1230–1306). The English translation is by Edward Caswall (1814–1878).

"The love of God, the sole object of Christian contemplation ..." Joseph Cardinal Ratzinger, *Orationis Formas*, "Letter to the Bishops of the Catholic Church on Some Aspects of Christian Meditation," §39, the Vatican, October 15, 1989, https://www.vatican.va/roman_curia/congregations/cfaith/documents/rc_con_cfaith_doc_19891015_meditazione-cristiana_en.html.

Saint Augustine (rightly, I think) suggested that in heaven ... See Augustine, *On Christian Teaching* 1.39.43.

In his *Symposium*, Plato famously describes love ... Plato, *Symposium* 211a–212a.

And I think Plato realized this ... The Athenian philosopher was very much aware of the limits of the ladder metaphor and recognized that universal Beauty is always present within particular beautiful things. Eric D. Perl makes this point in his scholarly discussion in *Thinking Being: Introduction to Metaphysics in the Classical Tradition*, AMMTC 17 (Leiden: Brill, 2014), 38–46.

"Revelation," he comments ... The quotation is from Cardinal Ratzinger's *Orationis Formas*, §6.

"By the law of charity we are ordered to welcome ..." Aelred of Rievaulx, *Spiritual Friendship*, trans. Lawrence C. Braceland, ed. Marsha L. Dutton, CFS 5 (Trappist, KY: Cistercian Publications, 2010), 1.32. I use this translation throughout.

friends are not "a burden and a bore" ... Aelred, *Spiritual Friendship* 2.19.

"accord in all things, human and divine ..." Cicero, *De Amicitia* 6.20, in *De Senectute*; *De Amicitia*; *De Divinatione*, trans. William Armistead Falconer, LCL 514 (Cambridge, MA: Harvard University Press, 1923).

"Friendship must begin in Christ ..." Aelred, *Spiritual Friendship* 1.10.

The better we are ... the more we are capable of friendship ... Aelred explains this in *Spiritual Friendship* 2.38.

he ties it directly to wisdom ... See Aelred's discussion on friendship and wisdom in *Spiritual Friendship* 1.61–66.

Scripture itself doesn't do it ... See Aelred, *Spiritual Friendship* 1.70.

"Among perfect friends ..." Aelred, *Spiritual Friendship* 3.48; cf. 3.86.

Thus rising from that holy love ... Aelred, *Spiritual Friendship* 3.134 (italics omitted).

when he thinks of the Trinity ... William speaks of this in Meditation 2.7–9, in *On Contemplating God; Prayer; Meditations*, trans. Penelope Lawson, CFS 3 (Kalamazoo, MI: Cistercian Publications, 1970).

"God forbid that I should glory ..." William, Meditation 10.1.

"Since I have not yet progressed ..." William, Meditation 10.4.

"We make a mental picture of your passion ..." William, Meditation 10.6; translation modified.

the soul "seems to see you as you are [1 John 3:2] ..." William, Meditation 10.7. The "you" addressed here in prayer is Christ. William applies both this biblical verse and 1 Cor 13:12 to Christ. In contemplation, the soul sees Christ and so anticipates the beatific vision.

"When we look more closely at the picture (*imaginem*) ..." William, Meditation 10.7.

contemplate the reality of love itself ... In Meditation 12.15, William explains that true saints "do not form pictures of your love, nor do they compare it to their own by any subtle reasoning; rather, your love itself, finding in them simple material on which to work ... forms them and conforms them to itself."

contemplation takes us from his humanity to his divinity ... William makes this point with particular clarity in *The Golden Epistle: A Letter to the Brethren at Mont Dieu* 43.173–75, trans. Theodore Berkeley, CFS 12 (Trappist, KY: Cistercian Publications, 1971).

CHAPTER II: ACROPHOBIA

"One day when I was busy working ..." Guigo II, *The Ladder of Monks* 2, in *The Ladder of Monks: A Letter on the Contemplative Life and Twelve Meditations*, trans. Edmund Colledge and James Walsh, CSS 48 (Collegeville, MN: Cistercian Publications, 1979), 2.

"Mounting step by step ..." John Chrysostom, Homily 83, in *Commentary on Saint John the Apostle and Evangelist: Homilies 48–88*, trans. Thomas Aquinas Goggin, FC 41 (Washington, DC: Catholic University of America Press, 1959).

Saint Augustine, in his *Confessions* ... See Augustine, *Confessions* 13.9.10.

"set up that ladder on which Jacob in a dream ..." RB 7.5. Throughout, I use the translation of Timothy Fry in *The Rule of Saint Benedict* (New York: Vintage–Random House, 1998).

Bernard of Clairvaux's *The Steps of Humility and Pride* ... See Bernard of Clairvaux, *The Steps of Humility and Pride*, trans. Jean Leclercq and Henri Rochais, rev. ed., CFS 13 (Kalamazoo, MI: Cistercian Publications, 1989).

"Twelve ladders ascend from the four corners ..." Hugh's booklet has been translated by Jessica Weiss in *The Medieval Craft of Memory: An Anthology of Texts and Pictures*, ed. Mary Carruthers and Jan M. Ziolkowski (Philadelphia: University of Pennsylvania Press, 2002), 41–70.

Demons manage to pick off ... For a fascinating scholarly book on demonology and asceticism, see Inbar Graiver, *Asceticism of the Mind: Forms of Attention and Self-Transformation in Late Antique Monasticism*, ST 213 (Toronto, ON: Pontifical Institute of Mediaeval Studies, 2018).

It is his book, *The Ladder of Divine Ascent* ... See John Climacus, *The Ladder of Divine Ascent*, trans. Colm Luibheid, CWS (Mahwah, NJ: Paulist Press, 1982).

"For Climacus the virtues are not so much qualities of man ..." The quotation comes from Kallistos Ware, introduction to John Climacus, *Ladder*, 18. Ware quotes from Dimitrije Bogdanović, *Jean Climaque dans la littérature byzantine et la littérature serbe ancienne* (Belgrade: Institut d'études byzantines, 1968), 218.

"We have Almighty God ..." John Climacus, *Ladder*, step 26.

"Our prayer has neither the power of access ..." John Climacus, *Ladder*, step 5.

The theme of brotherly love and mutual care ... For more detailed discussion of this theme, see Ware, Introduction, 34–43.

"An unbreakable bond of love ..." John Climacus, *Ladder*, step 4.

"It is not safe for an untried soldier ..." John Climacus, *Ladder*, step 4.

"some Moses ..." John Climacus, *Ladder*, step 1.

He derives the paradox from two biblical passages ... Benedict mentions these biblical passages in RB 7.2–3. Greg Peters offers insightful discussion of Benedict's "ladder of humility" in *The Story of Monasticism: Retrieving an Ancient Tradition for Contemporary Spirituality* (Grand Rapids, MI: Baker Academic, 2015), 75–78.

"we descend by self-exaltation ..." RB 7.7.

It's a paradox that Benedict keeps in mind ... Humility is a recurring theme in the Rule. Prayer requires humility and reverence (RB 20.1–2). When we receive guests, we must show humility—bowing our head and prostrating our body—since we receive Christ in our guests (53.6–7). A visiting priest should keep in mind that he is subject to the Rule and "give everyone an example of humility" (60.5).

William of Saint-Thierry, writing his *Golden Epistle* ... I take all references to William of Saint-Thierry from *The Golden Epistle: A Letter to the Brethren at Mont Dieu*, trans. Theodore Berkeley, CFS 12 (Trappist, KY: Cistercian Publications, 1971).

"exalted thoughts are death ..." William, *Golden Epistle* 1.6.17.

"Think of yourselves ... as wild beasts ..." William, *Golden Epistle* 1.6.18.

take Paul's words in 1 Timothy 1:15 to heart ... William, *Golden Epistle* 1.6.19.

"I would not then have you think ..." William, *Golden Epistle* 1.6.20.

"become of no worth ..." William, *Golden Epistle* 2.25.300.

"careful study (*inspectio*) of Scripture ..." Guigo II, *Ladder of Monks* 2.

"The good and the wicked alike ..." Guigo II, *Ladder of Monks* 6.

"the heart's devoted turning ..." Guigo II, *Ladder of Monks* 2.

"We can do nothing without Him ..." Guigo II, *Ladder of Monks* 8.

"and yet not entirely without us ..." Guigo II, *Ladder of Monks* 13.

"the mind is in some sort lifted up ..." Guigo II, *Ladder of Monks* 3.

"outstrips every faculty ..." Guigo II, *Ladder of Monks* 12.

we turn to numerous other Scripture passages ... Guigo recognizes the similarity with Matt 5:8 (1) in terms of the demand for purity in Pss 23:4–5; 51:10; 66:18;

Job 31:1; Ps 119:37; and (2) with regard to the reward for purity in Pss 27:8; 45:2; Isa 62:3; Sir 6:31; Ps 118:24.

"runs to meet" the soul "in all haste" ... Guigo II, *Ladder of Monks* 7.

"restores the weary soul ..." Guigo II, *Ladder of Monks* 7.

"one precedes another ..." Guigo II, *Ladder of Monks* 12.

CHAPTER III: PAYING ATTENTION

Jack never really does ... Robinson's earlier novel *Gilead* (2004) includes a scene where Jack allows the old Reverend John Ames to bless him just prior to leaving home, which instills some hope into Jack's attitude toward the faith of his youth.

Jack suffers from the vice of acedia ... Jack comes across much more sympathetically in Robinson's novel *Jack* (2020) than in *Home*, in part because *Jack* is written from his perspective. His romance with Della displays an occasional intentionality that seems at odds with the slothful Jack we know from the earlier novels. Most remarkably, perhaps, Jack here insists emphatically, "I guess I feel at home in a church. Not at ease, but at home." Yet also in *Jack*, Robinson hints at his sloth by repeatedly describing him as "resigned."

"In the Christian system of virtues ..." Pope Benedict XVI, *The Yes of Jesus Christ: Exercises in Faith, Hope, and Love*, trans. Robert Nowell (New York: Crossroad, 2005), 43. Cf. Jean-Charles Nault, *The Noonday Devil: Acedia, the Unnamed Evil of Our Times*, trans. Michael J. Miller (San Francisco, CA: Ignatius, 2015), 112.

Jean-Charles Nault, in his book *The Noonday Devil* ... See Nault, *Noonday Devil*, 57–81. Thomas offers the first definition in *ST* II-II, q. 35, a. 2, resp.; the second definition in *ST* II-II, q. 35, a. 1, sed contra.

"a break in the impetus ... Nault, *Noonday Devil*, 81.

"Press on, my mind, and pay strong attention (*adtende*) ..." Augustine, *Confessions* 11.27.34. The translation here largely follows Andrea Nightingale, *Once Out of Nature: Augustine on Time and the Body* (Chicago: University of Chicago Press, 2011), 80.

distinction between passing through (*passage*) and passing beyond (*dépassement*) ... Nault, *Noonday Devil*, 115. It originally comes from Joseph de Finance,

Essai sur l'agir humain, Analecta Gregoriana 126 (Rome: Pontificia Universitas Gregoriana, 1962).

the true source and reality of every temporal event… I purposely speak of God's eternal now as not only the true source but also the true reality of temporal events. God's eternal now functions somewhat like Plato's ideas. Just as Plato's ideas are the true reality of shadowy sense objects, so God's eternal now is the true reality of all temporal unfolding. Chiara Bertoglio helpfully writes of the eternal now as "the condition outside time, that transcends time, but which nonetheless embraces its totality." Bertoglio, *Musical Scores and the Eternal Present: Theology, Time, and Tolkien* (Eugene, OR: Pickwick, 2021), ix.

Acedia … "is the temptation to reject *passing beyond*…" The quotation is from Nault, *Noonday Devil*, 115.

"Love bridges the chasm between time and eternity…" Bertoglio, *Musical Scores*, 173.

warnings not to flee one's cell… See the discussion in Charles Cummings, *Monastic Practices*, rev. ed., MWS 47 (Collegeville, MN: Liturgical Press, 2015), 160–69.

"As your vocation demands…" William of Saint-Thierry, *The Golden Epistle: A Letter to the Brethren at Mont Dieu* 10.31, trans. Theodore Berkeley, CFS 12 (Trappist, KY: Cistercian Publications, 1971). The bracketed words are in the original.

the cell can turn into heaven at any time… William comments, "Both in a church and in a cell the things of God are practiced, but more continually in the cell. In a church at certain times the sacraments of Christian religion are dispensed visibly and in figure, while in cells as in heaven the reality which underlies all the sacraments of our faith is constantly celebrated with as much truth, in the same order, although not yet with the same untarnished magnificence or the same security that marks eternity." *Golden Epistle* 11.36; cf. 30.115–19.

a telltale sign of acedia from the fourth century on… The quotations that follow come from Evagrius of Pontus, *The Monk: A Treatise on the Practical Life* 7, in *Evagrius of Pontus: The Greek Ascetic Corpus*, trans. and ed. Robert E. Sinkewicz (Oxford: Oxford University Press, 2003); *The Anonymous Sayings of the Desert Fathers: A Select Edition and Complete English Translation*, trans. and ed. John Wortley (Cambridge: Cambridge University Press, 2013), 141; John Cassian, *The Institutes* 10.2, in *NPNF* 1.11. I take these references from Nault, *Noonday Devil*, 28, 44, 114.

"uprooting of man from his proper place…" Nault, *Noonday Devil*, 109.

a spatial as well as a temporal dimension... I borrow from Nault's discussion in *Noonday Devil*, 113–34.

Acedia, explains Evagrius, is a "noonday devil"... The expression *noonday devil* comes from Ps 90:6 (Douay-Rheims Bible), which is Ps 91:6 in most other English translations. Sinkewicz's translation speaks of the "noonday demon."

It is by *staying* home that we *go* home to God... Carl McColman's down-to-earth chapter on stability carries the great subtitle "Blooming Where We're Planted," in *Befriending Silence: Discovering the Gifts of Cistercian Spirituality* (Notre Dame, IN: Ave Maria Press, 2015), 127–39.

They "spend their entire lives drifting..." *The Rule of St. Benedict* (RB), ed. Thomas Fry (New York: Vintage–Random House, 1998), 1.10–11.

"perseverance in his stability"... RB 58.9.

"stability, fidelity to monastic life, and obedience..." RB 58.17.

William of Saint-Thierry explains to his novices... See William, *Golden Epistle* 1.26.97.

"To try to escape ill-health..." William, *Golden Epistle* 1.25.95 (translation modified).

Being temporalized means being removed from God's eternity... Andrea Nightingale, *Once Out of Nature: Augustine on Time and the Body* (Chicago: University of Chicago Press, 2011), 16.

"Suppose I am about to recite a psalm..." Augustine, *Confessions* 11.28.38, trans. Henry Chadwick (New York: Penguin, 1991). Cf. Nightingale, *Once Out of Nature*, 89.

"The *attentio* is a passive point of transit..." Nightingale, *Once Out of Nature*, 89.

"Suppose someone wished to utter a sound..." Augustine, *Confessions* 11.27.36. Cf. Nightingale, *Once Out of Nature*, 85.

the African bishop turns to Philippians 3:13–14... Here I benefit from the discussion in Nightingale, *Once Out of Nature*, 97–101.

"But 'For your mercy is better than lives' (Ps 61:3)..." *Confessions* 11.29.39. I have changed Chadwick's translation at several points.

"You are my eternal Father…" Augustine, *Confessions* 11.29.39.

not simply the negation of temporal distension… Sometimes Augustine does seem to treat God's eternal now as simply the opposite of created temporality. See, for example, his (beautiful) description of God's eternal now: "In the sublimity of an ever-present eternity (*praesentis aeternitatis*), you are before all things past and transcend all things future, because they are still to come, and when they have come they are past. 'But you are the same and your years do not fail' (Ps. 102:27). Your 'years' neither go nor come" (*Confessions* 11.13.16; translation slightly changed). But Augustine also maintains that God's eternal now holds creation within its providential embrace, and so eternity already contains, in some mysterious manner, the unfolding of time.

"Our personal stories," writes Chiara Bertoglio… See Bertoglio, *Musical Scores*, 41. Bertoglio also puts it this way: "If the unfolding of Time is wrapped in the atemporal reality of God's Eternal Present, similar to a music whose temporality is observable in a score, then the gift of the contemplation of God allows created beings to behold temporality in a single instant" (p. 83). In lectio divina, the aim is not to reject the transience of a biblical passage—say a psalm or a Gospel passage. The purpose is to behold its temporality in a single instant. The aim is to contemplate God in his eternal now.

CHAPTER IV: SWIRLING THOUGHTS

Columba Stewart, in his book *Cassian the Monk*… See Stewart's discussion on memory in *Cassian the Monk* (New York: Oxford University Press, 1998), 101–3.

striving "with constant repetition …" Conference 14 in *John Cassian: Conferences*, trans. Colm Luibheid (New York: Paulist Press, 1985).

"He had committed to memory the Old and New Testaments…" Palladius, *The Lausiac History*, trans. Robert T. Meyer, ed. Johannes Quasten, Walter J. Burghardt, and Thomas Comerford Lawler, ACW 34 (Mahwah, NJ: Paulist Press, 1964), 47.

Let her learn the Psalter first… I have taken the quotation of Jerome's *Epistle* 107 from *Select Letters of St. Jerome*, trans. F. A. Wright, LCL 262 (London: Heinemann, 1933), 365.

The fourth-century Rules of Pachomius… See the discussion in Stewart, *Cassian*, 103.

biblical lessons could be recited "by heart" ... Benedict's Rule speaks of reciting lessons "by heart" twice, in chapters 10.2 and 13.11. See *The Rule of Saint Benedict*, ed. Timothy Fry (New York: Vintage–Random House, 1998).

"the leisurely savoring of biblical texts..." The expression comes from *Benedict's Rule: A Translation and Commentary*, trans. and ed. Terrence G. Kardong (Collegeville, MN: Liturgical Press, 1996), 400.

"exegesis by concordance" ... Leclercq discusses the phrase in *The Love of Learning and the Desire for God: A Study of Monastic Culture*, trans. Catharine Misrahi, 3rd ed. (New York: Fordham University Press, 1982), 76–77.

Both the classical and the Christian traditions recognized this ... The next two paragraphs rely on my discussion in "Memory and Character Formation: The Ark in Hugh of Saint Victor," in *An Introduction to Child Theology*, ed. James M. Houston (Eugene, OR: Cascade, 2022), 139–64.

"Memory is the faculty by which the mind recalls..." Cicero, *On Invention* 2.53.160, trans. and ed. H. M. Hubbell, LCL 386 (Cambridge, MA: Harvard University Press, 1949).

"Experience," claims Aquinas... The quotation is from *ST* II-II, q. 49, a. 1.

"My child, knowledge is a treasury..." Hugh of Saint Victor, "Hugh of St. Victor: 'The Three Best Memory-Aids for Learning History,'" in Mary Carruthers, *The Book of Memory: A Study of Memory in Medieval Culture*, 2nd ed. (Cambridge: Cambridge University Press, 2008), 339–44, at 339.

Hugh reflected on the image of the ark in a series of lectures ... I offer a detailed discussion of Hugh's views on memory (and his use of "ark" terminology) in "Memory and Character Formation."

"The first is that which Noah made..." Hugh of Saint-Victor, *De Arca Noe Morali* 1.11, in *Selected Spiritual Writings*, trans. by a Religious of CSMV (1962; repr., Eugene, OR: Wipf & Stock, 2009).

"When I was one day sitting with the assembled brethren..." Hugh, *De Arca Noe Morali* 1.1. I have slightly changed the translation of the block quote. Boyd Taylor Coolman offers a solid theological reflection on *Noah's Ark* in *The Theology of Hugh of St. Victor: An Interpretation* (Cambridge: Cambridge University Press, 2010), 180–85.

"Make Him a temple, make Him a house..." Hugh, *De Arca Noe Morali* 1.5.

"When we let our hearts run after earthly things ..." Hugh, *De Arca Noe Morali* 4.4 (translation modified).

the three levels of the ark (Gen 6:16) refer to three kinds of thoughts ... Hugh, *De Arca Noe Morali* 2.9.

"unites us to God ..." Hugh, *De Arca Noe Morali* 2.8.

Mystic Ark as a thirteen-by-fifteen-foot mural ... Earlier scholars have doubted the existence of an actual painting, but the foremost scholar on the topic, Conrad Rudolph, makes the case for an actual copy to have existed. See his book *"First I Find the Center Point": Reading the Text of Hugh of Saint Victor's The Mystic Ark*, TAPS 94.4 (Philadelphia, PA: American Philosophical Society, 2004), 71–78.

detailed description of the painting in *The Mystic Ark* ... I take the text of *The Mystic Ark* from Hugh of St. Victor, *A Little Book about Constructing Noah's Ark*, trans. Jessica Weiss, in *The Medieval Craft of Memory: An Anthology of Texts and Pictures*, ed. Mary Carruthers and Jan M. Ziolkowski (Philadelphia: University of Pennsylvania Press, 2002), 41–70.

Hugh's diagram ... reproduced by art historian Conrad Rudolph ... The images that follow are taken from mysticark.ucr.edu, a website dedicated to Conrad Rudolph's images of *The Mystic Ark*. The website is well worth perusing.

"Scripture does not tell the number ..." Hugh, *Little Book* 13.26.

"I lead the river Jordan ..." Hugh, *Little Book* 13.26.

"I put Peter first ..." Hugh, *Little Book* 4.10.

thought (*cogitatio*), meditation (*meditatio*), and contemplation (*contemplatio*) ... Boyd Coolman discusses the three stages in *Theology of Hugh of St. Victor*, 166–67.

It is "the integrity of the soul ..." Hugh, *A Little Book* 9.22.

CHAPTER V: CHEWING AND BELCHING

"If you receive them well ... Augustine makes this comment in his famous Sermon 227, in *Sermons: On the Liturgical Seasons*, trans. and ed. Edmund Hill, WSA III.6 (Rochelle, NY: New City Press, 1993), 254.

"the crumbs of it compose the simple life…" Gregory the Great, *Homilies on the Book of the Prophet Ezekiel* 1.10.2, trans. Theodosia Tomkinson (Etna, CA: Center for Traditionalist Orthodox Studies, 2008).

inside the letter *E*… Ezekiel is seated inside the letter *E* not because of his name but because the Latin Vulgate of Ezekiel 1:1 begins with an *E*: *Et factum est in trigesimo anno* ("Now it came to pass in the thirtieth year").

we can simply drink the "plainer sayings"… Gregory has a similar lovely reflection on Job 1:4, which states that Job's sons would invite their sisters "to eat and drink with them." Gregory comments that Sacred Scripture "is food in its obscure passages, for it is broken in exposition, as it were, chewed, and swallowed. It is drink, however, in its easier passages." Gregory sees a reference to the explanation of difficult biblical passages in Lam 4:4 ("the little ones have asked for bread, and there was none to break it unto them") and a reference to easy commandments in Isa 55:1 ("All you that thirst, come to the waters") and John 7:37 ("If any man thirst, let him come to me and drink"). See *Moral Reflections on the Book of Job* 1.21.29, vol. 1, trans. Brian Kerns, CSS 249 (Collegeville, MN: Liturgical Press, 2014).

"For it is said of the elect…" Gregory, *Ezekiel* 1.10.7 (italics omitted).

knows "how to speak sweetly…" Gregory, *Ezekiel* 1.10.13.

"dyes the pen of his tongue…" Gregory, *Ezekiel* 1.10.13.

"Reading, as it were, puts food…" Guigo II, *The Ladder of Monks* 3, in *A Letter on the Contemplative Life and Twelve Meditations*, trans. Edmund Colledge and James Walsh, CSS 48 (Collegeville, MN: Cistercian Publications, 1981).

Guigo compares this beatitude to a grape… Guigo II, *Ladder of Monks* 4.

It is actually smell, not taste… Guigo II, *Ladder of Monks* 5.

"no more from without…" Guigo II, *Ladder of Monks* 6.

"He slakes its thirst…" Guigo II, *Ladder of Monks* 7.

The taste of the grape's sweetness inebriates… Guigo II, *Ladder of Monks* 7.

Guigo here borrows an ancient paradox… See Jean Daniélou's in-depth discussion in his introduction to *From Glory to Glory: Tests from Gregory of Nyssa's Mystical Writings*, trans. Herbert Musurillo (1961; repr., Crestwood, NY: St Vladimir's Seminary Press, 1979), 33–46.

four rows of vines form a square (*pagina*) ... Pliny, *Natural History* 17.25.169, vol. 5, trans. H. Rackham, LCL 371 (Cambridge, MA: Harvard University Press, 1950). Cf. the discussion in Ivan Illich, *In the Vineyard of the Text: A Commentary to Hugh's Didascalicon* (Chicago: University of Chicago Press, 1993), 57–58.

Scripture's "thoughts, like so many sweetest fruits ..." Hugh of Saint Victor, *The Didascalicon of Hugh of Saint Victor: A Medieval Guide to the Arts* 5.5, trans. and ed. Jerome Taylor (New York: Columbia University Press, 1961).

Bernard of Clairvaux offers numerous examples ... Marsha L. Dutton comments, "Eating and drinking appear throughout [Bernard's] sermons and spiritual treatises as the central metaphor for coming to the understanding of God." Dutton, "Eat, Drink, and Be Merry: The Eucharistic Spirituality of the Cistercian Fathers," in *Erudition at God's Service*, ed. John R. Sommerfeldt, SMCH 11, CSS 98 (Kalamazoo, MI: Cistercian Publications, 1987), 1–31, at 6.

He begins his first sermon on the Song of Songs ... Bernard's first sermon on the Song of Songs can be found in Bernard of Clairvaux, *Select Works*, trans. G. R. Evans, CWS (Mahwah, NJ: Paulist Press, 1987), 210–15.

"You have already tasted these two ..." Bernard, Sermon 1.1.2.

"Know the Lord in the breaking of bread ..." Bernard, Sermon 1.2.4.

"I should not dare to do it ..." Bernard, Sermon 1.2.4.

"'The eyes of us all are turned upon you ...'" Bernard, Sermon 1.2.4. I have changed the psalm reference between brackets.

"Consider again the strength of your salvation ..." Anselm, *Meditation on Human Redemption*, in *The Prayers and Meditations of Saint Anselm with the Proslogion*, trans. Benedicta Ward (London: Penguin, 1973), 230.

For Anselm, lectio divina involves hard work ... Bernard of Clairvaux recognizes the same: "Food tastes sweet in the mouth, a psalm in the heart. But the faithful and wise soul will not neglect to tear at the psalm with the teeth of its understanding. If you swallow it whole without chewing it the palate will miss the delicious flavor which is sweeter than honey from the honey-comb." Sermon 7.4.5.

Anselm's prayers, comments R. W. Southern ... R. W. Southern, *Saint Anselm: A Portrait in a Landscape* (Cambridge: Cambridge University Press, 1990), 103. I have benefited here also from Alex Michael Robert Trew, "*Ratio fidei*: Anselm of Canterbury's Theological Hermeneutics" (MA thesis, Regent College, 2019), 37.

Classical Roman philosophers such as Seneca and Quintilian… See Fiona J. Griffiths, "A Bee in the Garden of the Lord," in *The Garden of Delights: Reform and Renaissance for Women in the Twelfth Century* (Philadelphia, PA: University of Pennsylvania Press, 2007), 82–107, at 92–98.

especially those within the Cistercian tradition… Henri de Lubac shows that the prominence of *sweetness* language among the Cistercians was tied to a "pronounced interiorization of the mystery in the soul." *Medieval Exegesis*, vol. 2, *The Four Senses of Scripture*, trans. E. M. Macierowski (Grand Rapids, MI: Eerdmans, 2000), 173.

Henri de Lubac and Fiona Griffiths both offer discussions… In what follows, I rely especially on de Lubac, *Four Senses*, 162–77, for the first point; and on Griffiths, "Bee in the Garden," 91–105, for the remaining three points.

"The honeycomb is honey in the wax…" Honorius of Autun, *Expositio in Cantica canticorum* 4.11; quoted in de Lubac, *Four Senses*, 164.

"Expert in the task of making honey…" This translation from *The Aberdeen Bestiary* can be found at the University of Aberdeen website, https://www.abdn.ac.uk/bestiary/ms24/f63r.

Saint Ambrose … heaps similar praise… See Ambrose, *Hexameron* 5.21.66–72, in *Hexameron, Paradise, and Cain and Abel*, trans. John J. Savage, FC 42 (Washington, DC: Catholic University of America Press, 1961).

"Scripture rightly commends the bee…" Ambrose, *Hexameron* 5.21.70.

"taking the things we have gathered…" Lucius Annaeus Seneca, *Letters on Ethics: To Lucilius* 84.5, trans. Margaret Graver and A. A. Long (Chicago: University of Chicago Press, 2015).

murmuring lips resembled the buzzing of bees… Jean Leclercq, *The Love of Learning and the Desire for God: A Study of Monastic Culture*, trans. Catharine Misrahi, 3rd ed. (New York: Fordham University Press, 1982), 73.

"Divine Scripture is a honeycomb…" Rabanus Maurus's comment from *De universe* 22.1 as quoted in Griffiths, "Bee in the Garden," 98.

"The act of generation is common to all…" Ambrose, *Hexameron* 5.21.67.

"The virgin is a little bee…" Hildebert of Lavardin, *In Festo Purificationis Beatae Mariae sermo primus* (*PL* 171.611), as quoted in Griffiths, "Bee in the Garden," 101.

"**Some part of your daily reading …**" William of Saint-Thierry, *The Golden Epistle: A Letter to the Brethren at Mont Dieu* 1.31.122, trans. Theodore Berkeley, CFS 12 (Trappist, KY: Cistercian Publications, 1971).

"**Students of any age …**" Quintilian, *The Orator's Education: Books 11–12*, 11.2.41, trans. and ed. Donald A. Russell, LCL 494 (Cambridge, MA: Harvard University Press, 2001).

"**stomach of the mind**" … Augustine, *Confessions* 10.14.21.

"**deposit it in the memory as though swallowing it …**" Augustine, *The Trinity* 12.14.23, trans. and ed. Edmund Hill, WSA I.5 (Hyde Park, NY: New City Press, 1991).

"**For camels indeed chew the cud …**" Gregory the Great, *Job* 1.15.22.

The mind, explains Gregory, "is not cloven footed …" Gregory the Great, *Job* 1.28.40.

"**As your clean beasts …**" William, Meditation 8.5, in *On Contemplating God; Prayer; Meditations*, trans. Penelope Lawson, CFS 3 (Kalamazoo, MI: Cistercian Publications, 1970).

St. Albans Psalter … Jane Geddes offers extended discussion of this psalter in *The St Albans Psalter: A Book for Christina of Markyate* (London: The British Library, 2005).

we cannot understand this incomplete sentence … Cf. the helpful reflections on the inarticulate nature of the belch in Philip Liston-Kraft, "Bernard's Belching Bride: The *affectus* That Words Cannot Express," *MMT* 26 (2017): 54–72.

"**Why would you seek in such a spontaneous outburst …**" Bernard of Clairvaux, Sermon 67, in *St. Bernard's Sermons on the Canticle of Canticles*, trans. a priest of Mount Melleray (Dublin: Browne and Nolan, 1920), 2:278–93, at 282–83.

she "belches forth rather than utters …" Bernard, Sermon 67, in *Sermons*, 282.

she is "belching (*eructabunt*) the memory …" Bernard, Sermon 67, in *Sermons*, 282. My translation of Ps 145:7 (144:7 in the Vulgate) closely follows Bernard.

CHAPTER VI: TREES

Cruciformity is the heart of biblical teaching...   I am thinking here particularly of the fruitful work of New Testament theologian Michael J. Gorman—for example, his book *Inhabiting the Cruciform God: Kenosis, Justification, and Theosis in Paul's Narrative Soteriology* (Grand Rapids, MI: Eerdmans, 2009). Rachel Davies also highlights the theme of cruciformity in her careful discussion of Bonaventure's *The Tree of Life: Bonaventure, the Body, and the Aesthetics of Salvation* (Cambridge: Cambridge University Press, 2019).

Saint Bonaventure's *The Tree of Life* (*Lignum vitae*)...   I would like to express my indebtedness to my former student Kasey Kimball, whose excellent MA thesis on Bonaventure inspired this chapter. See Katherine McLennan Kimball, "Cultivating Christlikeness in and through Suffering: St. Bonaventure's *The Tree of Life* and *The Mystical Vine*" (MA thesis, Regent College, 2018).

"Trees," explains Sara Ritchey...   See Sara Margaret Ritchey, "Spiritual Arborescence: The Meaning of Trees in Late Medieval Devotion" (PhD diss., University of Chicago, 2005), 2.

Figures 6.1 and 6.2...   The two images come from *Speculum Virginum* in the Walters Art Museum. The Tree of Virtues is discussed in some detail in https://en.wikipedia.org/wiki/File:Virtues_Speculum_Virginum_W72_26r.jpg. For discussion of the Tree of Vices, see https://en.wikipedia.org/wiki/File:Vices_Speculum_Virginum_W72_25v.jpg.

Speculum virginum...   For scholarly discussion on the *Speculum virginum*, see Constant J. Mews, ed., *Listen, Daughter: The* Speculum virginum *and the Formation of Religious Women in the Middle Ages*, The New Middle Ages (New York: Palgrave, 2001). The book contains an appendix with a partial translation of the *Speculum*.

"Leaving the left side..."   *Speculum virginum* 4.383–85, quoted in Morgan Powell, "The *Speculum virginum* and the Audio-Visual Poetics of Women's Religious Instruction," in Mews, *Listen Daughter*, 111–35, at 124.

Gospel scenes to be "imprinted" (*imprimatur*)...   Bonaventure, *Tree of Life,* Prologue, 1, in *The Soul's Journey into God; The Tree of Life; The Life of St. Francis*, trans. Ewert Cousins, CWS (New York: Paulist Press, 1978).

I have endeavored to gather this bundle...   Bonaventure, *Tree of Life,* Prologue, 2.

four fruits or branches… The prologue distinguishes branches from leaves, flowers, and fruit: the leaves are for healing (Ezek 47:12; Rev 22:2); the flowers are beautiful and have a sweet smell; and the fruit satisfies our taste. The rest of the treatise itself, however, does not speak of leaves or flowers, but instead refers to twelve fruits, which seem to be identical to the twelve branches. Many medieval art images draw twelve branches and place the individual Gospel scenes on separate leaves that hang from the branches, with four scenes (four leaves) hanging from each branch.

Bonaguida's painting follows Bonaventure's book fairly closely… My discussion of Bonaguida's painting relies especially on Philip Esler, "Pacino di Bonaguida's *Tree of Life*: Interpreting the Bible in Paint in Early Fourteenth-Century Italy," *BRe* 3 (2014): 1–29. Esler highlights the elements of Bonaguida's painting that differ from Bonaventure.

a this-worldly, human, and physical Jesus… Amanda Donna Quantz insightfully comments: "In the *Tree of Life* and several other texts, Bonaventure uses his imagination to reflect on Gospel events in order to bring to light Jesus' emotional vulnerability. This approach helps him to explore Jesus' human experience while using language that fills the reader with greater compassion for the suffering Lord." Quantz, "Bonaventure's Tree of Life in Image and Word: An Interdisciplinary Study of Transformation through Christ" (PhD diss., University of St. Michael's College, 2003), 21.

the following four sections… Here and elsewhere, the Latin original comes from the *Opera Omnia*, ed. Aloysius Lauer, vol. 8 (Rome: Quaracchi, 1898).

Bonaventure probably wrote three additional stanzas… I follow the suggestions of Lauer, the editor of the Latin edition of Bonaventure's works. For details, see *Opera Omnia* 8.xxxix.

which allowed it to serve as a kind of refrain… I am taking my cue here from Lauer, *Opera Omnia* 8.86. Bonaventure gives this stanza in the prologue.

An additional two stanzas… Bonaventure, *Tree of Life*, Prologue, 6.

prefer "faith to reason, devotion to investigation…" Bonaventure, *Tree of Life*, Prologue, 5.

"We can best understand the *Lignum vitae*…" Richard S. Martignetti, *Saint Bonaventure's Tree of Life: Theology of Mystical Journey* (Rome: Quaracchi, 2004), 82.

"we use the Lignum vitae…" Martignetti, *Saint Bonaventure's Tree of Life*, 88.

On a certain morning... Bonaventure, *Life of Saint Francis* 13.3, in *The Soul's Journey into God; The Tree of Life; The Life of St. Francis*, trans. Ewert Cousins, CWS (New York: Paulist Press, 1978).

no biblical text was more important... Cf. Kimball, "Cultivating Christlikeness," 42–44.

"Now fixed with Christ to the cross [Gal 2:20]..." Bonaventure, *Life of Saint Francis* 14.1 (italics omitted).

"This love also so absorbed the soul of Francis..." Bonaventure, *The Soul's Journey into God*, Prologue, 3.

"With Christ I am nailed to the cross..." Bonaventure, *Tree of Life*, Prologue, 1.

"Thrown roughly upon the wood of the cross..." Bonaventure, *Tree of Life* 26.

Francis, in some sense, *was* the tree of life... I have in mind here the felicitous title of one of the chapters of Ritchey's dissertation—namely, "Francis as the *Lignum vitae*."

"not by the martyrdom of his flesh..." Bonaventure, *Life of St. Francis* 13.3. Here, Bonaventure has in mind Francis himself, but the comment applies equally to the reader of *The Tree of Life*.

Jesus as the "superessential Ray" of light... Bonaventure, *Tree of Life* 47. Bonaventure is quoting from Dionysius, a hugely influential early sixth-century mystical theologian.

"Rejoice, then, with that blessed old man..." Bonaventure, *Tree of Life* 7 (italics omitted).

composition of place... Nicholas Standaert discusses this imaginative form of meditation in "The Composition of Place: Creating Space for an Encounter," *The Way* 46, no. 1 (January 2007): 7–20. Ewert H. Cousins talks of "mysticism of the historical event," where "one recalls a significant event in the past, enters into its drama and draws from it spiritual energy, eventually moving beyond the event towards union with God." Cousins, "Francis of Assisi: Christian Mysticism at the Crossroads," in *Mysticism and Religious Traditions*, ed. Steven T. Katz (New York: Oxford University Press, 1983), 163–90, at 166–69. Cousins traces the origins of this approach to Francis and Bonaventure, and links it to the early Franciscan attention to the humanity of Jesus. I owe a thank-you to Kasey Kimball for pointing me to Cousins's article. As we will see in the next chapter, the English Cistercian abbot Aelred of Rievaulx already made use of this rhetorical strategy before Bonaventure.

CHAPTER VII: BREAD OF TEARS

"We should keep in mind…" Mary Carruthers, *The Craft of Thought: Meditation, Rhetoric, and the Making of Images, 400–1200* (Cambridge: Cambridge University Press, 1998), 102. Carruthers's entire discussion of memory and the demanding, rough character of spiritual compunction is illuminating (pp. 100–103).

compunctio—**which marks the discourse on lectio divina from the time of John Cassian…** To be sure, prior to Cassian's treatment, Origen, the Cappadocians, Evagrius of Pontus, and John Chrysostom all dealt with compunction in one form or another. Cassian is particularly noteworthy here because of his unparalleled influence on Western monasticism and spirituality. See the discussion on the origins of mourning (*penthos*) in Irénée Hausherr, *Penthos: The Doctrine of Compunction in the Christian East*, trans. Anselm Hufstader, CSS 53 (Kalamazoo, MI: Cistercian Publications, 1982).

the various types of prayer… John Cassian, *Conferences* 9.15, trans. Colm Luibheid, CWS (Mahwah, NJ: Paulist Press, 1985).

"by the contemplation of God alone…" Cassian, *Conferences* 9.18.

"fullness of perfection"… The quotations in this sentence are from Cassian, *Conferences* 9.25.

different activities can bring on this prayer of fire… Cassian, *Conferences* 9.26.

step seven of *The Ladder of Divine Ascent*… John Climacus, *The Ladder of Divine Ascent*, trans. Colm Luibheid, CWS (New York: Paulist Press, 1982).

Climacus even invents a new word… See Kallistos Ware, introduction to Climacus, *Ladder of Divine Ascent*, 24.

"Today we read the book of experience…" Bernard of Clairvaux, Sermon 3.1.1, in *Select Works*, trans. G. R. Evans, CWS (Mahwah, NJ: Paulist Press, 1987).

"Why do we try to express in everyday language…" Guigo II, *The Ladder of Monks* 8, in *The Ladder of Monks: A Letter on the Contemplative Life and Twelve Meditations*, trans. Edmund Colledge and James Walsh, CSS 48 (Collegeville, MN: Cistercian Publications, 1981).

Instead, it is the book of experience… Bernard's understanding of experience as a commentary on Scripture goes back to Cassian, who in the early fifth century writes, "The meaning of the words comes through to us not just by way of commentaries but by what we ourselves have gone through. Seized of the identical feelings in which the psalm was composed or sung we become, as it were, its author." *Conferences* 10.11.

Bernard, for his part, clearly worried about this... Where Bernard worried about his *own* lack of experience, Cassian, in *Conferences* 14, warns *others* against teaching without experience: "So have a care that you do not rush to teach something you have not done yourself. Otherwise, you will be counted among those in regard to whom Jesus had the following to say to his disciples: 'Do what they tell you and listen to what they say, but do not act as they do. They talk and do not act [Matt 23:3]' " (*Conferences* 14.9). He insists a little later, "How can someone pass on what he is incapable of perceiving? And if he is presumptuous enough to teach, his words will come to the ears of those listening to him as being worthless and useless" (14.14).

"A soul like mine," he comments... Bernard, Sermon 3.1.1.

"Sometimes it has happened to me..." Cassian, *Conferences* 9.28.

the grief wasn't matched by tears... Though he greatly valued the gift of tears, John Climacus refused to judge by appearances. We have to keep in mind that some people weep more easily than others: "I have seen small teardrops shed like drops of blood, and I have seen floods of tears poured out with no trouble at all." *Ladder of Divine Ascent*, step 7. It is not the tears that matter, but the inward struggle.

"to stir up the mind of the reader..." Anselm, *The Prayers and Meditations of St Anselm with the Proslogion*, trans. Benedicta Ward (London: Penguin, 1973), 89.

he fails to "dissolve entirely in tears..." Anselm, "Prayer to St Paul," line 81, in *Prayers and Meditations*.

"When truly, because of my wretchedness..." Anselm, "Prayer to St Paul," lines 86–90, in *Prayers and Meditations*.

"Grief, sorrow, groans, sighs..." Anselm, "Prayer to St John the Evangelist (1)," lines 83–85, in *Prayers and Meditations*.

"If they are concealed they cannot be healed..." Anselm, "Prayer to St Mary (1)," lines 61–62, in *Prayers and Meditations*.

"If I look within myself, I cannot bear myself..." Anselm, "Prayer to St John the Baptist," lines 122–31, in *Prayers and Meditations*.

he "cannot reveal his sins ..." Eileen Sweeney, *Anselm of Canterbury and the Desire for the Word* (Washington, DC: Catholic University of America Press, 2002), 24.

The so-called Anselmian transformation ... R. W. Southern discusses this transformation in chapter 5 of *Saint Anselm: A Portrait in a Landscape* (Cambridge: Cambridge University Press, 1990).

It took Augustine a long time ... Augustine recounts his conversion in book 8 of his *Confessions*. I quote from Henry Chadwick's translation, slightly modified here and there (Oxford: Oxford University Press, 1991).

"Ingrained evil had more hold over me ..." Augustine, *Confessions* 8.11.25.

"from a hidden depth of profound self-examination ..." Augustine, *Confessions* 8.12.28.

a "massive downpour of tears ..." Augustine, *Confessions* 8.12.28.

"To pour it all out with the accompanying groans ..." Augustine, *Confessions* 8.12.28.

"weeping in the bitter agony" of his heart ... Augustine, *Confessions* 8.12.29.

"Pick up and read ..." Augustine, *Confessions* 8.12.29.

Abba Isaac explains to Cassian and Germanus the different types of tears ... Cassian reports Abba Isaac's five types of tears in *Conferences* 9.29.

"His bodily progress is our spiritual progress ..." Aelred of Rievaulx, *Jesus at the Age of Twelve* 11, trans. Theodore Berkeley, in *Treatises; The Pastoral Prayer*, CFS 2 (Kalamazoo, MI: Cistercian Publications, 1971).

As he turns to the meaning of the name Bethlehem ... Aelred, *Jesus at the Age of Twelve* 11.

Only angels can eat this bread ... Aelred, *Jesus at the Age of Twelve* 12.

"Then," comments Aelred, "will you eat bread with ashes ..." Aelred, *Jesus at the Age of Twelve* 12.

"tears of repentance" ... Aelred, *Jesus at the Age of Twelve* 26.

"Kiss, kiss, kiss ..." Aelred, *Jesus at the Age of Twelve* 26.

"What are you about, my soul ..." Aelred, *Jesus at the Age of Twelve* 27.

Peter "comes to his right mind ..." Aelred of Rievaulx, *Rule of Life* 3.31, trans. Mary Paul Macpherson, in *Treatises; The Pastoral Prayer*, CFS 2 (Kalamazoo, MI: Cistercian Publications, 1971).

"It is not surprising if when the sun mourns ..." Aelred, *Rule of Life* 3.31.

"At this utterance ..." Aelred, *Rule of Life* 3.31.

"Why may I not touch you? ..." Aelred, *Rule of Life* 3.31.

An introspective conscience ... In 1963, the New Testament scholar Krister Stendahl published his influential essay "The Apostle Paul and the Introspective Conscience of the West," *HTR* 56 (1963): 199–215. The essay has deeply shaped theological studies since that time. My conclusion here is in part a polemic against such a dismissal of an introspective conscience.

"Even though I also had been privileged ..." Bernard makes the comment in Sermon 85, in *St. Bernard's Sermons on the Canticle of Canticles*, trans. a priest of Mount Melleray (Dublin: Browne and Nolan, 1920), 2:503–21, at 521.

CHAPTER VIII: THE BETTER PART

Bernard of Clairvaux reflected on this search ... I am consulting Sermon 86 from *St. Bernard's Sermons on the Canticle of Canticles*, trans. a priest of Mount Melleray (Dublin: Browne and Nolan, 1920), 2:503–21.

"The soul is sometimes rapt in ecstasy ..." Bernard, Sermon 86, p. 520.

"as rare as it is delightful ..." Bernard, Sermon 86, p. 520.

For Augustine, action and contemplation ... The following discussion benefits greatly from Kimberly Baker's dissertation "Augustine on Action, Contemplation, and Their Meeting Point in Christ" (PhD diss., University of Notre Dame, 2007). The key passages in Augustine are *Reply to Faustus the Manichean* 22.52–58 (Leah and Rachel); *Questions on the Gospels* 2.20; Sermons 103, 104, 179, and 255 (Martha and Mary); and Tractate 124 on the Gospel of John (Peter and John).

If that's really the case ... Augustine, Sermon 104.2 in *Sermons 94A–147A*, trans. and ed. John E. Rotelle, WSA III.4 (Brooklyn, NY: New City Press, 1992); translation slightly modified, following Baker, "Augustine on Action," 39.

Martha, explains Kimberly Baker ... Baker, "Augustine on Action," 37.

It is as if they are small sacraments… I discuss the sacramental character of the relationship between present (partial) vision and future (beatific) vision in Augustine in *Seeing God: The Beatific Vision in Christian Tradition* (Grand Rapids, MI: Eerdmans, 2018), 96–126. Baker, similarly, argues, "There is a sacramental dimension to the hope that infuses the present life." Baker, "Augustine on Action," 42.

The hard work of preaching… See Augustine, *Reply to Faustus* 22.54.

earthly things must be used for the sake of the enjoyment of God… See Augustine, *On Christian Teaching* 1.3.3–1.5.5.

Now we are still pilgrims… See Augustine, Sermon 103.1.

All Christians, even Martha, will arrive at the contemplative rest… See Augustine, Sermon 103.2. Cf. Baker, "Augustine on Action," 37.

the text speaks of eyes and ears of the heart… Gregory the Great, *Homilies on the Book of the Prophet Ezekiel* 2.2.2, trans. Theodosia Tomkinson, 2nd ed. (Etna, CA: Center for Traditionalist Orthodox Studies, 2008).

the wall… Gregory discusses the wall in *Ezekiel* 2.2.5.

the "measuring reed"… See Gregory's discussion in *Ezekiel* 2.2.6–8.

"we taste the mere beginnings…" Gregory, *Ezekiel* 2.2.8.

Behold Martha's part is not censured… Gregory, *Ezekiel* 2.2.9.

Leah's life as "laborious"… Gregory, *Ezekiel* 2.2.10.

"Just as a good order is to strive…" Gregory, *Ezekiel* 2.2.11.

two additional biblical illustrations… Gregory, *Ezekiel* 2.2.12–15.

"grazes the hem of the uncircumscribed light"… Gregory, *Ezekiel* 2.2.12.

God "withers every carnal desire…" Gregory, *Ezekiel* 2.2.13.

"Whatever is seen of Him…" Gregory, *Ezekiel* 2.2.14.

Aelred of Rievaulx's sermon on Martha and Mary… Aelred's "Sermon 19: For the Assumption of Saint Mary" is found in *The Liturgical Sermons: The First Clairvaux Collection*, trans. Theodore Berkeley and M. Basil Pennington, CFS 58 (Kalamazoo, MI: Cistercian Publications, 2001), 263–74. For brief discussions of this sermon, see David Grumett, "Action and/or Contemplation? Allegory and

Liturgy in the Reception of Luke 10:38–42," *SJT* 52 (2006): 125–39, at 132–33; Domenico Pezzini, "The Sermons of Aelred of Rievaulx," in *A Companion to Aelred of Rievaulx (1110–1167)*, ed. Marsha Dutton, BCCT 76 (Leiden: Brill, 2017), 73–97, at 84–85.

This takes his mind ... Aelred discusses the moat, wall, and tower in Sermon 19.7&8–14.

The east gate of her castle remained shut ... See Aelred, Sermon 19.16.

"all this pertains to physical activity ..." Aelred, Sermon 19.23.

"all this pertains to Mary ..." Aelred, Sermon 19.23.

"If Mary alone were in this home ..." Aelred, Sermon 19.18.

"subdue the flesh with vigils ..." Aelred, Sermon 19.21.

"At the time of *lectio* ..." Aelred, Sermon 19.28.

"put up with these labors ..." Aelred, Sermon 19.30.

In his *Rule of Life for a Recluse* ... I quote *A Rule of Life for a Recluse* from Mary Paul Macpherson's translation in Aelred of Rievaulx, *Treatises; The Pastoral Prayer*, CFS 2 (Kalamazoo, MI: Cistercian Publications, 1971).

"as it were the edge and border ..." Aelred, *Rule of Life* 2.26.

"She did not walk about to run hither and thither ..." Aelred, *Rule of Life* 2.28. While I appreciate Marsha Dutton's reflections on the Marth-and-Mary trope in Aelred, I do not agree that Aelred offers these comments to his sister so as to balance her life with service and contemplation. See Marsha L. Dutton, "The Sacramentality of Community in Aelred," in *A Companion to Aelred of Rievaulx (1110–1167)* (Leiden: Brill, 2017), 246–67, at 253.

"Idleness (*otiositas*) is the enemy of the soul ..." RB 48.1, quoted from *The Rule of Saint Benedict*, trans. Timothy Fry (New York: Vintage–Random House, 1998).

Greg Peters, in *The Story of Monasticism* ... See Peters's discussion in *The Story of Monasticism: Retrieving an Ancient Tradition for Contemporary Spirituality* (Grand Rapids, MI: Baker Academic, 2015), 155–69.

Hugh added an additional one ... See *The Didascalicon of Hugh of Saint Victor: A Medieval Guide to the Arts* 5.9, trans. and ed. Jerome Taylor (New York: Columbia University Press, 1961). As we saw in chapter 4, Hugh also used a threefold program of *cogitatio*, *meditatio*, and *contemplatio*.

he too affirmed diverse callings... See the discussion in *ST* II-II, q. 188, a. 1.

religious orders may be established specifically for the active life... Aquinas makes this point in *ST* II-II, q. 188, a. 2.

military religious orders, orders for preaching... See *ST* II-II, q. 188, aa. 3–5.

None, however, teased out their relationship ... as did Aquinas... *ST* II-II, q. 188, a. 6, is key in this discussion of the active and the contemplative life. Olivier-Thomas Venard offers a helpful discussion of this article in *A Poetic Christ: Thomist Reflections on Scripture, Language and Reality*, trans. Kenneth Oakes and Francesca Aran Murphy (London: T&T Clark, 2019), 161–64.

"It is better to enlighten... *ST* I-II, q. 188, a. 6.

The longing for contemplation makes us restless... This paragraph is mostly taken from my earlier book *Five Things Theologians Wish Biblical Scholars Knew* (Downers Grove, IL: IVP Academic, 2021), 113.

"I have lost the profound joys..." Gregory the Great, Epistle 1.5, in *The Letters of Gregory the Great*, trans. and ed. John R. C. Martyn, MST 40 (Toronto, ON: Pontifical Institute of Mediaeval Studies, 2004), 1:122. Cf. Gavin Ortlund, *Theological Retrieval for Evangelicals: Why We Need Our Past to Have a Future* (Wheaton, IL: Crossway, 2019), 188–96.

the Lord has seen him and that he has seen the Lord... Many translations have "provide" rather than "see." The Hebrew verb *raah* literally means "to see," though the derived meaning of "provide" is implied in this passage. Both the Greek Septuagint and the Latin Vulgate use verbs for "seeing."

"Yearnings, strivings, longings..." William of Saint-Thierry, *On Contemplating God* 1, in *On Contemplating God; Prayer; Meditations*, trans. Penelope Lawson, CFS 3 (Kalamazoo, MI: Cistercian, 1970).

"Worries and anxieties..." William, *On Contemplating God* 1.

"I do have in me the desire to desire you..." William, *On Contemplating God* 4.

"But now the ass is braying again..." William, *On Contemplating God* 12.

CHAPTER IX: INTO GREAT SILENCE

Benedict "returned to his beloved place of solitude (*solitudinis*)..." Gregory the Great, *The Life of Saint Benedict* 3.5, trans. and ed. Terrence G. Kardong (Collegeville, MN: Liturgical Press, 2009).

wandering "here and there" ... Gregory, *Life of Saint Benedict* 3.5.

"Either we sink..." Gregory, *Life of Saint Benedict* 3.9.

The prodigal ... did not experience true solitude... Gregory doesn't quite say it, but he seems to suggest that when the prodigal son joined his father at home, he finally lived in solitude, since he was now "with himself" (*secum*) again.

Figure 9.1: The Prodigal and Peter... The chart uses the preposition *ad* (to) for the return both of the prodigal son and Peter. This is in line with the block quote from Gregory. He wants to emphasize that both returned to (*ad*) themselves. Gregory, therefore, ignores the slight difference between the two biblical texts, with Luke 15:17 using the preposition *in* and Acts 12:11 using the preposition *ad*.

The eulogy on the solitary life, which concludes the *Consuetudines*... The eulogy is found in *The Consuetudines of Guigo I, 5th Prior of the Carthusian Order*, trans. Ugo-Maria Ginex, 3rd ed. (Canterbury: St Mary's Hermitage, 2020), 63–66. *Ancrene Wisse* closely follows Guigo's eulogy. *Ancrene Wisse*, in *Anchoritic Spirituality: Ancrene Wisse and Associated Works*, trans. and ed. Anne Savage and Nicholas Watson, CWS (Mahwah, NJ: Paulist Press, 1991), 105–9.

Isaac went out "to meditate in the field" ... *Consuetudines* 80.5.

When Jacob was left all alone... *Consuetudines* 80.5.

Moses, Elijah, and Elisha... *Consuetudines* 80.6.

Jeremiah "sat alone" ... *Consuetudines* 80.7.

John the Baptist... *Consuetudines* 80.9.

Even Jesus ... left us an example... *Consuetudines* 80.10.

One is never less alone than when alone... According to Cicero, the saying goes back to the Roman general Scipio Africanus (236/235–183 BC). *On Duties* 3.1, trans. Walter Miller, LCL 30 (Cambridge, MA: Harvard University Press, 1913). In Christian tradition, we find the saying in Ambrose, Epistle 26 (to Sabinus), in *Letters*, trans. Mary Melchior Beyenka, ed. Roy Joseph Deferrari, FC 26 (Washington, DC: Catholic University of America Press, 1954); Jerome, *Against*

Jovinianus 1.47, in *NPNF* II.6 (New York: Christian Literature Company, 1893); William of Saint-Thierry, *The Golden Epistle: A Letter to the Brethren at Mont Dieu* 10.30, trans. Theodore Berkeley, CFS 12 (Trappist, KY: Cistercian Publications, 1971); Aelred of Rievaulx, *A Rule of Life for a Recluse* 1.5, trans. Mary Paul Macpherson, in *Treatises; The Pastoral Prayer*, CFS 2 (Kalamazoo, MI: Cistercian Publications, 1971).

The solitary life should not be undertaken lightly ... Warnings against solitude, especially for beginners, abound. See, for example, John Climacus, *The Ladder of Divine Ascent*, step 4, trans. Colm Luibheid (New York: Paulist Press, 1982); William, *Golden Epistle* 35.141; 35.145; Aelred of Rievaulx, *Spiritual Friendship* 2.11, trans. Lawrence C. Braceland, ed. Marsha L. Dutton, CFS 5 (Trappist, KY: Cistercian Publications, 2010).

one out of many ... Aelred, *Spiritual Friendship* 1.21; 3.48; 3.86.

"The silence of eternity ..." Robert Cardinal Sarah with Nicolas Diat, *The Power of Silence: Against the Dictatorship of Noise*, trans. Michael Miller (San Francisco, CA: Ignatius, 2017), 98. The French edition was published in 2016.

"When we are face to face ..." Dom Dysmas de Lassus's comment is found in Sarah, *Power of Silence*, 221.

In Conference 9, Abba Isaac discusses four types of prayer ... John Cassian, *Conferences* 9.14–15, trans. Colm Luibheid, CWS (Mahwah, NJ: Paulist Press, 1985).

"Looking with purest gaze ..." Cassian, *Conferences* 9.14.

"Aflame with all this ..." Cassian, *Conferences* 9.15.

The notion of ineffability or indescribability ... The Latin actually contains the terms *ineffabilis* and *ineffabiliter* three times.

Si enim comprehendis, non est Deus ... Augustine, Sermon 117.5, in *Sermons 94A–147A*, trans. and ed. John E. Rotelle, WSA III.4 (Brooklyn, NY: New City Press, 1992).

"Theological negation does not grow out of a fastidiousness ..." See Rowan Williams, *Understanding and Misunderstanding "Negative Theology"* (Milwaukee, WI: Marquette University Press 2021), 40–41.

"Wherever God's word is translated ..." Joseph Ratzinger, *A New Song for the Lord: Faith in Christ and Liturgy Today*, trans. Martha M. Matesich (New York: Crossroad, 1996), 137.

"There is only one language spoken ..." Thomas Merton, *Bread in the Wilderness* (1953; repr., New York: New Directions, 1997), 129. Saint John of the Cross's first maxim on love is similar: "The Father uttered one Word; that Word is His Son: and He utters Him for ever in everlasting silence, and the soul to hear It must be silent." John of the Cross, Maxim 284, in *Spiritual Maxims*, in *The Complete Works of Saint John of the Cross, of the Order of Our Lady of Mount Carmel*, trans. David Lewis, vol. 2 (London: Longman, Green, Longman, Roberts, & Green, 1864). Cf. Sarah, *Power of Silence*, 143.

compulsive and incessant chattering and babbling ... Aelred of Rievaulx cautions against choosing a verbose person as a friend. He appeals to Job 11:2 ("Shall not he that speaketh much, hear also? or shall a man full of talk be justified?") and Proverbs 29:20 ("Hast thou seen a man hasty to speak? folly is rather to be looked for, than his amendment"). *Spiritual Friendship* 3.30.

"You, my beloved sisters, follow our Lady ..." *Ancrene Wisse*, 73.

Mary spoke only four times ... *Ancrene Wisse*, 76–77.

***Ancrene Wisse* appeals to Psalm 140:11 ...** The biblical appeals are found in *Ancrene Wisse*, 78.

a nun "opens her mouth ..." *Ancrene Wisse*, 78.

the anchoress as the lone sparrow ... *Ancrene Wisse*, 105. Medieval spiritual writings commonly use the solitary sparrow of Psalm 102:7 (as well as other birds) to dwell on themes of solitude, meditation, ascent, and silence. For an interesting scholarly discussion, see Mary Agnes Edsall, "'True Anchoresses Are Called Birds': Asceticism as Ascent and the Purgative Mysticism of the *Ancrene Wisse*," *Viator* 34 (2003): 157–86, at 174–82.

"Because many anchoresses have this same vice ..." *Ancrene Wisse*, 105.

"Words often bring with them ..." Sarah, *Power of Silence*, 125.

Eugene Peterson goes so far as to insist ... See Eugene Peterson, *Eat This Book: A Conversation in the Art of Spiritual Reading* (Grand Rapids, MI: Eerdmans, 2006), 109–16.

"The Word was made flesh ..." M. Basil Pennington, *Lectio Divina: Renewing the Ancient Practice of Praying the Scriptures* (New York: Crossroad, 1998), 12.

"Listen carefully, my son ..." RB, Prologue, 1.

"first step of humility" ... RB 5.1.

Twice quoting Luke 10:16 ... RB 5.6; 5.15.

the abbot speaks with the authority of Christ ... RB 2.2.

"Speaking and teaching are the master's task ..." RB 6.6–7.

Outlining twelve steps ... RB 7.10–66.

Pope Gregory tells the story ... Gregory the Great, *Life of Saint Benedict* 7.1–3.

"When he had asked ..." Gregory the Great, *Life of Saint Benedict* 7.2.

"that the thing was not due to his [i.e., Benedict's] merits ..." Gregory the Great, *Life of Saint Benedict* 7.3 (translation slightly modified).

"When I was being hauled from the water ..." Gregory the Great, *Life of Saint Benedict* 7.3.

Cardinal Sarah points to Saint Paul's famous words ... Sarah, *Power of Silence*, 62–63.

"The washing of their feet," explains Sarah ... Sarah, *Power of Silence*, 63.

Jesus deliberately enacts the silence and humility of God ... This paragraph is inspired by references in Sarah, *Power of Silence*, 63, 80, 199.

CONCLUSION

Christ, explains Bernard ... Bernard of Clairvaux, "On the Intermediate Coming and the Threefold Renewal," in *Sermons for Advent and the Christmas Season*, trans. Irene Edmonds, Wendy Mary Beckett, and Conrad Greenia, ed. John Leinenweber, CFS 51 (Athens, OH: Cistercian Publications, 2008), 33–34.

"I am wounded with love ..." This follows the Old Latin version of the Song of Songs, which in turn is based on the Septuagint. The Vulgate reads *amore langueo* (I languish with love).

One patristic preacher after the other ... I am relying here on Robert Louis Wilken, ed., *Isaiah: Interpreted by Early Christian and Medieval Commentators*, trans. and ed. with Angela Russell Christman and Michael J. Hollerich, The Church's Bible (Grand Rapids, MI: Eerdmans, 2007); and J. Robert Wright, ed., *Proverbs, Ecclesiastes, Song of Solomon*, Ancient Christian Commentary on Scripture (Downers Grove, IL: InterVarsity Press, 2005), 313.

"praises the accurate archer…" Gregory of Nyssa, *Homilies on the Song of Songs*, trans. and ed. Richard J. Norris (Atlanta: Society of Biblical Literature, 2012), Homily 4, p. 141.

"What do we understand by 'arrows'…" Gregory the Great, *Morals on the Book of Job* (Oxford: Parker, 1950), 3.2:633.

"From heaven the arrow was aimed…" Augustine, *Expositions of the Psalms 33–50*, trans. Maria Boulding, ed. John E. Rotelle, WSA 16 (Hyde Park, NY: New City Press, 2000), 293.

"For [Christ] is after all the chosen arrow…" *The Song of Songs: Interpreted by Early Christian and Medieval Commentators*, trans. and ed. Richard J. Norris, The Church's Bible (Grand Rapids, MI: Eerdmans, 2003), 105.

Subject Index

Scripture Index

Old Testament

New Testament